The Visual Investor

Founded in 1807, John Wiley & Sons is the oldest independent publishing company in the United States. With offices in North America, Europe, Australia and Asia, Wiley is globally committed to developing and marketing print and electronic products and services for our customers' professional and personal knowledge and understanding.

The Wiley Trading series features books by traders who have survived the market's ever changing temperament and have prospered—some by reinventing systems, others by getting back to basics. Whether a novice trader, professional or somewhere in-between, these books will provide the advice and strategies needed to prosper today and well into the future.

For a list of available titles, visit our Web site at www.WileyFinance.com.

The Visual Investor

How to Spot Market Trends

Second Edition

JOHN J. MURPHY

WILEY

John Wiley & Sons, Inc.

Library of Congress Cataloging-in-Publication Data:

Murphy, John J.
    The visual investor : how to spot market trends / John J. Murphy. – 2nd ed.
        p. cm. – (Wiley trading series)
    Includes index.
    ISBN 978-0-470-38205-9 (cloth)
 1. Investment analysis.   2. Portfolio management.   I. Title.
    HG4529.M863 2009
    332.63'22–dc22

                                                                    2008048202

Printed in the United States of America

10 9 8 7 6 5 4 3

To Clare and Brian

Contents

Preface   xv

Acknowledgments   xix

SECTION ONE   INTRODUCTION   1

What Has Changed?   1
Fund Categories   2
Global Funds   2
Investors Need to Be Better Informed   3
Benefits of Visual Investing   3
Structure of the Book   3

CHAPTER 1   What Is Visual Investing?   5

Why Market Analysis?   5
The Trend Is to Blend   6
What's in a Name?   6
Why Study the Market?   7
Chartists Are Cheaters   7
It's Always Just Supply and Demand   7
Charts Are Just Faster   8
Charts Do Look Ahead   8
Pictures Don't Lie   9
Picture Anything You Want   9
The Market's Always Right   9
It's All About Trend   10
Isn't the Past Always Prologue?   10

Timing Is Everything 13

Summary 13

CHAPTER 2 The Trend Is Your Friend **15**

What Is a Trend? 15

Support and Resistance Levels 18

Role Reversal 18

Short Versus Long Term 25

Daily, Weekly, and Monthly Charts 28

Recent versus Distant Past 28

Trendlines 31

Channel Lines 34

Retracing Our Steps by One-Third, One-Half, and Two-Thirds 34

Weekly Reversals 38

Summary 38

CHAPTER 3 Pictures That Tell a Story **41**

Chart Types 41

Time Choices 46

Scaling 46

Volume Analysis 50

Chart Patterns 52

Measuring Techniques 61

Even the Fed Is Charting 65

The Triangle 65

Point-and-Figure Charts 66

Chart Pattern Recognition Software 70

SECTION TWO INDICATORS **73**

CHAPTER 4 Your Best Friend in a Trend **75**

Two Classes of Indicators 75

The Moving Average 76

The Simple Average 76

Weighting the Average or Smoothing It?	77
Moving Average Lengths	77
Moving Average Combinations	78
Summary	95

CHAPTER 5 Is It Overbought or Oversold?	**97**

Measuring Overbought and Oversold Conditions	97
Divergences	97
Momentum	99
Welles Wilder's Relative Strength Index	100
The Stochastics Oscillator	110
Combine RSI and Stochastics	113
Summary	119

CHAPTER 6 How to Have the Best of Both Worlds	**121**

MACD Construction	121
MACD as Trend-Following Indicator	123
MACD as an Oscillator	123
MACD Divergences	125
How to Blend Daily and Weekly Signals	125
How to Make MACD Even Better—The Histogram	128
Be Sure to Watch Monthly Signals	130
How to Know Which Indicators to Use	130
The Average Directional Movement (ADX) Line	133
Summary	135

SECTION THREE Linkage	**137**

CHAPTER 7 Market Linkage	**139**

The Asset Allocation Process	140
The Relative Strength Ratio	142
2002 Shift from Paper to Hard Assets	142
Commodity/Bond Ratio also Turned up	144
Turns in the Bond/Stock Ratio	144

2007 Ratio Shifts Back to Bonds   147
Bonds Rise as Stocks Fall   147
Falling U.S. Rates Hurt the Dollar   147
Falling Dollar Pushes Gold to Record High   150
Commodity-Related Stocks   153
Foreign Stocks Are Linked to the Dollar   153
Commodity Exporters Get Bigger Boost   156
Global Decoupling Is a Myth   156
Rising Yen Threatens Global Stocks   158
Review of 2004 Intermarket Book   159
Summary   161

CHAPTER 8   Market Breadth   163

Measuring Market Breadth with NYSE AD Line   163
NYSE AD Line Violates Moving Average Lines   164
Advance-Decline Shows Negative Divergence   164
Where the Negative Divergences Were Located   166
Retail Stocks Start to Underperform During 2007   169
Retailers and Homebuilders Were Linked   171
Consumers are also Squeezed by Rising Oil   173
Dow Theory   173
Transports Don't Confirm Industrial High   175
Percent of NYSE Stocks above 200-Day Average   175
NYSE Bullish Percent Index   179
Point-and-Figure Version of BPI   181
Summary   182

CHAPTER 9   Relative Strength and Rotation   183

Uses of Relative Strength   183
Top-Down Analysis   186
Relative Strength versus Absolute Performance   187
Using Relative Strength between Stocks   190
Comparing Gold Stocks to Gold   190
How to Spot New Market Leaders   193
Where the Money Came from   193
Spotting Rotation Back into Large Caps   196

Trend Changes Are Easy to Spot 198
Rotation within Market Sectors 198
Chinese Stocks Lose Leadership Role 200
Summary 202

SECTION FOUR   MUTUAL FUNDS AND EXCHANGE TRADED FUNDS   205

CHAPTER 10   Sectors and Industry Groups   207

Difference between Sectors and Industry Groups 208
Performance Charts 209
Sector Carpets 211
Using Market Carpet to Find Stock Leaders 212
Industry Group Leader 213
Sector Trends Need to Be Monitored 214
Information on Sectors and Industry Groups 214
Spotting Natural Gas Leadership 215
Natural Gas Components 215
CBOE Volatility (VIX) Index 217
Summary 221

CHAPTER 11   Mutual Funds   227

What Works on Mutual Funds 227
Open- versus Closed-End Funds 228
Charting Adjustments on Open-End Funds 228
Blending Fundamental and Technical Data 229
Relative Strength Analysis 229
Traditional and Nontraditional Mutual Funds 229
Keep It Simple 230
200-Day Moving Average and Housing 230
Natural Gas Breakout 232
Consumer Discretionary Breakdown 232
Bear Crossing Sinks Chips 235
Negative ROC Hurts Technology 235
Consumer Staples Hold Up Okay 235

Retail Ratio Plunges   235
Energizing a Portfolio   240
Latin America Leads   240
Real Estate Is Global   240
Profunds Rising Rates Fund   244
Profunds Falling U.S. Dollar Fund   244
Commodity Mutual Funds   247
Inverse Stock Funds   247
Summary   250

CHAPTER 12 Exchange-Traded Funds   251

ETFs versus Mutual Funds   252
Using ETFs to Hedge   253
Using a Bear ETF   253
Trading the Nasdaq 100   255
Using Sector ETFs   258
Inverse Sector ETFs   260
Using Technology as a Market Indicator   260
Commodity ETFs   263
Foreign Currency ETFs   263
Bond ETFs   267
International ETFs   269
Summary   275

Conclusion   279

Why It's Called *Visual Investing*   279
The Media Will Always Tell You Why Later   279
Media Views Keep Shifting   280
Visual Analysis Is More User Friendly   280
Keep It Simple   280
Visual Tools Are Universal   281
The Stock Market Leads the Economy   281
Prices Lead the Fundamentals   282
Sector Investing   282
Exchange-Traded Funds   283
A Year After the 2007 Top   283
Warning Signs were Clearly Visible   284

APPENDIX A Getting Started — **285**

Find a Good Web Site — 285
Use the Readers Choice Awards — 285
StockCharts.com — 286
ChartSchool — 286
Online Bookstore — 287
Investor's Business Daily — 288
Stock Scans — 288
Bullish Percent Indexes — 289
DecisionPoint.com — 294
McClellan Breadth Indicators — 294

APPENDIX B Japanese Candlesticks — **295**

Candlestick Patterns — 297
Bullish Engulfing Pattern — 298
Stock Scan Candlestick Patterns — 300
Recommended Reading — 300

APPENDIX C Point-and-Figure Charting — **301**

Triple and Quadruple Signals — 302
How to Vary P&F Charts for Sensitivity — 304
There's No Doubt about P&F Signals — 305
Recommended Reading — 306

Index — **307**

Preface

T his may come as a surprise, but I don't really think of myself as a writer. I think of myself as a market analyst who writes about things that I see on charts. Fortunately, I've achieved some success in both fields. My first book, *Technical Analysis of the Futures Markets* (New York Institute of Finance/Prentice Hall, 1986) was described by many as the bible of technical analysis and was translated into a half dozen languages. A second edition was published under the title *Technical Analysis of the Financial Markets* (Prentice Hall, 1999) and, as the newer title implies, broadened its coverage to include all financial markets. I authored *Intermarket Technical Analysis* (John Wiley & Sons, 1991) which was described as a landmark publication since it was the first book to emphasize linkages between financial markets and asset classes. A second edition of that book, *Intermarket Analysis* (John Wiley & Sons, 2004) was published 12 years later.

The first edition of *The Visual Investor* (John Wiley & Sons, 1996) was my favorite of the books written thus far—and still is. While my other two books were written primarily for market professionals, or investors with some degree of charting experience, *The Visual Investor* was for the general public with little or no charting experience. The genesis for the book came while I was the technical analyst for CNBC. I usually had three or four short segments on the air each day to discuss some aspect of the financial markets. And I used a lot of charts. Unfortunately, there wasn't a lot of time to explain how the charts were constructed and exactly how to interpret them. I received an awful lot of mail from viewers asking me to explain what all the lines on the charts meant. The first edition of *The Visual Investor* was my answer to all of those viewer requests.

We decided to call the book *The Visual Investor* for a couple of reasons. What I did on TV (and still do in my market commentary) is show pictures of markets in much the same way that meteorologists look at weather maps. It's all visual. There was no point calling it anything else. Besides, a lot of people are intimidated by the term "technical analysis." Even I still don't understand what that means. So we decided to call it what it really was in an attempt to get more people to consider this valuable form of market analysis without all the unnecessary technical baggage and jargon.

I also started calling what I did *visual analysis* to lessen the fear factor of TV producers who seemed terrified by the subject (despite the fact that TV is a visual medium). It seems like every TV story has some chart attached to it these days. It still seems, however, that TV producers are reluctant to interview someone who actually knows how to read a chart. They'll ask economists, security analysts, and sometimes one of their own commentators what the charts mean. They seem reluctant, however, to ask a card-carrying chart analyst (yes, professional chartists now carry cards). They seem afraid that would be "too technical" for them or their audience. That's probably just as well because you don't need to watch TV to find out what markets are going up and which are going down. One of the purposes of this second edition is to convince you that you're perfectly capable of doing your own visual analysis of the various financial markets. And it's not as hard as you might think.

One of the things that happens to most market veterans over the years is that they tend to simplify their work. Part of the reason for that may simply be lack of energy as one gets older. I prefer to think of the tendency to simplify things as a sign of experience and, hopefully, some increased maturity and wisdom. When I first started my career as a chartist 40 years ago, I studied (and tried to apply) every technical tool and theory that I found. Believe me, there were a lot of them. At one time or another, I studied and used virtually every one of them. And I found some value in each one of them. As my intermarket work forced me to broaden my horizon to include all financial markets all over the world, however, there simply wasn't time to perform in-depth chart analysis on each and every one of them (especially with as many as 80 technical indicators in some charting packages). Then I found something else out. It wasn't really necessary to do so anyway. All one really needs to do is find out which markets are rising and which ones aren't. It's really as simple as that.

On an average day, I scan hundreds of financial markets. I don't necessarily look at each chart however. We now have screening tools (which I'll show you later) that help us to quickly determine which markets are rising and which ones are falling. Within the stock market, for example, we can usually tell at a glance which market sectors and industry groups are the strongest and which ones are the weakest on any given day. We can then look to see which individual stocks are driving those groups higher or lower. Only after we've uncovered the leaders (or laggards) do we actually look at the charts. We can do the same for foreign stocks and other financial markets such as bonds, commodities, and currencies. The Internet makes all of that easy to do.

One advantage of scanning so many markets is that it gives me a feeling for the big picture. Since all financial markets are linked in some fashion, it's helpful to get a sense of what the main theme is. Rising stock prices, for example, are usually associated with falling bond prices. A falling dollar usually coincides with rising commodities and stocks tied to those commodities. Strong foreign markets usually signal a higher U.S. market and vice versa. A strong stock market usually favors economically sensitive stock groups like technology and transportation. In a weaker market, defensive groups such as consumer staples and health care usually do better. No market trades in a vacuum. Traders who look at only a handful of markets miss out on valuable information. By the time you finish this book, you'll have a better grasp of how the big picture works.

The second edition of *The Visual Investor* follows the same theme as the first edition. I've tried very hard to keep it simple. I've chosen only those few indicators that I believe the most useful. If you can read a line on a chart and learn to tell up from down, you won't have any trouble grasping what visual analysis is all about. Knowing why a market is going up or down is interesting, but not crucial. The media is full of people telling you why they think a market is going up or down. It really doesn't matter. The media is also full of people telling you what the markets should be doing. All that matters is what the markets are actually doing. Visual analysis is the best way to determine that. And that's what this book is all about.

As you begin to understand the principles of visual analysis, you may notice an increase in your own sense of self-reliance. You may find that you don't really need to listen to all those analysts and economists who like to explain why the markets did what they did yesterday (which they didn't know or didn't bother tell you about the day "before" yesterday). You'll begin to realize that all those financial "experts" aren't that expert after all. Remember all those experts who didn't see the housing bubble bursting in 2007 until it was too late. Or those experts who assured us that the subprime mortgage mess wasn't all that serious in summer 2007. Even the Federal Reserve Board kept insisting during the second half of 2007 that the economy was in fine shape and inflation was well contained. While they were saying that, the stock market and the U.S. dollar were falling while bond prices and commodities were rising—a recipe for stagflation. By the middle of 2008, the Fed admitted that it was trying to battle a weakening U.S. economy and rising inflation at the same time. It took those experts several months to recognize what the markets were telling us all along. That's why we prefer looking at the markets instead of listening to the experts.

When I first started writing about intermarket principles more than a decade ago, it wasn't that easy to implement many of the strategies. Commodities, for example, were the hottest asset class over the past five years.

In the past, the only way to benefit from that was through the futures markets. The advent of exchange-traded funds have made access to commodities much simpler for the average investor. ETFs have also made sector trading much easier as well as access to foreign stocks. I'll show you how ETFs have made the life of the visual investor easier.

I started out to make this a "visual" book. I wanted to show you a lot of pictures of markets that could tell a story on their own. As a result, you're going to see a lot of charts. The charts I chose were taken from recent market data. They weren't chosen to depict perfect textbook examples, but to show real-life examples of visual principles at work in the current market environment. I hope I've chosen wisely. Please keep in mind there's only one question you have to continually ask yourself: Is the market I'm looking at going up or down? If you can answer that, you'll do okay.

—JOHN MURPHY
June 2008

Acknowledgments

I n the first edition of this book, I recommended that an investor have charting software and access to an online data service to perform visual analysis. Thanks to the increasing number of Internet resources, all one needs now is a good charting website, which eliminates the need for a separate data service. In other words, all you need to do is log on and start charting. One such charting service is StockCharts.com. As the chief technical analyst (and part owner) for that award-winning site, I've had some say in its development. Needless to say, I'm very proud of the result. All of the charts (and visual tools) in this book are taken from that website. I'd like to thank Chip Anderson, president of StockCharts.com, for giving me permission to do that. I'd also like to thank Mike Kivowitz of Leafygreen.info for his help in producing the artwork. More information on StockCharts.com can be found at the end of the book. It's a good place to start your own visual analysis.

Introduction

T raders and investors have been using a visual approach to investing for over a century. Up until the past decade, the use of visual analysis as a serious method of trading and investing was pretty much limited to professionals and full-time traders. Most successful traders would never think of making a trade without first consulting the pictures on their charts. Even the Federal Reserve Board now uses price charts.

WHAT HAS CHANGED?

For the average investor, however, the world of visual trading had been largely closed. The intimidating jargon and complicated formulas were beyond the reach and, indeed, the interest of the nonprofessional investor. A couple of important factors have changed that in the past decade. The most important is the availability of inexpensive *computers* and Internet charting services. The investing public now has an impressive array of technological and visual tools that weren't available to the professional community 30 years ago.

The second development has been the dramatic expansion of the *mutual fund* industry to the point where more mutual funds exist than stocks now traded on the New York Stock Exchange. This phenomenal growth has produced both benefits and challenges for the average investor. The challenge lies in the fact that the job of choosing among mutual funds has been greatly complicated. In a very real sense, the mutual fund growth has made the task of the individual investor more difficult. The original purpose of mutual funds was to *simplify* investing. If someone didn't have the time or expertise to pick stocks, that task could be turned over to a mutual fund manager. Besides professional management, instant diversification was provided. An investor could buy one fund and be in the market. Now, however, mutual funds are so segmented that the investor has a bewildering set of choices to make. In the past decade, the arrival of *exchange-traded funds* (ETFs) has replaced many mutual fund choices.

FUND CATEGORIES

Domestic stock funds are categorized by goal and style—*aggressive growth*, *growth*, *growth and income*, and *equity income*. Funds are also divided by the size or capitalization of the stocks included in their portfolios. *Large-cap stock funds* limit their portfolios to those stocks included in the Standard & Poor's 500 stock index. *Midsize funds* focus on stocks included in the S&P 400 Mid-Cap Index or the Wilshire Mid-Cap 750. *Small-cap funds* choose their portfolios from the Russell 2000 or the S&P 600 Small-Cap Index. Stock funds can be further identified by their specialization in various stock market sectors, such as *Technology*, *Basic Industry*, *Health Care*, *Financial Services*, *Energy*, *Precious Metals*, and *Utilities*. Stock *sectors* can be further subdivided into *industries* with even more specified funds. The Technology sector, for example, would include funds that emphasize *computers*, *defense and aerospace*, *communications*, *electronics*, *software*, *semiconductors*, and *telecommunications*. Fidelity Investments offers as many as 40 sector funds for the individual to choose from.

GLOBAL FUNDS

Another dimension has been the growing popularity of global investing. Investors can now trade in individual foreign countries or geographic regions by selecting the appropriate stock fund. As a result, investors are forced to keep abreast of market developments not just in the United States, but all over the world. While overseas investing carries more risk than domestic funds, the rewards are well worth it. From 2003 through the end of 2007, foreign stocks rose more than twice as much as U.S. stocks.

During these same four years, emerging markets gained four times as much as the U.S. market. Overseas investing provides diversification from the U.S. market, which is why financial advisors recommend leaving as much as a third of one's portfolio abroad to improve returns and lessen risk.

INVESTORS NEED TO BE BETTER INFORMED

For many investors, *fund* investing has replaced *individual stock* selection. However, with the degree of segmentation that has taken place in the stock fund industry, investors have little choice but to become better informed and more actively involved in the fund selection process. Investors must be aware of what different sectors of the American market are doing as well as how global markets are faring. The number of choices available to the investor is a mixed blessing.

So, too, are the technological advances of the past decade. The problem is knowing how to select and use the resources available. The technology has outpaced the public's ability to use the new data in the most efficient way. Which brings us to the purpose of this book—to help the average investor quickly acclimate to visual trading; and then show how these relatively simple principles can be applied to the problem of sector investing primarily through exchange-traded funds.

BENEFITS OF VISUAL INVESTING

The bright side of the increased specialization among funds is that the investor has never before been provided with so many vehicles to choose from. Individuals who favor a certain market sector or industry, but don't want to choose which stocks to buy, can now buy the whole group. Sector funds also provide additional ways to diversify one's core stock holdings and to pursue more aggressive growth opportunities with a portion of one's assets. That's where visual analysis comes in.

The tools explained in this text can be applied to any market or fund anywhere in the world. With the aid of a computer and easy access to price data, the task of monitoring and analyzing funds has been made immeasurably easier. The power of the PC can also be harnessed for such things as *monitoring* portfolios, *back-testing* rules for buying and selling decisions, *scanning* charts for attractive opportunities, and *ranking* funds by relative performance. While the challenges of learning how to apply new technology to fund and sector investing are there, so are the rewards. If you're in the market, you've already accepted the challenge. This book will show you how to reap the rewards.

STRUCTURE OF THE BOOK

The book is divided into four sections. Section One explains what visual analysis is and how it can be blended with more traditional forms of investment analysis. The critically important subject of *market trend* is explained, along with some visual tools to help identify the trend. You may be surprised to discover how much value lies in some of the simplest tools that are covered in the first section. Throughout the book, a special emphasis is placed on ETFs. Exchange-traded funds have greatly simplified the asset allocation and sector rotation process.

Section Two covers some of the more popular market indicators in use today. We stress the *concepts* behind the various indicators and how they are *interpreted*. We limit our coverage to only the most useful tools. For those wishing to explore the world of indicators more fully, reference sources are given at the end of the book.

Section Three introduces the idea of *market linkages*. This is especially important in order to appreciate why stock market investors should also monitor movements in commodity prices, bond prices, and the dollar. *Intermarket analysis* is also helpful in understanding asset allocation and the process of sector rotation within the stock market. Along the way, you'll gain some insight into policy-making decisions of the Federal Reserve. You'll be able to watch many of the same things the Fed watches.

Section Four focuses on sector analysis. *Relative strength* analysis is shown to play an important role in the selection process. We also show you how to analyze the global markets.

I'll pull things together in the Conclusion with the admonition to keep things simple, along with some final thoughts. The Appendices will offer advice on getting started and where to find valuable resources to help you do so. The Appendices will also introduce some increasingly popular charting styles you might want to incorporate into your visual analysis.

CHAPTER 1

What Is Visual Investing?

They say a picture is worth a thousand words. Maybe they should have said a thousand dollars. After all, we're talking here about using pictures to make money. And that's really what this book is about. It's that simple. A stock either goes up or down. If it goes up, and you own it, that's good. If it goes down, and you own it, that's bad. You can talk all you want about what a stock *should* be doing or *why* it isn't doing what it *should* be doing. You can talk about inflation, interest rates, earnings, and investor expectations. Ultimately, however, it comes down to the picture. Is the stock going up or down? Knowing the reasons behind a stock's movement is interesting, but not critical. If your stock goes up on a given day, they won't take the money away from you if you don't know why it went up. And if you can explain why it went down, they won't give you back your lost money. All that really matters is a picture, a simple line on a chart. The trick to visual investing is learning to tell the difference between what is going up and what is going down. The goal of this book is to help you tell that difference.

WHY MARKET ANALYSIS?

As the various chapters unfold, you will be provided with some relatively simple visual tools to aid you in market analysis and timing. Notice our use of the term *market analysis*. Whatever you choose to call it, the bulk of this book deals with visual analysis of the financial markets by utilizing price and volume charts. Analysis of fundamental data, such as earnings expectations and the state of the economy, helps determine what a stock *should* be doing. Market analysis tells us what the stock actually *is* doing. The two approaches are very different. The use of earnings estimates comes under the general heading of *fundamental* analysis. The use of market analysis comes under the heading of *chart,* or *visual,* analysis. Most investors are more familiar with the fundamental approach because that is what they are taught in school and read about in the media. There's no question that the fundamentals are what ultimately move a stock or group of stocks. It's just a question of how one goes about studying those fundamentals and their effect on the stock.

THE TREND IS TO BLEND

The fact of the matter is that most successful traders and money managers use some blend of the visual and the financial. The more recent trend is toward a blending of the chart and fundamental disciplines. The use of *intermarket analysis,* the study of *market linkages* (discussed in Section Three), blurs the line between those two disciplines even further. The intention here is simply to explain how the two approaches differ and increase the reader's understanding of why the charting (or visual) approach should be a part of any investment or trading decision.

WHAT'S IN A NAME?

Visual analysis (also called *chart* or *technical analysis*) refers to the study of the market itself. Price charts can show individual stocks, industry groups, major stock averages, international markets, bond prices, commodity prices, and currencies. Visual analysis of various types of funds can also be accomplished. Many people are intimidated by the term *technical analysis.* As a result, they deprive themselves of the benefits of a very useful form of analysis. If that is the case with you, simply call it *visual analysis* because that's what it is. The dictionary defines *visual* as "capable of being seen by the eye; visible." *Technical* is defined as "abstract or theoretical." Believe me, there's nothing abstract or theoretical about this form of analysis. I'm often amazed at the number of people who are terrified by technical analysis but look at price charts all the time. They're scared more by the name than the analysis. To relieve that anxiety, we'll use the terms *visual analysis, market analysis,* and *chart analysis* throughout this book.

WHY STUDY THE MARKET?

Let's suppose an investor has some money to invest in the stock market. The first decision is whether or not this is a good time to put new funds into the market. If it is, which sector of the market would be most suitable? An investor has to study the market in order to make an informed decision. The question is how to accomplish that task.

An investor can read the newspapers, plow through a lot of earnings reports, call up his or her broker on the phone, or subscribe to some financial publication or web site. All of those things should probably be done as part of the process anyway. But there's a quicker and easier way: Instead of wondering what the market should be doing, why not look at what it is doing? Begin by studying the price trend of major stock averages. Then, look at the charts of the various stock sectors to see which way they're trending. Both steps can be accomplished in a matter of minutes by looking at the appropriate chart pictures.

CHARTISTS ARE CHEATERS

In a way, using chart analysis is a form of cheating. After all, why does a stock go up or down? It goes up because its fundamentals are bullish. It goes down because its fundamentals are bearish. Or, at least, that is how the market perceives a stock's fundamentals. How many times have you seen a stock fall in price in the face of a bullish piece of news? What matters isn't always the actual news, but what the market was expecting and what it thinks of that news.

Why, then, is chart analysis cheating? Because it is a shortcut form of fundamental analysis. It enables a chartist to analyze a stock or industry group without doing all of the work of the fundamental analyst. And how does it do that? Simply by telling the chartist whether the fundamentals of a stock are bullish or bearish by the direction its price is moving. If the market perceives the fundamentals as bullish, the stock will be rewarded with a higher price. A negative market evaluation of a stock's inherent fundamental value will punish the stock by pushing its price lower. All the chartist has to do is study the direction of the stock to see if it is going up or down. It almost seems like cheating, but it really isn't. It's just smart.

IT'S ALWAYS JUST SUPPLY AND DEMAND

The simplest way to understand the difference between the two approaches is to consider *supply and demand*. Simple economics tells us that when demand increases relative to supply, prices rise. When supply exceeds demand, prices fall. The same principle applies to stocks, bonds, currencies, and commodities. However, how does one tell what those supply and demand figures are? The ability to tell which is greater is obviously the key to price forecasting. The hard way is to actually study all of the supply and demand factors, individually and collectively, to determine which is greater. The easier way is to let the price itself tell us. If the price is rising, demand is greater. If the price is falling, supply is probably greater.

CHARTS ARE JUST FASTER

An excellent example of the difference between the two approaches was provided to me early in my career as a market analyst. Our portfolio manager called me and a fundamental analyst into his office one day and gave us both the same assignment: to analyze the historic value levels for a list of stocks that he was considering purchasing for the company's investment portfolio. He wanted to know at what level each stock was overvalued and which were at more reasonable historic levels and more suitable for purchase.

I went back to my office and got out a long-term chart book showing price histories, going back several decades, for each stock. I simply noted the price levels where the stocks had peaked and troughed in the past, and which stocks were closest to those peaks and troughs. The entire project was completed the same afternoon.

However, my report wasn't submitted for another two weeks, which was how long it took my fundamental counterpart to complete his report. When both lists were submitted, the funny thing was that we both came up with essentially the same results. He had taken all of the fundamental factors, including historic price/earnings ratios and the like, into consideration to determine his numbers for historic valuations. I simply looked at the price histories of the stocks. We came up with the same numbers, but my task took two hours while his took two weeks. I learned two things from that. First, both approaches often give us the same results, demonstrating the enormous overlap between the two. Second, the chart approach is much quicker and doesn't require much knowledge of the stocks in question.

CHARTS DO LOOK AHEAD

The market is always looking ahead. It is a *discounting mechanism*. We don't always know why a market is rising or falling. When we do find out, the market often goes in the opposite direction. The tendency of markets to lead fundamental data accounts for most of the discrepancies between the two approaches.

PICTURES DON'T LIE

Since fundamentals are discounted in the market, market analysis is just another form of fundamental analysis—a more visual approach, if you will. Often when I'm asked why a market is rising, I respond by saying that the fundamentals are bullish. I may have no idea what those fundamentals are. But I can feel confident that a rising price signals that the market is taking a bullish view of its fundamentals. It is this very point that makes the case for market analysis so compelling.

It also demonstrates why studying the market visually is such a vital part of the investing process. It suggests why fundamental analysis shouldn't be used in a vacuum. Market analysis can alert an investor to changes in a market's supply/demand equation, which would then prompt a reevaluation of that market's fundamentals. Or, market analysis can be used as a check or filter on fundamental assessments. Either way, there is plenty of room for both disciplines to complement each other's strengths.

PICTURE ANYTHING YOU WANT

One of the greatest strengths of the visual approach to market analysis is its ability to monitor a large number of markets at the same time and to cross over into other investment mediums. It is possible for an investor to chart markets all over the world. Global stock and bond markets, foreign currencies, stock sectors, individual stocks, bonds, and commodities can easily be monitored. In addition, the principles of chart analysis can be applied to any and all of those markets with little knowledge of the respective fundamentals of the markets themselves. Given the trend toward global investing, and the myriad investment choices now available to the individual investor, this is no small achievement. And the beauty of it is that one can do a creditable job of analyzing those markets by mastering a relative handful of visual tools.

THE MARKET'S ALWAYS RIGHT

Charts work for two reasons. First, they reflect the market's assessment of the value of a given stock. How many times have you heard the expression "You can't fight the tape"? If you're bullish on a stock, and it is falling, you're wrong in your opinion of that stock (or, as forecasters sometimes like to say, "early"). If you are short on the stock and it is rising, you're wrong again. The market gives us a daily report card. Analysts sometimes say that a market is rising or falling for the wrong reasons (usually when the analyst has been wrong on the stock's direction). There's no such thing as a market moving for the wrong reasons. The market is always right. It's up to us to get in sync with it. I've been told a few times in my career that I was right, but for the wrong reasons—usually by someone who was wrong for the right reasons. I'd rather be right for the wrong reasons than wrong for the right reasons any day. How about you?

IT'S ALL ABOUT TREND

The second reason that charts work is that markets trend. If you don't believe it, look at the chart of the Dow Jones Industrial Average in Figure 1.1. If you're still not convinced, all you have to do to prove it to yourself is buy a stock that is falling. The existence of a downward trend will be painfully apparent. The study of trend is what visual chart analysis is all about. From this point on, the tools and indicators that we employ will have one purpose in mind—to identify the trend of a stock or market, either up or down. Figure 1.2 shows why it's important to be able to tell up from down.

ISN'T THE PAST ALWAYS PROLOGUE?

Critics of charting claim that past price data can't be used to predict the future, or that charts work because of a "self-fulfilling prophecy." Consider whether the first claim makes any sense: What form of forecasting doesn't use past data? Doesn't all economic and financial forecasting involve the study of the past? Think about it. There is no such thing as future data. All anybody has is past data.

If you are concerned about the self-fulfilling prophecy, turn on CNBC or any other news outlet and listen to the conflicting opinions of market analysts. As with any method of forecasting, market analysts often differ as to how they interpret the same data. I'm often asked why charts work. Does it really matter? Isn't it enough that they do work? Keep in mind that charts are nothing more than a visual history of a stock's performance. It's virtually impossible for a stock to trend in any direction without that trend being revealed on the price chart. It naturally follows that if trends can be seen, they can also be acted upon.

$INDU (Dow Jones Industrial Average) INDX
23-May-2008　　**Open** 12985.41 **High** 13136.69 **Low** 12460.09 **Close** 12479.63 **Volume** 3.6B **Chg** -507.17(-3.91%) ▾
━ **$INDU (Weekly) 12479.63**

FIGURE 1.1 Anyone who doesn't believe that markets trend might want to study this chart of the Dow Industrials. A lot of money was made between 2003 and 2007 by investors who spotted and believed in that four-year uptrend.
Source: StockCharts.com.

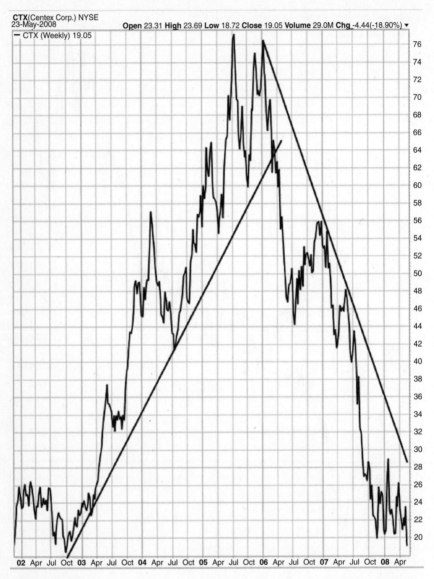

FIGURE 1.2 This chart shows an uptrend and a downtrend in one stock. After tripling in price between 2003 and 2005, the homebuilding stock fell a similar amount the following two years. It's important to be able to tell the difference between the two trends.
Source: StockCharts.com.

TIMING IS EVERYTHING

This first chapter intends not only to explain how the visual approach differs from traditional forms of financial analysis, but also to show how they can be blended together. Consider the problem of timing: Suppose your fundamental analysis identifies a stock that appears attractive for purchase. Do you just go in and purchase it? Maybe the analysis is right, but the timing is wrong. In such cases, the application of some basic charting can help determine if now is the best time to begin buying, or if purchases should be deferred until a more opportune time. In this way, the two disciplines can be combined quite nicely.

SUMMARY

The point of this chapter is to present some of the philosophical ground on which visual chart analysis is based and to demonstrate how and why it should be incorporated into one's analysis. The logic and simplicity behind the visual approach is both appealing and compelling. At the same time, it seems worthwhile for anyone just beginning a study of this approach to understand and appreciate its true value.

Consider the plight of someone who doesn't use any form of visual analysis: Picture a bus driver operating the vehicle without looking out the windows and at the rearview mirror. Imagine a surgeon operating on a patient blindfolded or without first looking at an X-ray. Have you ever seen a meteorologist do a weather forecast without maps? All these people are using visual tools and skills. Would you undertake any serious venture with your eyes closed? Would you go on a trip without a map? Why, then, would you consider investing your money in any stock or mutual fund without first looking at a picture of how it is doing?

In the next chapter, we begin showing you what you can see in that picture.

CHAPTER 2

The Trend Is Your Friend

A s we stated at the outset, markets trend. They usually move in a specific direction, either up or down. There are periods when a market will move sideways for a while in an apparently trendless fashion. Such cases represent interim periods of indecision, but are still important. Sideways movements are often nothing more than a pause in the existing trend, after which the prior trend resumes. At other times, a sideways movement can signal an important reversal of the trend in progress. It's important to be able to tell the difference between the two. But first, let's define just what a trend is and provide some guidelines for determining when a trend is in motion, when it is likely to continue, and when it is likely to reverse.

WHAT IS A TREND?

Since our primary task in visual analysis is the study of trend, we need to explain just what a trend is. Simply put, *trend* represents the direction a market is moving. It's important to recognize that no market moves in a straight line. If we observe the bull market in stocks that begin in 2003, it is easy to spot several periods of downward correction or sideways consolidation in the bull trend (see Figure 2.1). An uptrend is most often represented by a series of rising peaks (highs) and troughs (lows). As long as each succeeding peak is higher than the prior peak, and as long as each successive trough is higher than the preceding trough, the uptrend remains intact (see Figure 2.2). Any failure to exceed a previous high is an early

15

$INDU (Dow Jones Industrial Average) INDX
29-Dec-2008 **Open** 12500.48 **High** 12526.03 **Low** 12451.13 **Close** 12463.15 **Volume** 306.7M **Chg** .38.37 (.0.31%) ▼
— $INDU (Daily) 12463.15

FIGURE 2.1 Markets don't rise in a straight line. There were several pullbacks or consolidations in the market's bull run from mid-2003 to mid-2007.
Source: StockCharts.com.

$SPX (S&P 500 Large Cap Index) INDX
23-May-2008   Open 1425.28 High 1440.24 Low 1373.72 Close 1375.93 Volume 15.7B Chg -49.42 (-3.47%) ▾
─ $SPX (Weekly) 1375.93

FIGURE 2.2 The market uptrend from 2004 to mid-2007 was defined by rising peaks and troughs. The uptrend ended in January 2008 when the summer 2007 low was broken.
Source: StockCharts.com.

warning of a possible trend reversal. Any downside violation of a prior low is usually a confirmation that a trend reversal has in fact taken place (see Figure 2.3). A downtrend is just a mirror image of an uptrend and is characterized by a series of declining peaks and troughs (see Figure 2.4). The ability of a price to hold above a previous low point followed by an upside penetration of a prior high point is necessary to signal a reversal of the preceding downtrend.

SUPPORT AND RESISTANCE LEVELS

Fortunately, these peaks and troughs have names that are self-explanatory (see Figure 2.5). *Support* refers to a reaction low, or trough, that was formed sometime in the past. Analysts often speak of prices bouncing off a support level. They're usually referring to nothing more than a prior low formed sometime in the last week, month, or year. Remember that support is always *below* the market. What the market does at that support is very important. If the market closes below the support level (referred to as *breaking support*), the downtrend is resumed. The ability of prices to bounce off that support level (referred to as a successful *test of support*) is usually the first sign that the downtrend is ending and that prices are beginning to bottom.

Resistance is the name assigned to any previous peak. You may hear analysts speak of prices approaching an overhead resistance level. They are simply referring to some price level at which a prior peak was formed. The ability of prices to exceed that prior peak is critical. If prices close above the peak, the uptrend is maintained. If prices back off again from the prior peak, a warning signal is given of a possible trend failure (see Figure 2.6). Resistance is a barrier above the market.

ROLE REVERSAL

This is a market phenomenon that you should be aware of. After support and resistance levels are penetrated by a reasonable amount, they often reverse roles. In other words, a broken support level (prior bottom) becomes a resistance barrier above the market. During an uptrend, a broken resistance level (prior peak) usually becomes a new support level on subsequent market corrections. Figure 2.7 shows how this happens. Market analysts look for support to function near a prior market peak. Figure 2.8 shows what usually happens in a downtrend. Once a prior support level is broken, it becomes a resistance barrier above the market.

$SPX (S&P 500 Large Cap Index) INDX
23-May-2008   Open 1392.20 High 1392.20 Low 1373.72 Close 1375.93 Volume 2.9B Chg -18.42(-1.32%) ▾
— $SPX (Daily) 1375.93

Jun Jul Aug Sep Oct Nov Dec 2007 Feb Mar Apr May Jun Jul Aug Sep Oct Nov Dec 2008 Feb Mar Apr May

FIGURE 2.3 An example of an uptrend turning into a downtrend. The pattern of lower peaks and troughs starting in October 2007 ended the market's four-year bull run.
Source: StockCharts.com.

FIGURE 2.4 A downtrend is defined as a series of successively lower peaks and troughs. A downtrend is seen in the Financials Sector SPDR from mid-2007 to mid-2008.
Source: StockCharts.com.

XLF (Financials Select Sector SPDR) AMEX
23-May-2008   Open 24.91 High 24.92 Low 24.53 Close 24.65 Volume 72.3M Chg -0.37 (-1.48%) ▾
— XLF (Daily) 24.65

FIGURE 2.5 Previous peaks are called *resistance* levels, while previous lows are called *support*. Resistance is above the market, while support is below. In an uptrend, resistance is usually exceeded. In a downtrend, support is usually broken.
Source: StockCharts.com.

FIGURE 2.6   The failure of the Financials Sector SPDR in June 2007 to exceed its earlier peak was the first sign of a top. The subsequent drop below its spring 2007 low confirmed that a bearish trend reversal had taken place.
Source: StockCharts.com.

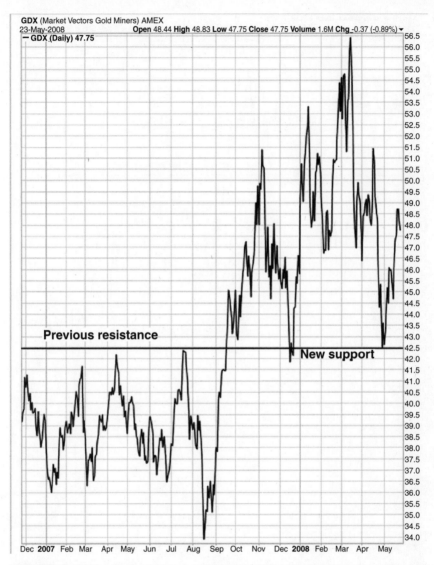

GDX (Market Vectors Gold Miners) AMEX
23-May-2008   **Open** 48.44 **High** 48.83 **Low** 47.75 **Close** 47.75 **Volume** 1.6M **Chg** -0.37 (-0.89%) ▼
— GDX (Daily) 47.75

Previous resistance

New support

Dec **2007** Feb Mar Apr May Jun Jul Aug Sep Oct Nov Dec **2008** Feb Mar Apr May

FIGURE 2.7 The Market Vectors Gold Miners ETF broke through a previous resistance barrier near 42 during September 2007. That broken resistance acted as a new support level during two later pullbacks. Broken resistance usually becomes new support.
Source: StockCharts.com.

FIGURE 2.8 During August 2007, Lehman Brothers fell below a previous support level near 67. That broken support level became a new resistance barrier over the market on subsequent rally attempts. Broken support levels usually become new resistance.
Source: StockCharts.com.

The rationale behind this tendency to reverse roles stems from investor psychology. If support exists at a prior low, that means investors have bought at that level. Once that level is decisively broken and investors realize they've made a mistake, they're usually anxious to break even. In other words, they will sell where they previously bought. Prior support becomes resistance. During an uptrend, investors who sold near a prior peak only to watch the stock trend higher are now anxious to take advantage of a second chance to buy where they once sold. Prior resistance becomes new support on market dips.

SHORT VERSUS LONG TERM

Many investors are confused by the terms *short term* and *long term*, which are so casually tossed around by market professionals. The distinction is actually fairly simple, but requires an understanding of the fact that there are many different degrees of trend interacting with each other. A *major trend*, as the name implies, refers to an important trend that lasts anywhere from six months to several years. When analysts speak of the major trend of the stock market, they are referring to the *longer-term trend* of the market, which is the most important to stock investors. The major trend is also called the *primary trend*.

The second most important trend is the *secondary*, or *intermediate*, *trend*. This refers to a correction in the major trend that can last from one to six months. In other words, it is not long enough to qualify as a major trend, but too long to be considered a short-term trend. The third degree of trend is the *short-term*, or *minor*, *trend*. This usually refers to a correction or consolidation phase that lasts less than a month and is measured in days or weeks. It usually represents nothing more than a pause in the intermediate or major trend. The short-term trend is generally of most importance to market traders as opposed to investors (see Figures 2.9 and 2.10).

Breaking down market trends into three categories is really an oversimplification. There are an infinite number of trends to measure at any one time, from an intraday chart showing hourly changes, to a 50-year trend measured on annual charts. However, for purposes of convenience and simplification, most analysts use some version of the three just mentioned. Bear in mind that different analysts may use different time parameters to determine trend significance. Some measure short-term trends in days, intermediate trends in months, and major trends in years. The precise definition isn't that important. What is important is that you understand the basic difference between the three degrees of trend.

GDX (Market Vectors Gold Miners) AMEX
1-Feb-2008   Open 50.54 High 50.93 Low 48.89 Close 49.15 Volume 3.3M Chg -1.20 (-2.38%) ▾
◄ｌGDX (Daily) 49.15

FIGURE 2.9 The six-week decline in the Gold Miners ETF during the fourth quarter of 2007 qualified as an intermediate correction in a major uptrend. The rally from August to early November was interrupted by a couple of short-term pullbacks. *Source:* StockCharts.com.

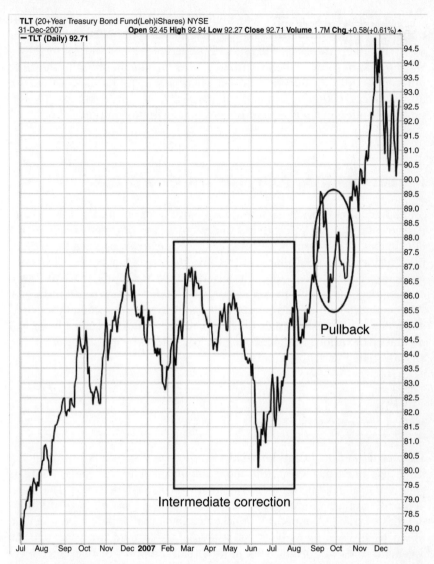

TLT (20+Year Treasury Bond Fund(Leh)iShares) NYSE
31-Dec-2007   **Open** 92.45 **High** 92.94 **Low** 92.27 **Close** 92.71 **Volume** 1.7M **Chg** +0.58(+0.61%) ▲
— **TLT (Daily) 92.71**

Pullback

Intermediate correction

Jul   Aug   Sep   Oct   Nov   Dec **2007** Feb   Mar   Apr   May   Jun   Jul   Aug   Sep   Oct   Nov   Dec

FIGURE 2.10 The 20-Year Treasury Bond ETF suffered a three-month intermediate correction during the first half of 2007 (see box). During September, it experienced a short-term pullback lasting less than a month (see circle).
Source: StockCharts.com.

For example, an analyst may be bullish on a stock, but bearish short term. That simply means that although the most important trend (the major trend) is still up, the stock will probably experience some short-term downward pressure (often called *volatility*). This may mean different things to different people. A short-term trader might sell a stock that is entering a downside correction. A longer-term investor would probably use a short-term correction in a major uptrend as a buying opportunity.

DAILY, WEEKLY, AND MONTHLY CHARTS

An appreciation of what each trend is doing is important. For this reason, it's necessary to use price charts that monitor the different trends. In order to gain a long-term perspective, *monthly charts* showing 10 years of price history are a good place to start. *Weekly charts* that cover at least five years are recommended to get a closer picture of the major trend. *Daily charts* going back a year are necessary to study the shorter-term trends. While monthly and weekly charts are most helpful in determining a generally bullish or bearish attitude on a market, daily charts are most helpful in the timing of various trading strategies. You'll see why it's important to use all three (see Figures 2.11 and 2.12).

RECENT VERSUS DISTANT PAST

Time is important in market analysis. Generally speaking, the longer a trend has been in motion, the more important it is. A five-day trend is clearly not as significant as a five-month or a five-year trend. The same is true of support and resistance levels, since they measure those different degrees of trend. A support or resistance level that was formed a couple of weeks ago is not nearly as important as one formed two years ago. As a general rule, the further back in time that a support or resistance level was formed, the more significant it becomes. As a second rule, the more times a support or resistance level has been "tested," the more important it becomes. Sometimes a market will back off from a resistance level three or four times. Clearly, any subsequent penetration of that barrier carries much more significance. The number of times a price tests support or resistance is also important in the identification of *price patterns*, which will be covered in the next chapter.

FIGURE 2.11 The 10-year monthly bar chart shows the S&P 500 during 2007 backing off from major resistance at its 2000 peak. Monthly trendlines help define major bull and bear trends. Monthly charts provide a valuable long-term perspective. *Source:* StockCharts.com.

$HGX (Housing Index - Philadelphia) INDX
23-May-2008   **Open** 145.64 **High** 147.15 **Low** 120.72 **Close** 130.02 **Chg** -14.72 (-10.11%) ▼
$HGX (Weekly)

FIGURE 2.12   The weekly chart of the PHLX Housing Index made the 2006 down-turn in homebuilding stocks much easier to spot (see circle). That downturn also warned that the housing boom was coming to an end.
Source: StockCharts.com.

TRENDLINES

The simple *trendline* is possibly the most useful tool in the study of market trends. And you'll be happy to know that it is extremely easy to draw. Chart analysts use trendlines to determine the slope of a market trend and to help determine when that trend is changing. Although horizontal trendlines can be drawn on a chart, the most common usage refers to up trendlines and down trendlines. An *up trendline* is simply drawn under the rising reaction lows. A *down trendline* is drawn above the declining market peaks. Markets often rise or fall at a given slope. The trendline helps us to determine what that slope is.

Once a valid trendline is drawn, markets will often bounce off it several times. For example, in an uptrend, markets will often pull back to the up trendline and bounce off it. Retests of up trendlines often present excellent buying opportunities (see Figure 2.13). Prices in a downtrend will often bounce back to the falling trendline, presenting a selling opportunity. Analysts often refer to *trendline support and resistance*.

How to Draw a Trendline

The most common way to draw a trendline is to make sure that it includes all of the price action. On a bar chart (where the price range is marked by a vertical bar), the up trendline is drawn in such a way that the trendline rests on the bottom of the bars. A down trendline touches the top of the price bars. Some analysts prefer to connect only the closing prices instead of the individual price bars. For longer-range trend analysis, it doesn't make too much difference. For shorter-term analysis, I prefer connecting the tops and bottoms of the individual price bars.

It takes two points to draw a line. An up trendline can't be drawn until two troughs are visible. Even then, the trendline is not necessarily a *valid* trendline. Prices should test the trendline, and bounce off it, to confirm that the trendline is valid. Preferably, prices should touch a trendline three times. (Sometimes, however, the market isn't as accommodating as we would like and a trendline is touched only twice.) The more times a trendline is tested, the more significant it becomes. Figure 2.14 shows a long-term down trendline being touched three times.

Most analysts draw several lines on their charts. Sometimes the original trendline proves to be incorrect, in which case a new trendline must be drawn. Another reason for having several trendlines is that they measure different trends. Some measure the short-term trend, some the longer trend. As with trends themselves, longer-term trendlines carry more significance than shorter-term trendlines (see Figures 2.13 and 2.14).

$GOLD (Gold - Continuous Contract(EOD)) INDX
23-May-2008   **Open** 903.20 **High** 935.40 **Low** 900.60 **Close** 925.80 **Chg** +25.90 (+2.88%) ▲
$GOLD (Weekly)

FIGURE 2.13   The price of gold bounced off a two-year rising trendline during the summer of 2007 (second arrow) which provided an excellent buying opportunity. *Source:* StockCharts.com.

FIGURE 2.14 A 13-year down trendline applied to the 10-Year T-Note Yield touches the top of the monthly bars. The mid-2007 plunge in bond yields began right at the falling trendline (see second arrow). Trendlines work very well on long-term charts.

Source: StockCharts.com.

CHANNEL LINES

Channel lines are easily drawn on price charts and often help identify support and resistance levels. Markets will often trend between two parallel trendlines, one above and one below the price action. During a downtrend, you must first draw a conventional down trendline along two market peaks. Then move to the bottom of the intervening trough and draw a line parallel to the declining trendline. You'll wind up with two declining trendlines, one above the price action and one (the channel line) below (see Figure 2.15). A stock will often find support when it touches the lower channel line.

To draw a rising channel (during an uptrend), you must first draw a conventional up trendline along two market lows. By moving to the peak between the two troughs, you can draw another rising trendline exactly parallel to the lower trendline—except that the channel line is rising above the price trend, while the conventional up trendline is below. It's usually a good idea to know where rising channel lines are located, since markets will often stall at that level.

While the channel technique doesn't always work, it's usually a good idea to know where the channel lines are located. A move above a rising channel line is a sign of market strength, while a decline below a falling channel line is a sign of market weakness. Some chart services refer to channel lines as *parallel lines*.

RETRACING OUR STEPS BY ONE-THIRD, ONE-HALF, AND TWO-THIRDS

One of the simplest and most useful market tendencies to be aware of is the *percentage retracement*. We've already stated that markets generally don't trend in a straight line. Trends are characterized by zig-zags, which are identified by successive peaks and troughs. Intermediate trends represent corrections to major trends, while short-term trends represent corrections to intermediate trends. Those corrections, or interruptions, usually retrace the prior trend by predictable percentage amounts. The best known is the *50-percent retracement*. A stock that's traveled from 20 to 40 will often retrace about 10 points (50 percent) before resuming its advance. Knowing this, an investor might consider purchasing a stock that has lost about half the amount of its prior advance. In a downtrend, stocks will often regain half of the prior losses before resuming their decline. This tendency for prices to retrace the prior trend by certain percentages is true in all degrees of trend.

MER (Merrill Lynch & Co., Inc.) NYSE
23-May-2008   **Open** 44.29 **High** 44.45 **Low** 42.57 **Close** 43.38 **Volume** 17.7M **Chg** -1.14 (-2.58%) ▼
MER (Daily)

FIGURE 2.15 From summer 2007 to spring 2008, Merrill Lynch bounced several times off its lower channel line. The channel line is drawn below the price trend and parallel to the basic trendline which is drawn over the declining peaks.
Source: StockCharts.com.

One-Third to Two-Thirds Retracements

Usually a market will retrace a *minimum one-third* of its prior move. A rally from 30 to 60 will often be followed by a 10-point correction (one-third of the 30-point gain). This minimum retracement tendency is particularly helpful in the timing of purchases or sales. In an uptrend, an investor can determine in advance where a one-third retracement lies, and use that level as a potential buy point. In a downtrend, a one-third bounce could represent a selling area. Sometimes a severe correction will retrace as much as *two-thirds* of the prior move. That level becomes very significant. If the correction is just that, prices rarely retrace more than two-thirds. That area represents another useful support area on the charts. If a market moves beyond the two-thirds point, then a total trend reversal is most likely taking place.

Most chart services allow the user to identify retracement levels on a chart. This is done in two ways. After the user has identified the beginning and end of a move with a cursor, a table appears which tells the user at what price levels the various percentage retracements will occur. A second option draws horizontal lines that highlight the levels on the price chart at which the various percentage retracements will occur. These retracement lines help function as support levels in an uptrend and resistance levels in a downtrend. The user can preset the percentage retracements to any levels desired. The levels most commonly used are 38 percent, 50 percent, and 62 percent.

Why 38 Percent and 62 Percent?

These two retracement levels are derived from a number series known as the *Fibonacci numbers*. This series begins with the number 1 and adds each two succeeding numbers together (e.g., $1 + 1 = 2$, $1 + 2 = 3$, and so on). The most commonly used Fibonacci numbers are 1, 2, 3, 5, 8, 13, 21, 34, 55, and 89. *Fibonacci ratios* are very important. The two most important are 38 percent and 62 percent. Each Fibonacci number is approximately 62 percent of the next higher number (e.g., $\frac{5}{8} = .625$); hence, the 62 percent retracement level. 38 is the inverse of 62 ($100 - 62 = 38$); hence, the 38 percent retracement number. This is probably all you need to know at this point about these numbers. They are very popular among professional traders and are widely used to determine how far corrections will retrace. Figure 2.16 shows the 38 percent, 50 percent, and 62 percent retracement lines applied to a chart.

FIGURE 2.16 Fibonacci retracement lines on the Market Vectors Gold Miners ETF show the fourth quarter 2007 correction retracing just over 50 percent of its prior uptrend before turning back up. The 38 percent, 50 percent, and 62 percent lines usually act as support in uptrends.
Source: StockCharts.com.

Doubling and Halving

This simple technique can prove useful in determining when to sell a rising stock and when to buy a falling stock. Consider selling at least a portion of a stock that has doubled in price. The flip side of that is to consider buying a portion of a stock that has lost half of its value. This is sometimes called the *cut in half rule*, which differs from the 50-percent retracement rule. The 50-percent retracement refers to a stock that loses half of its prior advance. A 50-percent retracement of a stock that has risen from 50 to 100 would be a decline to 75. The cut in half rule refers to a stock that loses half of its total value, which would mean a fall all the way to 50 in this example.

WEEKLY REVERSALS

The *weekly reversal* is another simple market formation that's worth looking out for. An *upside weekly reversal* occurs during a market decline and can be seen only on a weekly bar chart. A stock starts the week with a lot of selling and usually breaks under some type of support level. By week's end, however, prices have turned dramatically upward and close above the previous week's price range. The wider the weekly price bar, and the heavier the trading volume, the greater the significance of the turnaround.

A *downside weekly reversal* is just the opposite. Prices open the week sharply higher and then collapse at week's end. While that pattern alone isn't usually enough to turn the chart bearish, it is enough to warrant closer study of the situation and to consider taking some type of defensive action. Weekly reversals take on more significance if they occur in the vicinity of historic support or resistance levels. The daily version of the weekly reversal is referred to as a *key reversal day*. While daily reversals can be important, weekly reversals carry much more significance.

SUMMARY

The most important goal of the visual trader is to be able to identify the *trend* of a market and spot when that trend is changing. The entire point of visual analysis is to participate in significant uptrends and to avoid significant downtrends. There are different categories of trend, however. The *major trend* (usually more than six months) measures the most important trend of a market. The *intermediate trend* (lasting from one to six months) tracks less important trends that represent corrections within the major trend. The *minor trend* (usually lasting less than a month) is the least important of the three and measures shorter-term swings in a market. This shorter trend is extremely important for timing purposes. It's important to watch all three trends for a proper perspective. For this reason, it's necessary to utilize daily, weekly, and monthly charts.

An *uptrend* represents a series of rising peaks (resistance) and troughs (support). A *downtrend* represents a series of declining peaks (resistance) and troughs (support). *Resistance levels* are always above the market. *Support levels* are always below the market. *Trendlines* drawn along those peaks and troughs are one of the simplest ways to measure market trends. Another useful technique is *50-percent retracement.* Other important percentage retracements are 33 percent, 38 percent, 62 percent, and 66 percent. A *doubling in price* usually marks an *overbought* market. A *halving in price* usually signals that a market is *oversold.* The next chapter shows how simple trendlines, along with support and resistance levels, are combined to form predictive *price patterns.*

CHAPTER 3

Pictures That Tell a Story

Having learned how to identify a trend, to spot support and resistance levels, and to draw a trendline, the visual investor is ready to look for price patterns. Prices have a tendency to form patterns or pictures that often indicate which way a stock is going to trend. It should be obvious that the ability to distinguish between patterns that represent nothing more than an *interruption* in the primary trend and those that signal an impending trend *reversal* is a valuable skill to acquire. In order to accomplish a complete analysis of any chart, it is important to take both price and volume (trading activity) into consideration. We'll see how to incorporate volume into your chart analysis. But first, a quick word on the types of charts available for visual analysis.

CHART TYPES

The Bar Chart

We're going to confine our discussion to the most popular chart types, beginning with the bar chart. A daily *bar chart* represents each day's price action with a vertical bar and horizontal price ticks, one to the left and one to the right of the vertical bar (see Figure 3.1). The vertical bar connects the high price of the day to the low price. The vertical bar measures the stock's daily *price range*. A small horizontal tick is placed to the left of the bar, which represents the *opening price*. The small horizontal tick to the right of the vertical bar represents the *closing price*. The price bar tells us where the stock opened (left tick), where it closed (right tick), and the

41

FIGURE 3.1 A daily bar chart. Each price bar shows the daily price range. The tick to the left of each bar is the open and the tick to the right the closing price. *Source:* StockCharts.com.

highest and lowest prices reached during the day (top and bottom of the vertical price bar). On a weekly bar chart, the bar measures the price range for the entire week, with the left tick showing Monday's open and the right tick Friday's close.

The Line Chart

The most important price of the day is the closing price, because that is the market's final judgment for that day as to what a stock is worth. When you turn on your nightly news report to see what's happened to your stock portfolio, you will learn where a stock closed and its change from the previous day. They'll tell you that IBM, for example, closed at 110, down 2 points from the previous day; or that the Dow Jones Industrials rose 10 points to close at 9,000. To many analysts, the final price is all that really matters. Those analysts usually employ a simpler type of chart that uses just the closing prices. They simply draw a line that connects the successive closing prices for each day. They wind up with a single line, which is referred to as a *line chart*. (see Figure 3.2).

Both the bar chart and the line chart can be used to perform virtually any type of visual analysis. As mentioned in the previous chapter, it makes very little difference where longer-range price trends are being studied. However, for shorter time periods most analysts prefer the bar chart, which provides a more complete summary of the price action. The same holds true for trendline analysis. For shorter-term study, we'll employ bar charts most of the time. For longer-range trends, we'll use both types.

The Candlestick Chart

This is a Japanese version of the bar chart that has become extremely popular with market analysts in recent years. The candlestick chart uses the same price data as the bar chart—open, high, low, and close—but the candlestick presents the data in a more useful visual format (see Figure 3.3). In the *candlestick chart*, a thin bar represents the daily price range (called the *shadow*). The fatter portion of the bar (called the *real body*) includes the distance between the opening and closing prices. If the closing price is higher than the opening price, the fat portion of the candlestick is white. A white candlestick is bullish. If the closing price is lower than the opening, the fat portion is black. A black candlestick is considered bearish.

The Japanese place considerable importance on the relationship between the opening and closing prices. The attraction of the candlestick chart is that it provides the same information as the Western bar chart, but with an added dimension. Not only does the color of the bars reveal

FIGURE 3.2 A daily line chart. This chart shows a single line that connects each day's closing price. It's the simplest charting method.
Source: StockCharts.com.

FIGURE 3.3 A daily candlestick chart. The rectangle shows the difference between the open and closing prices. A white body (bullish) occurs when the close is higher than the open. A dark body (bearish) means the close is lower than the open. *Source:* StockCharts.com.

a bullish or bearish bias in a given market, but the shape of the candles reveals bullish or bullish patterns that aren't visible on the bar chart. In addition, all of the techniques that can be applied to the bar chart can also be applied to the candlestick. More information on candlesticks can be found in Appendix B.

TIME CHOICES

In the previous chapter, we pointed out that *monthly* and *weekly charts* can be constructed for longer-range trend analysis. *Daily charts* can be used for shorter-term study. *Intraday charts*, measuring hourly price changes, can even be employed for short-term trading purposes. We were primarily referring there to the line and bar charts. Candlestick charts can be time adjusted with each candlestick representing one hour, one day, one week, or one month in the same way as one would adjust a bar chart. Daily line charts connect daily closes, weekly line charts connect weekly closes, and so on. All of the chart types described can be adjusted for both short-term and long-term analysis simply by adjusting the time sensitivity (see Figures 3.4 and 3.5).

In addition, the basic charting principles are applied the same way in each time dimension. In other words, one would analyze a weekly chart in the same way as a daily chart. One of the real advantages of computer charting is the ability to shift between daily and weekly charts with a keystroke to gain a different time perspective, and to move back and forth between bar, line, or candlestick charts with another keystroke. Two choices then are which type of chart to employ and over what time period. But there are other choices to consider.

SCALING

The most commonly used price charts present two types of information—*price* and *time*. Time is shown horizontally, with dates along the bottom of the chart moving from left to right. The price scale is shown vertically, moving from the lower prices upward to higher prices. There are two ways to show the vertical price data. The most common is by using a linear, or arithmetic, scale. On a linear stock chart, for example, each price increment is measured equally. Each one-point advance looks the same as any other one-point advance. An advance from 10 to 20 looks the same as an advance from 50 to 60. Each represents a 10-point advance and takes up the same distance on the vertical scale. This is the chart scale most of us are familiar with. The other type is the log scale (see Figure 3.6).

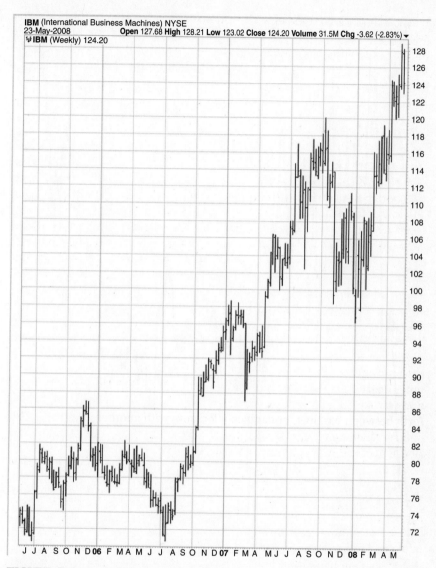

IBM (International Business Machines) NYSE
23-May-2008   **Open** 127.68 **High** 128.21 **Low** 123.02 **Close** 124.20 **Volume** 31.5M **Chg** -3.62 (-2.83%) ▾
ᴪ**IBM** (Weekly) 124.20

FIGURE 3.4 A weekly bar chart showing three years of IBM price action. Weekly charts can be shown for all chart types (bar, line, and candlestick) and are more useful than daily charts for studying long-term price trends.
Source: StockCharts.com.

FIGURE 3.5 A weekly line chart of IBM spanning ten years. Weekly charts can also be drawn for all chart types and portray very long-term trends.
Source: StockCharts.com.

$WTIC (Oil - Light Crude - Continuous Contract (EOD) INDX
23-May-2008   **Open** 126.15 **High** 135.09 **Low** 125.10 **Close** 132.19 **Chg** +6.15 (+4.88%) ▲
$WTIC (Weekly)

FIGURE 3.6 Logarithmic price scales show percentage price changes. That's why the scale looks squeezed as prices move higher. Long-term trendlines usually work better on log scales. This log chart shows a six-year up trendline in crude oil. *Source:* StockCharts.com.

Logarithmic or *semilog charts* measure price changes by percentages instead of by units. In other words, a move from 10 to 20 looks much larger than a move from 50 to 60. The reason is that, in percent terms, a rally from 50 to 60 is not nearly as significant as a move from 10 to 20. An investor who buys a stock at 10 and watches it rise to 20 has doubled his or her money—a 100 percent gain. An investor purchasing a stock at 50 and watching it rise to 60 has only gained 20 percent, despite the fact that both stocks rallied 10 points. In order to match the same 100 percent gain from 10 to 20, the other stock would also have to also double in price, rising from 50 to 100. Log charts, therefore, are constructed in such a way that the gain from 10 to 20 (100 percent) measures the same distance as the move from 50 to 100 (100 percent).

Generally speaking, the difference between the two scales isn't that significant for shorter time periods. Most traders still employ the more familiar arithmetic scale for that purpose, and there's no reason why you shouldn't do the same. The differences on longer range charts can, however, be significant. On a semilog chart, successive price increases look smaller in comparison to earlier moves. As a result, trendlines drawn on log charts will be broken much quicker. There's no absolute answer as to which technique is better. For most of our work in this text, we employ the simpler arithmetic scaling. However, it's usually a good idea to look at the chart both ways when doing longer-range work. The computer lets you switch back and forth quite easily.

VOLUME ANALYSIS

Most price charts also show *volume bars* along the bottom of the chart. On a bar chart, for example, the vertical volume bars along the bottom horizontal part of the chart correspond to each price bar in the upper end of the chart (see Figure 3.7). Heavier volume is shown by larger volume bars and, of course, lighter volume can be identified by smaller volume bars. By scanning the chart, the analyst can see which days (or weeks) had the heaviest volume. This is important because volume tells us a lot about the strength or weakness of the price trend. Generally speaking, when a stock price is in an uptrend, buying pressure should be greater than selling pressure. In a healthy uptrend, volume bars are generally larger when prices are rising and smaller when prices are falling. In other words, volume is confirming the price trend. When the analyst notices that price pullbacks are accompanied by heavier volume than is evident on rallies, that is an early warning that the uptrend is losing momentum. As a general rule of thumb, *heavier volume should be evident in the direction of the existing trend.*

FIGURE 3.7 It's generally a good sign when a price rise is confirmed by rising volume as was the case with Barrick Gold at the start of 2008. Heavy downside volume during March 2008, however, warned of a downside correction.
Source: StockCharts.com.

Granville's On-Balance Volume

This useful indicator was first described by Joseph Granville in his 1963 book, *Granville's New Key to Stock Market Profits*. What makes *on-balance volume* (OBV) so useful is that it presents a more visually helpful way to view the volume flow and to compare it with the price action (see Figure 3.8). Volume should increase in the direction of the price trend. Granville's indicator makes it easier to make sure that is happening. The construction of on-balance volume is extremely simple. Every day that a stock trades, it closes up or down on a certain amount of trading activity. If the stock closes higher, that day's volume is given a positive value and is added to the previous day's volume. If the stock drops, its volume is considered to be negative and is subtracted from the previous day's volume. On days when the stock is unchanged, the volume line also remains unchanged. In other words, *on-balance volume is a running cumulative total of positive and negative volume numbers.*

Eventually, the on-balance volume line will take a direction. If the direction is up, the line is bullish, meaning that there is more volume on up days than on down days. A falling OBV line signals that volume is heavier on down days, and is considered to be bearish. By including the OBV line along the bottom of the chart (or overlayed right on top of the price action), the analyst can easily see if the price and volume lines are moving in the same direction. If both are moving up together, the uptrend is still healthy. In that case, volume is *confirming* the price trend. However, if prices are moving higher while the volume line is dropping, a negative *divergence* exists, warning that the price uptrend may be in trouble. It is when the price and volume lines begin to diverge from each other and travel in opposite directions that the most important warning signals are given.

It is the direction of the OBV line that matters, not the numerical value of the line. The OBV values will change depending on when the line was begun (how far back you are looking). Concentrate on the trend, not the numbers. Chart services will compute and draw the OBV line for you.

CHART PATTERNS

Reversal or Continuation

A number of chart patterns that carry some predictive value have been identified by chart analysts over the years. We confine our comments here to a handful of the more easily recognizable and more reliable ones. Under the category of *reversal patterns*, the three most important are the *double top and bottom, the triple top and bottom,* and the *head and shoulders top*

FIGURE 3.8 The on balance volume (OBV) line rose faster than the price of Barrick Gold during the second half of 2007 and was a bullish sign for that stock. *Source:* StockCharts.com.

and bottom. These patterns can be spotted quite easily on most charts and, when properly identified, can warn that a trend reversal is taking place. Under the category of *continuation patterns*, we're going to study the *triangle*. When this pattern is clearly evident on the chart, it usually implies that a market is just consolidating within its prior trend and will most likely resume that trend. This is why it is called a *continuation* pattern. All you really need to spot these patterns is an ability to see peaks (resistance levels) and troughs (support levels) and the ability to draw some trendlines.

Volume

Volume is important in the interpretation of chart patterns. During a topping pattern, for example, volume will display a tendency to lighten during rallies and increase during pullbacks. During the latter stages of a downtrend, prices will display heavier volume bars during rallies and lighter volume during price dips. At important breakouts, particularly bullish breakouts, heavy volume is an essential ingredient. An upside breakout in any market that is not accompanied by a noticeable increase in trading activity is immediately suspect. During continuation patterns, such as the *triangle*, volume generally becomes much lighter, reflecting a period of indecision. Volume should pick up noticeably once the pattern has been resolved and prices break free of the prior trading range.

On-Balance Volume

On-balance volume can be very helpful in the study of price patterns. Since these sideways price patterns usually represent a period of indecision in the market, the analyst is never sure whether the stock in question is truly reversing or just resting. The volume line can often help answer that question by showing which way the heavier volume is flowing. That can help the analyst determine earlier on whether the stock is undergoing accumulation (buying) or distribution (selling). Many times, the on-balance line will break out before prices do (as happens in Figure 3.8). That's usually an early signal that prices will follow in the same direction. It's a good idea to keep an eye on the OBV line, especially in the study of price patterns, to confirm that the price chart is telling the true story and warn when it is not.

Double Tops and Bottoms

These patterns are self-explanatory. Picture an uptrend which is a series of rising peaks and troughs. Each time a stock rallies back to its old high at a previous peak, one of two things will happen: Either the price will go through that peak, or it won't. If price closes through the prior peak, the uptrend is resumed and everything is fine. If, however, the stock fails to exceed its prior peak and starts to weaken, caution flags are being waved. What the analyst then has is a possible *double top* in its earliest stages. A double top is nothing more than a price chart with two prominent peaks at about the same price level (see Figure 3.9).

Trading Ranges

The chart in Figure 3.10 shows why we never know for sure if that pullback is the beginning of a double top or just a natural hesitation at a prior resistance level. Prices will often do nothing more than trade sideways for a while between the prior peak and the prior trough before finally resuming the uptrend. We normally refer to that sideways pattern as a *consolidation* or a *trading range*. In order for an actual double top to be present, something else has to happen. Not only does the stock have to stall at a previous peak—the price also has to fall enough to close below its previous trough. Once that happens, the pattern of higher peaks and troughs has been reversed and the analyst is left with a double top reversal pattern. The double top is also referred to as an *M pattern* because of its shape (take another look at Figure 3.9).

Although we've described a topping pattern, the bottoming pattern is just a mirror image. A *double bottom* is present when a market forms two prominent lows around the same price level, followed by an upside close through the prior peak. A new uptrend has been started, especially if the upside breakout takes place on heavy volume. Here again, chartists like to see the on-balance volume line confirm whatever prices are doing. The double bottom is also called a *W pattern* (see Figures 3.11 and 3.12).

Triple Tops and Bottoms

As you might expect, *triple tops* show three prominent tops instead of two. This simply means that the sideways period of price movement is carried on much longer. However, the interpretation is the same. If prices that had been in an uptrend eventually close at a new high, the uptrend is resumed. If, however, three prominent peaks are visible around the same price level and prices break below the previous reaction low, then a triple top reversal pattern has probably occurred (see Figure 3.13). A *triple bottom* would naturally show three prominent troughs at about the same price level, followed by an upward penetration of the previous peals. As you can see, these patterns are pretty self-explanatory and are easily spotted. If you look at any library of market charts, you will spot countless examples of these patterns. Generally speaking, double tops and bottoms are much more frequent. Triple tops and bottoms are less frequent, but they can

FIGURE 3.9 A double top formation forms when prices turn down twice from the same price level as the Financials Sector SPDR did during 2007 (see circles). The bearish pattern was completed when the price fell below its spring 2007 low.
Source: StockCharts.com.

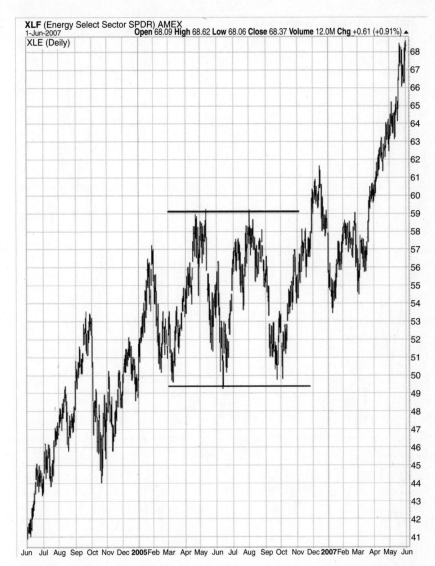

FIGURE 3.10 A trading range forms when prices trade sideways within an existing trend. The Energy Sector SPDR spent most of 2006 trading between two flat trendlines. Prices exceeded the upper line at the end of the year and resumed their major uptrend.

Source: StockCharts.com.

FIGURE 3.11 A very obvious double bottom formed between June 2006 and June 2007 in the price of the 10-Year Treasury Note which led to a new uptrend during the second half of that year. Most double bottoms are pretty easy to spot.
Source: StockCharts.com.

GG (Goldcorp, Inc) NYSE
23-May-2008   Open 42.45 High 43.22 Low 41.91 **Close 42.10 Volume 5.4M Chg** +0.14 (+0.33%) ▲

FIGURE 3.12 Goldcorp formed a bullish double bottom between October 2006 and October 2007. The upside breakout in the OBV line in September 2007 led the price breakout by a month.
Source: StockCharts.com.

$SOX (Semiconductor Index - Philadelphia) INDX
29-Feb-2008   **Open** 351.78 **High** 369.33 **Low** 347.20 **Close** 348.05 **Chg** -3.83 (-1.09%) ▾
$SOX (Weekly)

FIGURE 3.13 A triple top is clearly visible on the weekly chart of the Semiconductor (SOX) Index from 2004 to mid-2007. The final breakdown took place at the end of 2007. Although triple tops aren't that common, they're also pretty easy to spot.
Source: StockCharts.com.

be found. Another popular variation of the triple top and bottom is the *head and shoulders* reversal pattern.

Head and Shoulders Pattern

You've probably gotten the idea by now that there isn't anything terribly complicated about these price patterns and the names assigned to them. The same is true of the *head and shoulders* pattern. This bottoming pattern is basically the same as the triple bottom in the sense that there are three prominent lows. Where they differ is in how the three lows are formed. The triple bottom shows three lows at about the same price level. The head and shoulders pattern gets its name from the fact that it shows one prominent low in the middle (the head) surrounded on each side by two slightly higher lows (the shoulders) (see Figure 3.14). It resembles a person standing on his or her head.

In a bottoming pattern, a trendline (neckline) is drawn above the two intervening peaks. Once that line is broken on the upside, the pattern has been completed and a new uptrend has been signaled. The bottom version is called an *inverse* head and shoulders.

The top is just a mirror image of the bottom (see Figure 3.15). While a top is being formed, the middle peak (head) is slightly higher than the surrounding peaks (shoulders). A trendline (neckline) is drawn below the two intervening troughs. Once prices fall below that trendline, a new down-trend has been signaled (see Figure 3.16).

In all of these reversal patterns, it's important to study the volume pattern to confirm what prices are doing. An on-balance volume line is especially helpful while these patterns are forming and at their completion, to make sure that the volume flow is confirming the price action. Keep in mind that heavier volume is more critical on the upside than on the downside.

MEASURING TECHNIQUES

Price patterns often tell us how far a market will run. These measurements are simply meant to give an approximation of the minimum distance a market can be expected to travel after a pattern has been completed. The general rule of thumb for the three patterns covered here is that *the height of the pattern determines the market's potential.* In other words, simply measure the height of the sideways trading range and project that distance from the breakout point. If the height of a double or triple top is 20 points, that would imply that prices will probably drop at least 20 points from the point where the previous reaction low was violated. For example,

FIGURE 3.14 The British pound completed a head and shoulders bottom in mid-2002 as the U.S. dollar was peaking. The upside penetration of the neckline during June of that year completed that bullish price pattern.
Source: StockCharts.com.

FIGURE 3.15 A head and shoulders top in the U.S. Dollar Index that was completed in the spring of 2002 began a major descent that eventually took it to a record low.
Source: StockCharts.com.

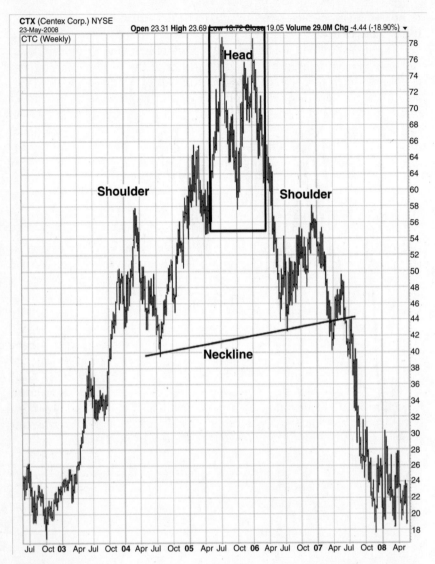

FIGURE 3.16 A three-year head and shoulders top in Centex was completed during 2007 when the homebuilding stock broke its neckline. The middle peak (the head) was itself a double top.
Source: StockCharts.com.

if the trading range measured from 50 to 70, a break to the downside would imply a target to 30.

The measurement for the head and shoulders is a bit more precise. At a top, the vertical distance from the top of the head to the neckline is subtracted from the level where the neckline is broken on the downside. At a head and shoulders bottom, the vertical distance from the bottom of the head to the neckline is added to the point where prices exceed the neckline. Bear in mind, however, that these are not precise measurements and only help to approximate the minimum potential for a market move.

EVEN THE FED IS CHARTING

During the summer of 1995, the central banks launched a successful intervention in support of the U.S. dollar. The financial press attributed part of that success to the fact that the central bankers had actually employed some technical trading methods on the markets. That the Federal Reserve Board was taking the chart approach more seriously was confirmed by the release of a staff report, "Head and Shoulders: Not Just a Flaky Pattern" (C.L. Osler and P.H.K. Chang, *Staff Report No. 4*, Federal Reserve Bank of New York, August 1995). I was also pleasantly surprised to see my first book, *Technical Analysis of the Futures Markets* (Prentice Hall, 1986), quoted frequently throughout the report as a primary source of information. The final conclusion of the report was that the head and shoulders pattern produces statistically and economically significant profits when applied to currency trading. The report's introduction states:

> *Technical Analysis ... has been shown to generate statistically significant profits despite its incompatibility with most economists' notions of "efficient markets."*

Who are we to argue with the Fed?

THE TRIANGLE

This pattern differs from the previous ones in that the *triangle* is usually a continuation pattern. Its formation signals that a trend has gotten ahead of itself and needs to consolidate for a while. Once that consolidation has been completed, the prior trend usually resumes in the same direction. In an uptrend, therefore, a triangle is usually a bullish pattern.

In a downtrend, a triangle is usually bearish. The shape of the triangle can take various forms. The most common is the *symmetrical triangle* (see Figure 3.17). This pattern is characterized by sideways movement on the chart where the price action gradually narrows. Trendlines drawn along its peaks and troughs appear to *converge* on each other. Each trendline is usually touched at least twice and often three times. Usually, about two-thirds to three-quarters of the way into the pattern, prices will break out in the direction of the prior trend. If the prior trend was up, prices will probably break out on the upside.

Ascending and Descending Triangles

These two variations of the triangle generally have a more decisive predictive quality. In an *ascending triangle*, the line drawn along the upper end of the price range is flat, while the line along the bottom of the range is rising (see Figure 3.18). This is considered to be a bullish pattern. A *descending triangle* has a flat lower line and a falling upper line, and is considered to be bearish (see Figure 3.19). The resolution of all three types of triangle takes place when one of the two trendlines (either above or below the pattern) is broken decisively. Here again, a pickup of volume is important, especially if the breakout is to the upside.

There are ways to determine how far prices will probably go after completion of the triangle. The simplest way is to measure the vertical height at the triangle's widest part (on the left) and project that distance from the point where the breakout actually occurs on the right. As in the case of the reversal patterns mentioned previously, the larger the vertical height (volatility) of the pattern, the greater the price potential.

One other measuring rule has to do with the horizontal size of all these patterns. A pattern that has been forming for two weeks isn't as significant (and doesn't carry the same potential) as a pattern that has been forming for two months or two years. Generally speaking, *the longer any price pattern has been forming, the more important it is.*

POINT-AND-FIGURE CHARTS

We can't leave the subject of chart types without mentioning the *point-and-figure* chart whose main advantage is that it provides more precise buy and sell signals. Uptrends and downtrends are marked by alternating X and O columns. An X column shows rising prices, while an O column shows declining prices. A buy signal is given when the last X column exceeds a previous X column. A sell signal is triggered when the last O column falls

ORCL (Oracle Corp.) Nasdaq GS
23-May-2008   **Open** 22.04 **High** 22.75 **Low** 21.87 **Close** 21.98 **Volume 142.3M Chg** +030 (+1.38%) ▲
ORCL (Weekly)

FIGURE 3.17 A bullish symmetrical triangle is visible on the weekly chart of Oracle between 2004 and 2006. An upside breakout in the spring of 2006 signaled resumption of the major uptrend. That's another reason to keep an eye on weekly charts.

Source: StockCharts.com.

SLV (iShares Silver Trust) AMEX
23-May-2008   **Open** 168.83 **High** 181.13 **Low** 166.66 **Close** 180.21 **Volume** 4.1M **Chg** +12.71 (+7.59%) ▲
SLV (Weekly)

FIGURE 3.18 An ascending triangle has a flat upper line and a rising lower line and is usually a bullish price pattern. This chart shows two bullish ascending triangles on the weekly chart of the Silver iShares between 2004 and 2007.
Source: StockCharts.com.

FIGURE 3.19 A descending triangle has a flat lower line and falling upper line and is usually a bearish pattern. This chart shows the U.S. Dollar Index completing a bearish descending triangle during February 2008 by falling below the lower line. *Source:* StockCharts.com.

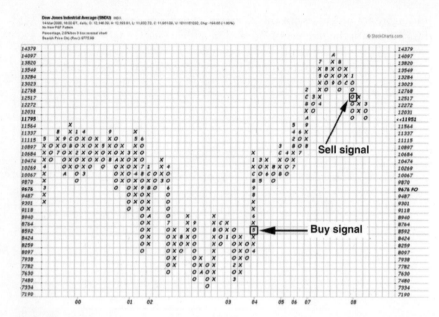

FIGURE 3.20   A point and figure chart of the Dow Industrials with a 2 percent box size is suitable for long-term trend analysis. A buy signal in May 2003 at 8592 lasted until the end of 2007. The first major sell signal in five years took place in January 2008 at 12517.
Source: StockCharts.com.

below a previous O column. The user can vary the box size to change the chart's sensitivity. A 1 percent box size is recommended in most cases. A .5 percent box size can be used for short-term trends, while a 2 percent box size is more suitable for longer-range trends (see Figure 3.20). For most investors, locating simple buy and sell signals should be sufficient. Chartists, however, have devised *point-and-figure* price patterns that can be employed as well. Appendix C provides more information on them. Appendix B does the same for candlestick patterns.

CHART PATTERN RECOGNITION SOFTWARE

Virtually all of the technical indicators that are discussed in this book are relatively objective (as you'll see in Section Two). A signal is either given or it isn't. These indicators also lend themselves to back-testing to determine their reliability and are very useful in building objective trading systems. That's not the case with the chart patterns. Pattern recognition is one of the most subjective elements in visual analysis and, up until now, didn't lend itself to objective computer analysis. In an attempt to remedy that situation, I got together with the engineers at Equis International to produce Chart Pattern Recognition software, which can be used as a plug-in with MetaStock charting software. The CPR software scans the library of stock charts and isolates those that appear to be forming the most important chart formations described in this chapter. It even provides price projections once those patterns are completed. You'll find more information on this software and other visual analysis products in Appendix A at the end of the book.

Indicators

CHAPTER 4

Your Best Friend in a Trend

T he first three chapters cover a fair amount of ground. You could stop reading here and still do a fair job of visual market analysis simply by studying the trend of the markets, knowing where the support and resistance levels are located, drawing some trendlines, and being able to spot important chart patterns. There are additional indicators, however, that help the analyst track existing trends and that signal when those trends are reversing or losing momentum. This brings us to the moving average, which works especially well in a trending market.

TWO CLASSES OF INDICATORS

Moving averages, like trendlines, help measure the direction of existing trends and can help determine when a trend change has taken place. Moving averages also act as support and resistance levels. Moving averages, as helpful as they are, are *lagging indicators*. They confirm that a trend change has occurred, but only after the fact. Another class of indicator—*oscillators*—helps determine when a market has reached an important extreme on either the upside or the downside. The oscillator tells us when a market is *overbought* or *oversold*. The major value of oscillators is that they are anticipatory in nature. They warn us in advance that a market has rallied too far, and are often able to anticipate a market turn before it actually happens.

In this chapter, we explain the various ways moving averages can be used as a trend-following indicator. You'll also learn how moving averages can be used to arrive at price objectives and to measure market extremes. The next two chapters in this section show how to use some of the more popular oscillators. That discussion is supplemented with coverage of another indicator that uses moving averages, while also functioning as an oscillator, to give you the best of both worlds.

THE MOVING AVERAGE

There's good news and bad news related to the moving average. The bad news is that it won't tell you in advance that a trend change is imminent. The good news is that it will help you determine if an existing trend is still in motion and help to confirm when a trend change has taken place. It may be helpful to think of a moving average as a *curving trendline*. A moving average can serve the same purpose as a trendline in the sense that it provides support during selloffs in an uptrend and resistance to bounces in a downtrend. The breaking of the moving average line usually carries the same meaning as the breaking of a trendline in the sense that it implies a trend change. The main advantage of the moving average over the trendline is the former's ability to combine more than one moving average line to generate additional trading signals.

THE SIMPLE AVERAGE

Chart services offer a wide variety of ways to plot moving averages. For example, the user can plot one moving average line by itself, or combine two lines to generate *crossover* signals. The *length* of the lines can also be varied, depending on whether the analyst is plotting shorter- or longer-term trends. The first choice to be made, however, is which *type* of moving average to employ. Let's explain why.

A moving average is simply an average of a market's closing prices over a selected time span. The best known example is the *200-day moving average*, which is applied to stock charts to monitor the *major trend*.

To construct the 200-day average, the computer adds the last 200 closing prices for a stock and divides that sum by 200. Each day, a new number is added to the total (the latest price) and an old number is dropped off (the price 201 days back). Since the average moves with each passing day, it is called a *moving* average. A 50-day average would use the last 50 days while a 10-day average would use the last 10 days. This is called a *simple average* because each day's price is given equal weight.

WEIGHTING THE AVERAGE OR SMOOTHING IT?

While the simple average is most commonly used, some analysts prefer giving extra weight to the more recent price action. This is the idea behind a *weighted* moving average. The weighted average assigns more weight to recent price data and lesser weight to prices further back in time. For that reason, the weighted average is more sensitive than the simple average and tends to hug the price trend more closely. The *exponentially smoothed average* is the most popular of the weighted averages. This average assigns a percentage value to the last day's price, which is then added to a percentage of the previous day's value. For example, the last day's close could be assigned a value of .10. This means that the last day's closing price would be given a value of 10 percent, which is then added to 90 percent of the previous day's value. A value of .05 would give the last day's price a smaller 5 percent weighting and the previous day's a larger 95 percent. The higher the percentage assigned to the last price, the more sensitive the line becomes to more recent price action.

Computers allow the user to convert these percentage weightings into time periods for easier comparison. For example, the 5 percent exponential weighting is equivalent to a 40-day moving average. A 10 percent weighting would be the equivalent of a more sensitive 20-day moving average. The person who wants to use a 40-day moving average, for example, can choose between a simple average, a weighted average, or an exponentially smoothed average by making a keystroke. If you do choose to experiment with weighted averages, this explanation should help you understand the differences. Another reason for explaining the exponentially smoothed average here is to prepare you for our discussion in Chapter 6 of a popular indicator, the MACD, that utilizes the exponential smoothing technique.

MOVING AVERAGE LENGTHS

What length moving average should one employ? That depends on what trend the analyst is tracking. For long-term trends, the 200-day average is most popular. The 50-day average is most commonly used on stock charts to track the intermediate trend. Traders who specialize in the futures markets, with a much shorter time horizon, like to employ a 40-day average. The 20-day average is also used in another popular indicator that we'll cover later in the chapter. These daily average lines can be translated onto weekly price charts by adjusting the time periods. For example, a 50-day average translates to a 10-week average, while a 200-day line corresponds to a 40-week average.

The trend is considered to be *up* as long as the price of the market is above the moving average line and the line is rising. A close below a moving average line is a warning of a potential price change (see Figure 4.1). If the moving line turns down as well, the negative signal becomes much stronger. A stock is considered to be strong if it is above its 50-and 200-day moving averages. A close below its 50-day average signals a short-term top and a possible drop to the 200-day average (see Figure 4.2). A close below a 200-day average is considered very bearish and hints of a major trend change. Many times prices will drop back to their moving average lines before resuming their uptrend. In these instance, moving average lines act as support levels and function like an up trendline (see Figures 4.3 and 4.4).

During the early stages of an upturn, the minimum requirement for purchase of a stock is usually a close over its 50-day (10-week) average. More conservative investors often require a close above the 200-day (or 40-week) line as further proof of a bullish trend change before committing funds to a stock. Most analysts employ a combination of averages.

MOVING AVERAGE COMBINATIONS

Two moving averages are commonly used to analyze market trends. How the two averages relate to each other tells a lot about the strength or weakness of a trend. Two commonly employed numbers among stock investors are the 50-day (10-week) and the 200-day (40-week) combination. The trend is considered bullish (upward) as long as the shorter average is above the longer (see Figures 4.5 and 4.6). Any crossing by the shorter average below the longer is considered negative. Some analysts use a 10-week and a 30-week average for the same purpose. In that case, a bullish case requires that the 10-week average crosses and stays above the 30-week average.

Whichever combinations are employed, the principle is always the same. *The shorter moving average must be above the longer to justify a bullish case.* Crossover *buy* and *sell* signals are given when the shorter average crosses above or below the longer moving average line, respectively. Figures 4.7 and 4.8 show a combination of two exponentially smoothed moving averages.

Since moving average lines are trend-following indicators, *they do best in a trending environment.* During an extended uptrend, for example, moving averages will get you aboard and keep you aboard the market

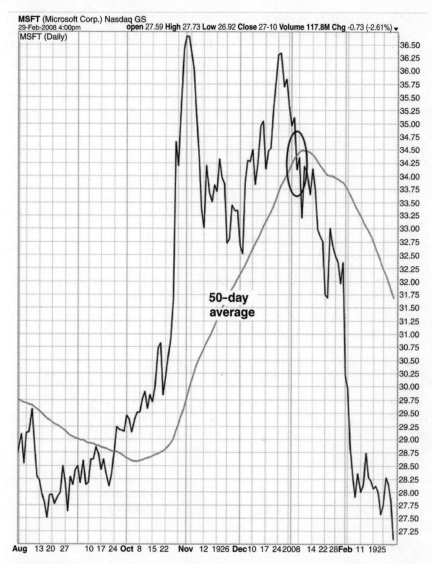

FIGURE 4.1 The January 2008 crossing by Microsoft below its 50-day average (see circle) signaled the start of a downtrend and was a good time to exit the stock. *Source:* StockCharts.com.

IEF (7-10 Year Treasury Bond Fund(Leh)iShares) NYSE
30-May-2008 11:31am   **open** 87.35 **High** 87.46 **Low** 87.24 **Last** 87.41 **Volume 1.2M Chg** +0.39 (+0.45%) ▲
− IEF (Daily) 87.41
− MA(50) 89.45
− MA(200) 87.34

50-day average

200-day average

FIGURE 4.2 The 7–10 Year T-Bond Fund violated its 50-day average in April 2008, which signaled a drop all the way down to its 200-day average a couple of months later.

Source: StockCharts.com.

FIGURE 4.3 The 40-week moving average acted as a support line for the CRB Commodity Index from 2003 to 2006. That's a sign of an ongoing bull market. *Source:* StockCharts.com.

FIGURE 4.4   The break of the 40-week average by the Financials Sector SPDR during the summer of 2007 (see circle) was the start of a major decline in that sector. *Source:* StockCharts.com.

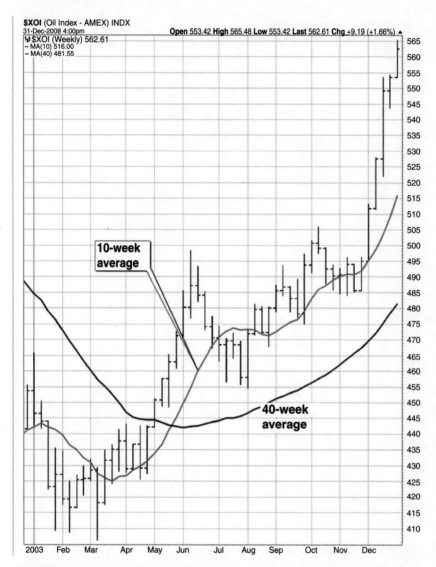

FIGURE 4.5 The upward crossing of the 10-week average over the 40-week average during the spring of 2003 signaled a new uptrend in the AMEX Oil Index, which lasted through the end of 2007. Moving average crossovers provide valuable timing signals.
Source: StockCharts.com.

$BKX (Bank Index - Philadelphia) INDX
30-May-2008 12:03pm   Open 76.21 **High** 77.39 **Low** 74.32 **Last** 76.10 **Chg** -0.10 (-0.13%) ▼
◍ $BKX (Weekly) 76.10
— MA(10) 80.61
— MA(40) 90.22

40-week average

10-week average

FIGURE 4.6 The downward crossing of the 10-week average below the 40-week average in mid-2007 (see circle) signaled a major downturn in the PHLX Bank Index. *Source:* StockCharts.com.

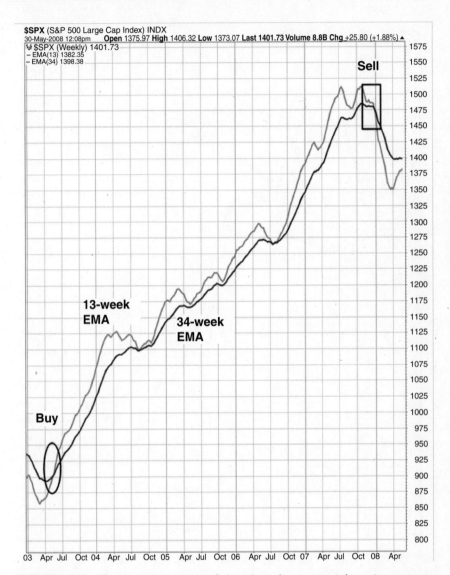

$SPX (S&P 500 Large Cap Index) INDX
30-May-2008 12:08pm   **Open** 1375.97 **High** 1406.32 **Low** 1373.07 **Last 1401.73 Volume** 8.8B **Chg** +25.80 (+1.88%) ▲
$SPX (Weekly) 1401.73
— EMA(13) 1382.35
— EMA(34) 1398.38

Sell

13-week EMA

34-week EMA

Buy

FIGURE 4.7 The upward crossing of the 13-week *exponential moving average* (EMA) over the 34-week EMA in spring 2003 was a major buy signal for the S&P 500 (see circle). The two EMAs didn't turn negative until the end of 2007 (see box). *Source:* StockCharts.com.

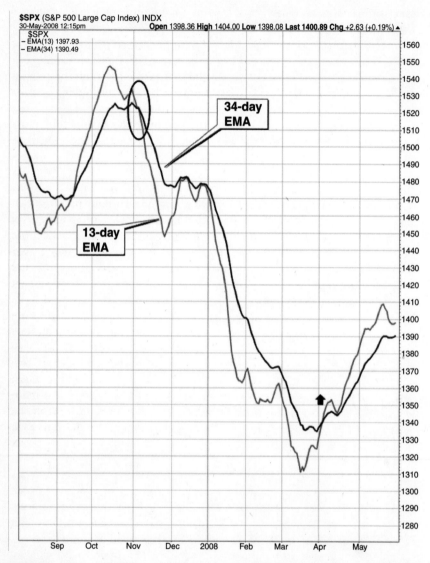

$SPX (S&P 500 Large Cap Index) INDX
30-May-2008 12:15pm　　　　Open 1398.36 **High** 1404.00 **Low** 1398.08 **Last 1400.89 Chg** +2.63 (+0.19%) ▲
　$SPX
− EMA(13) 1397.93
− EMA(34) 1390.49

FIGURE 4.8 The 13- and 34-day EMA lines crossed downward on the S&P 500 (not shown) in early November 2007 (see circle) and stayed negative until the following April (see arrow). The S&P lost 10 percent during that time span.
Source: StockCharts.com.

trend until it exhausts itself. By the same token, moving averages can act as a valuable filter to keep you from buying stocks in a downtrend. Moving averages, however, are not that helpful in an extended trading range or a period of sideways price action. They need a trend to function well.

Computers also allow you to plot the *difference* between the two averages. During a strong uptrend, for example, the shorter moving average rises faster than the longer average. The spread between the two averages will widen. When the spread between the two averages begins to narrow, that is usually an early warning that the uptrend is losing some momentum.

Put Envelopes around the Average

There are other ways to use the moving average to help monitor support and resistance levels and to determine market extremes. *Trading envelopes* are one example. This technique plots lines, called *envelopes*, at predetermined percentage amounts above and below a moving average line. The percentages may vary, depending on which trend and which market is being studied. Short-term traders, for example, often plot envelopes 3 percent above and 3 percent below a 20-day moving average (see Figure 4.9). Prices will often stall at the upper and lower envelope lines before correcting back to the moving average line in the middle. A longer-term version might entail plotting envelopes 5 percent around a 10-week average and 10 percent envelopes around a 40-week average (see Figures 4.10 and 4.11). A price move outside the envelopes warns that a market has reached a dangerous extreme and is vulnerable to a retracement in the other direction. Some experimentation is needed to tailor this technique to the market you're following and to the appropriate time span to suit your purposes.

Or Put Bands around It

Bollinger bands, developed by John Bollinger, blend a statistical concept with the envelope technique. Two bands are placed above and below the centered moving average, as with envelopes; but instead of using fixed percentage amounts (such as 5 percent or 10 percent) around the moving average line, Bollinger bands are plotted *two standard deviations* above and below a moving average line, which is usually 20 periods (see Figure 4.12). Bollinger bands also contract and expand depending on the market's degree of volatility.

Standard deviation is a statistical concept that describes how a set of data (prices) is dispersed (spread) around an average value. The concept of standard deviation has a very specific value in statistics. That is because 68 percent of the data values differ from the middle average by less than one

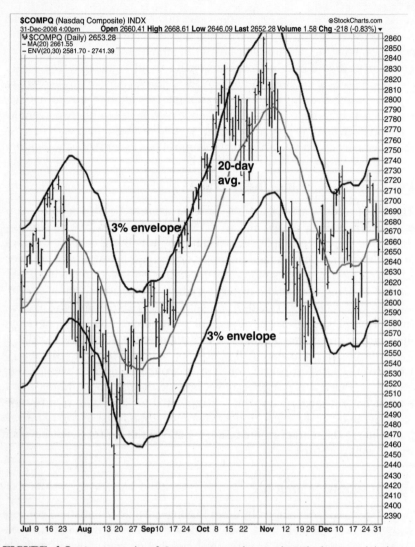

FIGURE 4.9 An example of 3 percent envelopes plotted above and below a 20-day average of the Nasdaq Composite Index during the second half of 2007. Three percent envelopes help determine short-term price extremes.
Source: StockCharts.com.

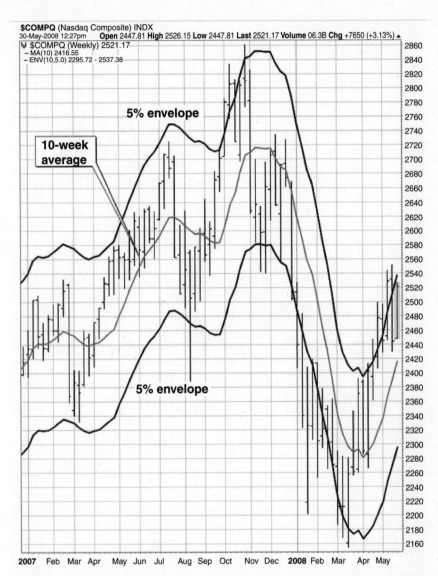

FIGURE 4.10 An example of 5 percent envelopes plotted above and below a 10-week average of the Nasdaq Composite Index from the start of 2007 to spring 2008. Five percent envelopes help determine intermediate price extremes.
Source: StockCharts.com.

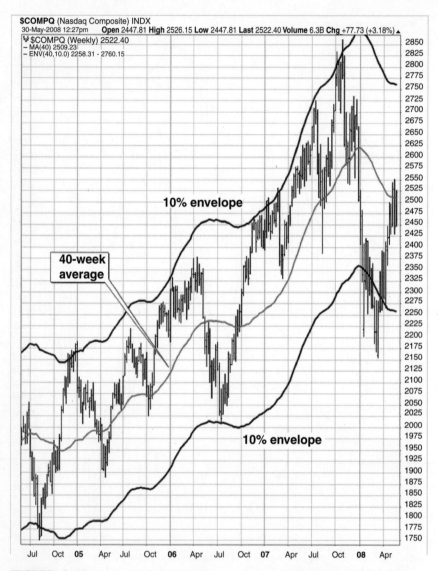

FIGURE 4.11 An example of 10 percent envelopes plotted above and below a 40-week average of the Nasdaq Composite Index from mid-2004 to mid-2008. Ten percent envelopes help determine major price extremes and possible turning points. *Source:* StockCharts.com.

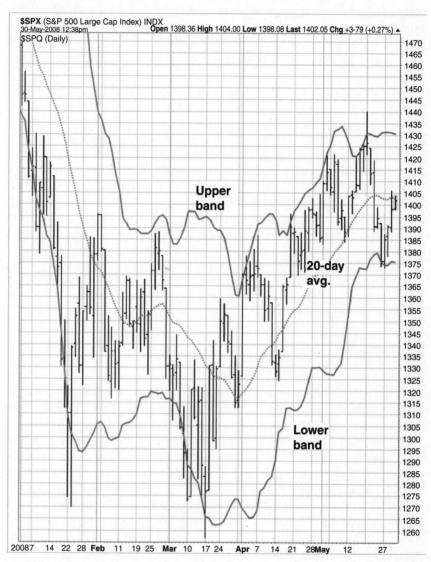

FIGURE 4.12 An example of Bollinger bands plotted two standard deviations above and below a 20-day average of the S&P 500 during the first half of 2008. Daily Bollinger bands help determine short-term support and resistance levels. *Source:* StockCharts.com.

standard deviation. *Ninety-five percent of the data values differ from the middle average by less than two standard deviations.* Since the Bollinger bands are placed two standard deviations above and below the 20-period moving average, 95 percent of all price action should be contained by the two bands.

The interpretation is the same, however. Prices will usually meet resistance at the upper band and support at the lower band. As in the case of envelopes, three lines are overlaid on the price chart. On a daily chart, the middle line is usually a 20-day average. In a bullish environment, prices will rise above and stay above the 20-day line, which acts as support. However, upward price surges will usually stall at the upper band. The opposite is true in a downtrend. Prices will usually trade below the 20-day average, which will function as resistance to price advances. Prices will usually bounce off the lower band. The simplest way to interpret Bollinger bands is that the upper band represents overhead resistance, while the lower band represents support below.

These bands are also helpful in determining price objectives. During a downward price correction, for example, prices can be expected to find support either at the 20-day average or at the lower band if prices fall below the 20-day average line.

Band Width Is Important, Too

There is another important distinction between trading envelopes and Bollinger bands: The width of the envelopes stays constant at all times. For example, in the case of 3 percent envelopes, the two envelopes will always be 6 percent apart (3 percent above and 3 percent below the moving average line). The Bollinger bands, by contrast, are constantly contracting and expanding in order to adjust to market volatility. *Volatility* refers to the degree of movement in prices. The bands will contract during periods of low volatility and expand during periods of high volatility. You can track the width of the bands to determine market volatility. Unusually narrow bands (reflecting low volatility and a quiet market) are usually followed by a period of high volatility (rapid and substantial price moves). Conversely, unusually wide bands (reflecting high volatility and a strong trend) usually warn of a possible slowing in the existing trend (or a return to a trading range environment [see Figure 4.13]).

Bands Work on Weekly and Monthly Charts

While many traders apply Bollinger bands to daily charts, they work equally well on weekly charts for longer-term perspective. All you have to do is to switch from a 20-day to a 20-week moving average. In the case of the

FIGURE 4.13 Bollinger band width (below chart) measures the distance between the two bands. Upward spikes in band width signals increased volatility and lower stock prices (see arrows). The decline in band width during the first half of 2008 led to higher prices.
Source: StockCharts.com.

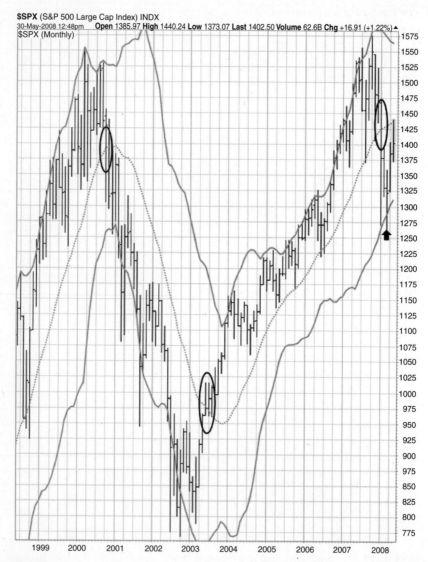

$SPX (S&P 500 Large Cap Index) INDX
30-May-2008 12:48pm   **Open** 1385.97 **High** 1440.24 **Low** 1373.07 **Last** 1402.50 **Volume** 62.6B **Chg** +16.91 (+1.22%) ▲
$SPX (Monthly)

FIGURE 4.14   Bollinger bands applied to a monthly S&P 500 chart over ten years shows that crossings above and below the 20-month average help define bull and bear markets (see circles). The early 2008 decline found support at the lower band (see arrow).
Source: StockCharts.com.

weekly chart, the 20-week moving average usually functions as support during an uptrend or resistance in a downtrend. The *weekly* bands also help to identify price targets and market extremes in the same way that they do on *daily* charts. The same principles hold true on monthly charts (see Figure 4.14).

SUMMARY

Like trendlines, *moving averages* help identify potential support and resistance levels and alert us when a trend change is taking place. It is important to tailor the *length* of the average to the length of the trend being followed. Moving averages can be used by themselves or in combination to generate trading signals. Trading *envelopes* and *bands* determine market extremes by measuring how far prices have traveled from a moving average centerline. Moving averages work best in trending markets and usually lag the price action. In the next chapter, we show some indicators that can anticipate market turns and that also work well in a less trendy and more choppy market environment.

CHAPTER 5

Is It Overbought or Oversold?

MEASURING OVERBOUGHT AND OVERSOLD CONDITIONS

There are several ways to determine when a market is overbought or oversold. The most effective way is to use an indicator called an *oscillator*. Oscillators tell us when a market has reached an extreme in either direction, which makes it vulnerable to a countertrend correction. When a stock has gone up too far, analysts will often say that the stock is *overbought*. That simply means that the stock may have to pause for a while to digest those gains, or possibly have to correct downward before resuming its uptrend. At a stock's most extreme highpoint, some traders will take profits and temporarily halt the advance. Other buyers will reemerge during the ensuing price setback, and the stock will eventually be pushed higher. An *oversold* condition is just the opposite, and implies that a stock has fallen too far and is probably due for a short term bounce. It's generally better to buy a market when it's oversold and sell when it's overbought (see Figure 5.1).

DIVERGENCES

There's a second element in oscillator analysis that is extremely valuable. Not only do oscillators help us determine when a market is overbought or oversold, but they also warn us in advance when a *divergence* is building up in a stock. Divergences usually warn of an impending trend reversal. We've encountered the idea of divergence in our discussion of on-balance volume in Chapter 3. In other words, we study two lines that

97

FIGURE 5.1 This chart demonstrates that it's better to buy when an oscillator is in an oversold condition and to sell when it's overbought.
Source: StockCharts.com.

usually trend in the same direction. When they start to diverge from one another, the analyst begins to suspect that the trend is losing momentum. Oscillators are especially helpful for this purpose. There are two elements, then, to oscillator analysis: One is to spot when a market has reached a dangerous extreme (either overbought or oversold) and the other is to identify divergences while prices are in that extreme oscillator range. We'll show you how this is done.

MOMENTUM

This is the most basic concept in oscillator analysis. A price chart tells us whether prices are rising or falling. An oscillator chart tells us more about the *momentum*, or pace, of a market. An oscillator tells us the *rate* (also called *rate of change*) at which a market is rising or falling. This type of oscillator tells us whether the current trend is gaining or losing its momentum. In the latter stages of an advance, the momentum of the advance (or the rate of change) usually begins to slow. That slowing in the momentum may not show up on the price chart, but will usually be seen on the oscillator that accompanies the price chart. Oscillators that measure momentum and rate of change are the most basic kind. There are other more sophisticated oscillators, which we'll deal with a bit later in this chapter. But let's begin with the basics.

Momentum or Rate of Change Oscillators

There are various ways to construct these two oscillators, but their interpretation is basically the same. The trader is comparing the latest closing price to a price in the past. Depending on which variation is chosen, the computer will take either the *difference* between the latest price and the price in the past or a *ratio* of the two. Let's use a 10-day period as an example. In the first case, the computer subtracts the price 10 days ago from the latest price. If the latest price is higher than the old price, the oscillator value will be positive. If the latest price is lower, the oscillator value will be negative. Using that construction, the oscillator will fluctuate above and below a midpoint line which is called a *zero line*.

Using the *ratio* method, the computer *divides* the latest price by the price 10 days ago. It matters little which formula is used, because both charts look exactly alike and are interpreted in the same way. Chart programs sometimes differ in the way these two oscillators are named and constructed, even though the basic principles are always the same. To prevent any confusion, read the user manual for the software package that you are using to make sure that you know exactly how your software defines and constructs *momentum* and *rate of change* (ROC) oscillators.

Interpretation of Rate of Change

The midpoint line (zero line) is the key to this type of oscillator. A crossing above the midline is considered to be positive (a buy signal). A crossing below the midline is negative (a sell signal). Many analysts use these oscillators just to generate that type of buy and sell signal. However, they can also be used to spot market extremes. When the oscillator line has traveled too far above or too far below the midline, the market is considered to be overbought (above) or oversold (below). If the oscillator line starts to move back toward the midline, it is an early signal that the current trend is losing momentum (see Figure 5.2).

Longer-Range Momentum

The 10-day period used in the prior example would only be useful for very short term trading purposes. Analysts generally employ longer time spans for longer-range momentum analysis. For example, the analyst might compare the last closing price to the price 13 weeks, 26 weeks, or even 52 weeks in the past (see Figure 5.3). Naturally, the longer the time span used, the more significant the signals will be, although they will be much fewer. This oscillator does have one drawback.

Market Extremes Are Too Subjective

By studying the historical pattern of momentum oscillators, it is possible to estimate what values marked overbought or oversold extremes in the past. However, there are no *preset* values that can be used universally. For that reason, many analysts prefer other types of oscillators that preserve the benefits of the momentum and rate of change lines but solve the problem just mentioned. One of the most popular is the *relative strength index* (RSI).

WELLES WILDER'S RELATIVE STRENGTH INDEX

This popular oscillator was first described by J. Welles Wilder, Jr., in his 1978 book, *New Concepts in Technical Trading Systems*. The main value of this oscillator is that it presents the analyst with upper and lower boundaries to determine overbought and oversold conditions. The values of the RSI oscillator range from 0 to 100. Readings over 70 are considered to be overbought. Readings below 30 are considered to be oversold. Applying those two boundaries to any market environment greatly simplifies the search for markets that have reached dangerous extremes. It's also worth noting that the midpoint value of 50 can serve the same purpose as the zero

FIGURE 5.2 This chart shows three Dow sell signals during the second half of 2007 when the 10-day *rate of change* (ROC) line fell below its zero line (see circles). *Source:* StockCharts.com.

FIGURE 5.3 The 52-week ROC line fell below its zero line at the end of 2007 for the first time in five years and signaled the start of a bear market. The upside crossing in the spring of 2003 signaled the start of a major bull market (see circles). *Source:* StockCharts.com.

line in the momentum oscillator, and crossings above and below that value can generate trend signals. (Figure 5.4 shows an example of 70 and 30 lines identifying an overbought and oversold condition.)

Which Time Spans to Use for the RSI

The two values most commonly used for the relative strength index are 14 and 9. Most software programs offer one of those numbers as the default value. (*Default value* simply means that the software program will suggest the most commonly used value for an indicator.) A daily RSI will be based on price data covering the last 9 or 14 days. A weekly chart will include the past 9 or 14 weeks. Since the computer does the calculation for you, it's not necessary to memorize the formula. Still, it's always helpful to know what you're studying.

The relative strength index uses a ratio of the average points gained on *up* days during the past x number of days (usually 9 or 14) divided by the average points lost on *down* days over the same time span. That value (*RS*) is then inserted into a formula.

$$RSI = 100 - \frac{100}{1 + RS}$$

$$RS = \frac{\text{Average of } x \text{ days' up closes}}{\text{Average of } x \text{ days' down closes}}$$

$$x = \text{Usually 9 or 14 periods}$$

The fact that 9 or 14 are most commonly used doesn't limit you to those values. But they do provide a good starting point as you learn to use this indicator. Later on, you may choose to experiment with other values. Most software packages allow you to *optimize* values for all indicators by testing for best time span to use in each market. However, the benefit of starting with the default value is that it provides a number you can apply universally to all markets. Also keep in mind that whether you are using daily, weekly, or monthly charts, it's a good idea to use the same numbers. For example, use a nine-day, a nine-week, and a nine-month value.

Modifying Values to Suit Market

The main value of the RSI oscillator is to determine when a given market has reached an overbought (over 70) or an oversold (below 30) region. In a very quiet market with low volatility (movement), you may notice that the swings in the RSI line stay between 70 and 30. In that case, the RSI line has little value. You might want to try increasing its amplitude (wideness) by *shortening* the time span. Try a seven-day RSI line, for example. The idea

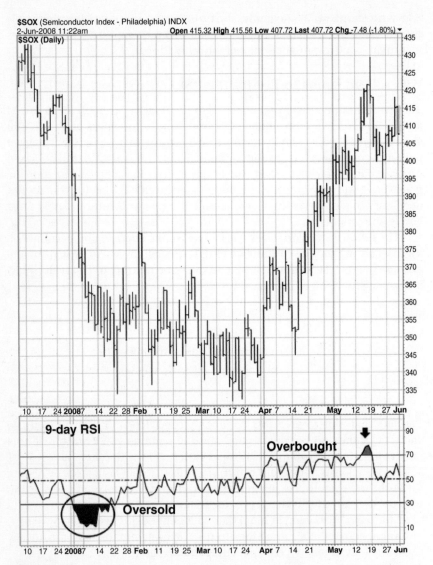

FIGURE 5.4   The nine-day RSI line shows an oversold condition (below 30) in the Semiconductor (SOX) Index at the start of 2008. The RSI line crossed over 70 four months later during May which warned of an overbought condition.
Source: StockCharts.com.

is to widen the fluctuations in the RSI line to the point that it moves either above 70 or below 30. The way to do that is to shorten the time span.

The opposite case involves a situation where the RSI line is *too* volatile. In a very active market, the RSI line may be too sensitive. Frequent moves above 70 and below 30 become less meaningful. It's hard to distinguish between the valid signals and market noise. In that case, it's necessary to reduce the amplitude of the RSI line by *lengthening* the number of days used. Try 21 days, for example. That will eliminate many of the meaningless moves and help identify those that really matter. Fortunately, the computer lets you vary the time span with a keystroke.

RSI Divergences

The fact that a market has reached an overbought or oversold extreme in any oscillator does not necessarily mean that a trend reversal is imminent. It just alerts you to the fact that prices have entered a *potentially* dangerous area. During a strong uptrend, for example, prices may signal an overbought reading by moving above 70 on the RSI line and stay above 70 for some time. Sale of a rising stock at that point could prove to be premature. This brings us to the second necessary ingredient in oscillator analysis—the existence of divergence.

Quite often, prices will hit a new high accompanied by a value in the RSI line above 70. Prices will then consolidate for a while or experience a short downward correction, before setting a new high. Meanwhile, the RSI line will fail to rise above its prior peak (still above 70). The presence of a double top in the RSI line (above 70) or a pattern of descending RSI peaks while a stock is at a new high is a warning of a possible negative divergence. But there's more.

At that point, the RSI line has two peaks and a trough in between those peaks. If the RSI line then drops below the trough, a *failure swing* has been given. In other words, when the RSI line forms its own double top (above 70) and starts to fall, a potential sell signal is given—even though the stock may still be rising. Many times the sell signal will coincide with an RSI drop back below the 70 line. At a bottom, the situation is reversed. A double bottom in the RSI line (below 30) followed by an upward penetration of the prior peak (or a move back above the 30 line) usually signals a potential buying situation, even if the stock continues to drop. (See Figure 5.5 for an example of a negative divergence.)

There's More Value in the 70 and 30 Lines

The crossings of the 70 and 30 lines should always be watched closely. During a strong uptrend, it's not unusual for an RSI oscillator line to rise above 70 and stay there. That is usually the sign of a strong uptrend. Prices

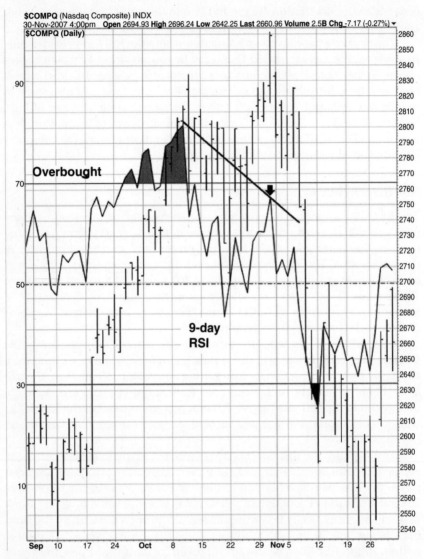

FIGURE 5.5 The nine-day RSI (solid line) shows a negative divergence from the Nasdaq Composite Index during October 2007 (see falling trendline). That divergence warned of a potential rally failure.
Source: StockCharts.com.

may stay above the 70 line for weeks. In such instances, it's probably best to ignore the oscillator for the time being, as long as it stays above 70. A crossing below 70, especially if it happens after a long period of time, often signals a change in trend. Many traders treat a crossing below the 70 line as a sell signal and a crossing above the 30 line as a buy signal (see Figure 5.6).

Crossings of the 50 Line Are Important, Too

Although most of the attention in the RSI oscillator is focused on the 70 and 30 lines, the 50 line is also important. Since it is the *midpoint* value on the RSI line (which ranges from 0 to 100), the 50 line often serves the same function as the zero line in the rate of change oscillator. In that case, buy and sell signals are often given by crossings above and below the midpoint line. You'll notice, for example, that during a correction in an uptrend, the RSI line will often find support at the 50 line before turning back up again. During a downtrend, bounces in the RSI line will halt near the 50 line. Crossings of the 50 line, therefore, do carry some significance and should be monitored. That's especially true on weekly and monthly charts.

Use Weekly and Monthly Charts

We've been talking mainly about daily charts. It's important, however, to monitor the RSI line on weekly charts as well. Daily charts tend to be the most volatile and are geared for short-term timing purposes. Weekly charts carry much more significance and should always be used as a filter on the daily charts. The most potent buy signals, for example, are given when both the daily and weekly lines are turning up from below 30. If the daily RSI line turns up while the weekly RSI line is dropping, the buy signal is much weaker and is probably not very trustworthy. It's preferable to use the weekly chart for *major trend* analysis and the daily chart for *timing* purposes.

Monthly charts are also valuable, but only for very long-term analysis. Once you have asked the computer to show you a 14-day RSI oscillator on a stock chart, for example, a simple keystroke switches you to a 14-week oscillator. Another keystroke switches you to a 14-month oscillator. Short-term traders, utilizing intraday data, can shorten the time span to a 14-minute or 14-hour RSI for day-trading purposes. Although oscillators are generally placed along the bottom of the chart for comparison with the prices located in the upper half of the chart, most charting programs allow you to overlay the RSI line right on top of the price action for easier comparison. Doing that makes divergence analysis a good deal easier (see Figure 5.7).

Let's take a look at another popular oscillator that can be used along with the relative strength index.

FIGURE 5.6 A downward crossing of the 70 line by the nine-day RSI gave a sell signal in Oil Service Holders during September 2007. The RSI crossed back over its 30 line four months later, which generated a new buy signal.
Source: StockCharts.com.

FIGURE 5.7 A 14-month RSI line overlaid on monthly S&P 500 bars helped spot major turning points in 2000, 2002, and 2007 (see arrows).
Source: StockCharts.com.

THE STOCHASTICS OSCILLATOR

This oscillator, popularized by George Lane, has many of the same features as the RSI line. The time span for both indicators is usually 9 or 14. *Stochastics* is also plotted on a scale from 0 to 100. However, its overbought and oversold boundaries are slightly wider than the RSI in the sense that stochastic readings above 80 are overbought and below 20 are oversold. This is because the stochastic oscillator is more volatile than the RSI. The other major difference is that the stochastics oscillator utilizes two lines instead of one. The slower *%D line* is a moving average of the faster *%K line*. It is the presence of two lines instead of one that distinguishes the stochastics from the RSI line and gives the former greater value in the eyes of many traders. That is because precise trading signals on the stochastics oscillator are given *when the two lines cross* and when their value is above 80 or below 20 (see Figure 5.8).

What Does Stochastics Mean?

The American College Dictionary defines *stochastic* as an adjective "based on one item in the probability distribution of an ordered set of observations." The use of the term as a market indicator has a much more specific meaning, which may be a loose adaptation of the true meaning of the word. In the way that we are using it here, *stochastics* refers to the location of a current stock price in relation to its range over a set period of time. The time span most often used is 14 days. The stochastics oscillator determines where the current price is located on a percentage scale from 0 to 100, in relation to its price range over the past 14 days. The formula for stochastics is quite simple:

$$\text{Fast line } (\%K) = 100[(\text{close} - \text{low}_{14})/(\text{high}_{14} - \text{low}_{14})]$$

$$\text{Slow line } (\%D) = \text{3-day average of } \%K$$

where *Close* represents the latest closing price and *high* and *low* are the respective highest and lowest values for the past 14 days. The slower *%D* line is a three-day moving average of the faster *%K* line.

Fast Versus Slow Stochastics

The formula just described is referred to as *fast stochastics*. If plotted on a chart, the two lines will look very jagged. As a result, most traders employ a smoother version of this indicator, referred to as *slow stochastics*. The slow stochastics formula simply takes the slower *%D* line and smooths it

FIGURE 5.8 An upward crossing by the two stochastic lines from oversold territory near 20 gave a buy signal for the StreetTracks Gold ETF in November 2007 (see
circle).
Source: StockCharts.com.

one more time. The result is three lines. Fast stochastics uses the two faster lines while slow stochastics uses the two slower (smoother) lines. It is recommended that you utilize slow stochastics. The default values for slow stochastics are 14, 3, and 3. You'll find the slower stochastic lines much smoother and more reliable.

Stochastic Line Crossings

The interpretation of stochastics is similar to that of the RSI line. Look for overbought and oversold situations (in this case, however, the values are 80 and 20). Then look for potential divergences, as with the RSI. What distinguishes stochastics is the *crossing* of the two lines, which adds a valuable ingredient to this oscillator. Given an oversold condition (below 20), especially where a positive divergence exists, a crossing by the faster %K line above the slower %D line constitutes a buy signal. In an overbought condition (above 80), any crossing by the faster %K line below the slower %D line constitutes a sell signal. Therefore, the stochastics oscillator provides not only a warning of a dangerously extended market, but provides an action signal as well.

What about Running Markets?

As discussed previously, a strong uptrend will often provide stochastic readings that rise above 80 and stay there. In those cases, it's usually best to wait for the stochastic lines to drop below 80 to give a sell signal. There are going to be periods during strong trending markets when this oscillator is not very helpful. That is why some judgment is always involved, and why it's important to use this and all oscillators in conjunction with other indicators. It's foolish to slavishly follow all buy and sell crossings in this indicator without consideration of the overall trend of the market. Which brings us to our final point—the use of longer-range signals.

Weekly Signals Determine Position

Perhaps the greatest weakness in the oscillator approach is the absence of a *trend filter*. Daily stochastics charts fluctuate endlessly from overbought to oversold and back to overbought again. Successive buy and sell signals are given. It's silly to attempt to follow each signal. For example, during an uptrend, buy signals are much more important than sell signals. During a downtrend, sell signals are much more important than buy signals. The overall trend of the market must always be taken into consideration. Why would you want to sell a stock that is in an uptrend or buy a stock in a downtrend? One way to get around this problem is to employ other trend-following techniques, such as the moving average, to determine the direction of the market. Another is to employ a weekly stochastics chart as a trend filter on the daily stochastic chart.

Use the weekly stochastic indicator to determine the trend of the market and which side of that market you will be trading from. As long as the weekly stochastic lines are positive (the faster %*K* line above the slower %*D*), operate only from the buy side. Utilize oversold readings on the daily chart for buying opportunities while ignoring the short-term sell signals. When the weekly stochastics lines are negative (faster line below the slower), ignore buy signals on the daily chart and utilize short-term overbought readings for selling purposes. What you're doing then is buying dips in uptrends and selling rallies in downtrends. (Figures 5.9 and 5.10 show why it's better to combine weekly and daily signals.)

Time Filter Signals

Monthly stochastics charts are also recommended for longer-range analysis and confirmation. At the other extreme, short-term traders often utilize 14-hour charts and 14-minute stochastic charts for day-trading purposes. Whatever time period you are trading (14 hours, 14 days, or 14 weeks), always use the *next longer* time period to determine the direction of the market you will be trading from. If you are trading 14-hour stochastics, use 14 *days* to determine the trend. If you are trading 14-day stochastics, use 14 *weeks* as a trend filter. Why not use the 14-month stochastics as a filter on the 14-week chart as well? (see Figure 5.11).

It's also a good idea to use the same time span on all of your charts. For example, if you use 14 on your dailies, use 14 on your weeklies and monthlies as well.

COMBINE RSI AND STOCHASTICS

It's always best to combine indicators. Each of these oscillators can be used by itself, but their value is enhanced when they are used together. For one thing, the stochastics oscillator (being more volatile) tends to reach overbought and oversold areas much faster than the RSI line. Stochastics also tends to provide many more divergences than the RSI line. As a result, the stochastics signals are earlier, but often less reliable than those given by the relative strength index. I like to keep both oscillators on the bottom of the chart. When the stochastics lines are giving overbought or oversold readings, I generally like to wait for the slower RSI line to confirm the stochastic reading by moving above 70 or below 30. I find that the most

FIGURE 5.9 The daily stochastic lines gave short-term buy signals in the Semiconductor Index during August and November 2007. It's usually better to ignore short-term buy signals when the weekly version of that indicator is pointing down. *Source:* StockCharts.com.

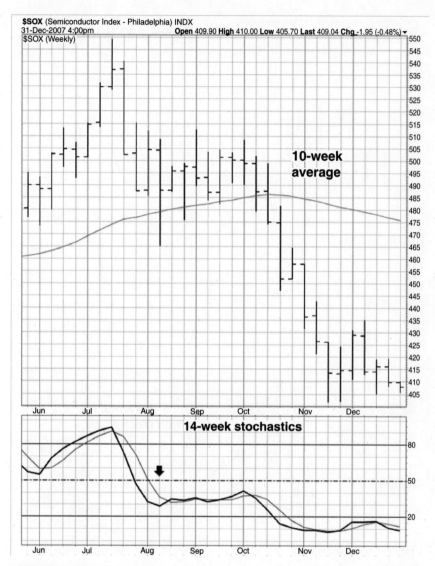

FIGURE 5.10 The weekly stochastic lines for the Semiconductor Index were falling between July and November 2007, which negated any buy signals on the daily chart.
Source: StockCharts.com.

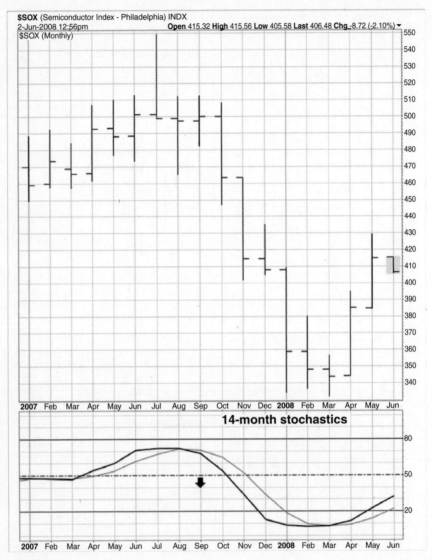

FIGURE 5.11 The monthly stochastic lines for the Semiconductor Index turned down during August 2007 and didn't turn positive until March 2008. Daily and weekly buy signals are suspect while the monthly lines are still falling.
Source: StockCharts.com.

FIGURE 5.12 The daily stochastic lines gave a premature buy signal for the Energy Sector SPDR during November 2007. It wasn't until the RSI and stochastic lines dropped into oversold territory together during January 2008 that a true buy signal was given.

Source: StockCharts.com.

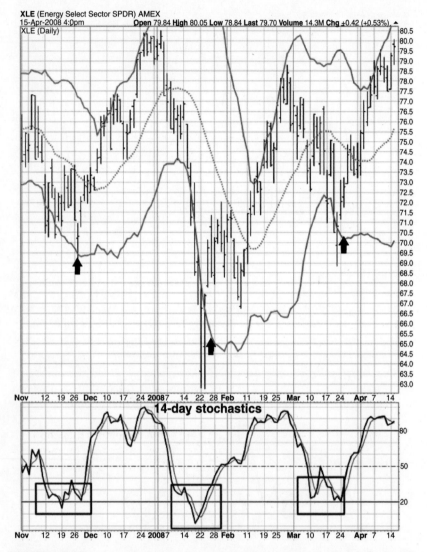

FIGURE 5.13 It's a good idea to combine Bollinger bands with oscillators. This chart shows three stochastic buy signals on the Energy SPDR (see boxes). Each buy signal occurred while the XLE was testing the lower Bollinger band (see arrows). *Source:* StockCharts.com.

reliable signals are given when both oscillators are in overbought or oversold territory simultaneously. Then one can switch to the stochastic lines to generate the actual buy or sell signal with much more confidence (see Figure 5.12).

Combine Other Indicators

The best way to enhance the value of any indicator is to combine it with other indicators. Signals on oscillators take on greater meaning if prices are also touching one of the Bollinger bands. Another possibility is to combine oscillators with moving averages. Why not use a 40-week moving average to determine whether you wish to emphasize buy or sell signals on the oscillator charts? The possibilities are endless. Use your computer power to combine indicators for better results (see Figure 5.13).

SUMMARY

Charting programs offer many types of oscillators to help determine market extremes and potential turning points. The most basic are *momentum* and *rate of change* indicators. The two most popular, and probably most valuable, are the *relative strength index* and *stochastics*. This type of indicator is most useful during choppy market periods and when a trend is nearing completion. They are much less valuable in the middle of a strong trend. Therefore, oscillators should not be overused and should be deemphasized during strong trending markets. For example, a moving average is more helpful during a strong trend. There are some indicators that combine the trend-following properties of a moving average system with the overbought/oversold properties of an oscillator. The next chapter discusses one of the better ones.

CHAPTER 6

How to Have the Best of Both Worlds

T he most critical problem facing the visual investor is knowing when to emphasize each class of indicator. During a strong trending period, moving averages will outperform most other indicators. During choppy market periods, when prices swing back and forth in an essentially trendless manner, oscillators are much better than moving averages. Fortunately, there is one indicator that combines the best of both worlds in the sense that it is both a trend-following system and an oscillator. It employs moving averages to generate trend-following signals, but also helps to determine when a trend is overbought or oversold. It is also helpful in spotting divergences, one of the greatest strengths of an oscillator. After showing you how to use it, we'll show you an even better way to use it. We're speaking of the *moving average convergence divergence* (MACD) indicator.

MACD CONSTRUCTION

This indicator, developed by Gerald Appel, utilizes three moving averages in its construction although only two lines are shown on the chart. The first line (called the *MACD line)* is the difference between two *exponentially smoothed* moving averages of the price (usually 12 and 26 periods). The computer subtracts the longer average (26) from the shorter (12) to obtain the MACD line. A moving average (usually nine periods) is then used to smooth the MACD line to form a second (signal) line. The result is that two lines are shown on the chart, the faster MACD line and the slower *signal line* (see Figure 6.1). Some analysts prefer to use the preceding

FIGURE 6.1 Example of a daily MACD buy signal (up arrow) for the Dow Industrials in August 2007 and an MACD sell two months later during October (down arrow). *Source:* StockCharts.com.

moving average values for buy signals and another set of values for sell signals, as Appel originally recommended. The problem with doing that is that you need to construct two different MACD indicators with two different sets of numbers. Perhaps for this reason, or for purposes of simplicity, most analysts seem content to employ the previously mentioned default values (9, 12, and 26) in all situations. By doing it that way, the same moving average values can be used for buy and sell signals on all markets, as well as on daily, weekly, and monthly charts.

MACD AS TREND-FOLLOWING INDICATOR

Interpretation of the two lines in the MACD system is relatively straightforward and is similar to the *crossover* technique described in the discussion of moving averages in Chapter 4. In other words, buy signals are registered when the faster MACD line crosses *above* the slower signal line. Sell signals occur when the faster line crosses *below* the slower. By using it in that fashion, valuable trading signals are given that will keep you on the right side of a trend (i.e., on the *long* side during uptrends, and on the *short* side or out of the market during downtrends). Naturally, signals given on daily charts are more frequent and of shorter duration than those given on weekly charts. That is why it is best to place more reliance on the MACD crossover signals given on weekly charts, and to utilize the daily charts for timing purposes or for shorter-term trading signals (see Figure 6.2).

MACD AS AN OSCILLATOR

Being able to use this same indicator to determine overbought and oversold conditions gives it a particularly unique quality. This is possible because the MACD and signal lines fluctuate above and below a zero line, just like the rate of change oscillator described in Chapter 5. The best buy signals are given when the two lines are below the zero line (oversold) and the best sell signals when the two lines are above the zero line (overbought). Some analysts use crossings above and below the zero line as an additional way to find buy and sell signals. A bullish crossing of the MACD lines that takes place below the zero line, for example, would be confirmed when both lines cross above the zero line themselves.

Studying the MACD system, you will observe that when the lines rise too far above the zero line, a potential *overbought* signal is given. Conversely, when the lines drop too far below the zero line, a possible *oversold* condition is signaled. Unfortunately, the MACD lines have no predetermined overbought and oversold levels as exist with the relative strength

FIGURE 6.2 An MACD weekly sell signal on the Nasdaq 100 Power Shares at the start of November 2007 (down arrow) lasted five months until the following April. Weekly MACD signals last longer than daily signals and are more important for trend trading.
Source: StockCharts.com.

index (70 and 30) or stochastics (80 and 20). It is up to the user to compare where the MACD lines are presently located to their extreme upper and lower boundaries in the past. In this way, the MACD system can be used much the same as an oscillator to determine when markets have risen or fallen too far. But there's another way in which this indicator resembles an oscillator.

MACD DIVERGENCES

The previous chapter discussed how to spot divergences on oscillator charts. This can also be done with the MACD system. You will notice that after the MACD lines have risen far enough above the zero line, they will begin to diverge from the price action. In other words, prices will continue to advance while the MACD lines form a double top or a series of declining peaks. This is an early warning that the uptrend is losing momentum. A sell signal given when the MACD lines are stretched too far above the zero line and after a negative divergence has been formed is usually worth paying attention to (see Figure 6.3). The situation is reversed at bottoms. A double bottom in the MACD lines while they are too far below the zero line warns that prices may be nearing a trough. This potentially bullish warning is confirmed by a bullish crossing of the two lines from that oversold placement. Here again, weekly signals carry much more weight than daily signals (see Figure 6.4).

HOW TO BLEND DAILY AND WEEKLY SIGNALS

Signals given on weekly charts always carry more trend significance than those given on daily charts. It also follows that signals on weekly charts are less important than those on monthly charts, while signals on daily charts carry more significance than those on hourly charts. The universal guiding price in all market analysis is that a longer-range chart is always more significant than a shorter-time chart. Our primary concern here is how to blend weekly and daily signals. Let's say that your computer flashes a bullish crossing of the MACD lines from below the zero line on a daily chart. Do you jump in and buy the stock in question? Not necessarily.

You should always check to see what the weekly indicator looks like. If that is also in an oversold condition (or already in a bullish alignment), then the buy signal on the daily chart may provide a good entry point. If the weekly chart is too far above the zero line (or in a bearish alignment), then it's probably best to ignore the buy signal on the daily chart. It's generally best to start with the weekly chart to determine major buying and selling

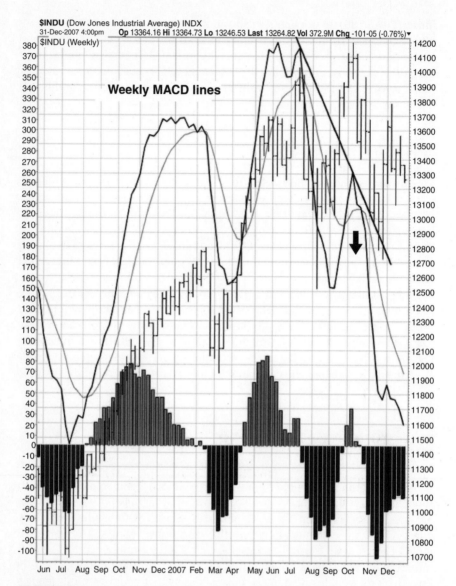

FIGURE 6.3 The weekly MACD lines show a negative divergence (falling trendline) during October 2007 as the Dow Industrials temporarily hit a new record high. A weekly MACD sell signal after a negative divergence is more bearish.
Source: StockCharts.com.

FIGURE 6.4 Example of a bullish MACD divergence. The daily MACD lines formed a higher bottom in January 2007 as the price of crude oil hit a new low (see arrow). An MACD buy signal after a positive divergence is a much stronger signal.
Source: StockCharts.com.

zones. The daily chart can be used for earlier trend warnings and to fine-tune entry and exit points.

HOW TO MAKE MACD EVEN BETTER—THE HISTOGRAM

As good as the MACD indicator is in the form just described, there's a way to make it even better. That technique is called the *MACD histogram*. The MACD histogram provides even earlier warnings of potential trend changes and greatly enhances the value of the indicator. Since the histogram shows the MACD crossover signals (in a slightly different way), nothing is lost in its use. What is gained is a way to generate action signals much sooner. The histogram simply plots the *difference* between the MACD line and the signal line. It's called a *histogram* because vertical bars are used to show the difference between the two lines (see Figure 6.5).

The MACD histogram fluctuates above and below a zero line of its own. When the histogram value is above the zero line, it simply means that the two MACD lines are in bullish alignment (MACD over signal line). As long as the histogram value is above its zero line, the MACD signals are still bullish. When the faster MACD line crosses below the slower signal line (registering a sell signal), the histogram value falls below its zero line as well. Crossings above and below the zero line by the histogram always coincide with bullish and bearish crossings by the two MACD lines themselves. As stated earlier, this is just another way of viewing the same system. Here's where the advantage of the histogram comes in.

If the histogram is above its zero line (bullish), but begins to drop toward the zero line, that tells us that the positive relationship (or spread) between the two MACD lines, although still positive, is beginning to weaken. Remember that the histogram measures the *difference* between the two MACD lines. The plus or minus value of the histogram (above or below its zero line) tells us if the MACD lines are bullish or bearish. The *direction* of the histogram tells us whether that bullish or bearish relationship is gaining or losing momentum.

Let's take a market in a downtrend. The histogram is below zero, which means that the MACD line is below its signal line. In other words, the stock is in a downtrend. For a while, the histogram is also dropping. Suddenly, the histogram lines start to rise toward the zero line. This tells us that although the MACD system is still negative (no buy signal yet), the downtrend is losing momentum. Many traders will cover short positions in this instance. An actual buy signal to initiate a long position doesn't take place until the histogram moves above its zero line. The pattern is just the opposite in an uptrend.

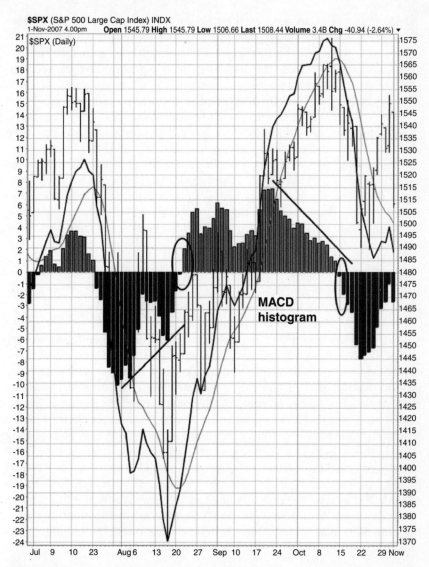

FIGURE 6.5 During August 2007, the S&P 500 histogram bars bottomed three weeks before the actual MACD buy signal (first circle). The histogram bars peaked in September a month before the actual MACD sell signal in October (second circle). *Source:* StockCharts.com.

During an uptrend, a positive histogram reflects a bullish MACD alignment. For a while, the histogram will be above its zero line and rising. At some point, however, the histogram will begin dropping toward its zero line. Traders will often use the decline in the histogram as an early signal to begin taking some profits in the rising stock. No actual sell signal is given, however, unless and until the histogram actually drops below the zero line.

The signals can be applied to the both weekly and daily charts, although the latter has less reliability. Weekly charts are preferable. But, here again, it's important to blend the two. The first buy and sell signals are always given on the daily chart, since it's the more sensitive. Check to see what the weekly chart is doing. If the daily MACD histogram is giving a buy signal while the weekly MACD histogram is beginning to rise toward its zero line (or already above it), the daily buy signal is probably a good one. It's always good to have the daily and weekly charts agree with each other (see Figure 6.6).

BE SURE TO WATCH MONTHLY SIGNALS

Most of your work with MACD lines will probably involve daily and weekly charts. Weekly signals determine trend direction, while daily signals provide short-term entry and exit points. Make sure, however, that both point in the same direction, Don't forget to watch the monthly MACD lines as well. Although monthly signals are infrequent, they are the most important of all. Figure 6.7 overlays monthly MACD lines on the S&P 500 from the start of 2000 to early 2008. Only three monthly MACD crossings took place in those eight years. The two lines turned down at the start of 2000 and stayed down through the ensuing three-year bear market. They turned bullish in the spring of 2003 and stayed bullish until the end of 2007. In December of that year, the monthly lines turned negative for the first time in nearly five years. Fortunately, you don't have to consult the monthly MACD lines often because monthly signals don't change direction that much. But make sure you know which way they're pointing.

HOW TO KNOW WHICH INDICATORS TO USE

There is one more critical problem that still hasn't been resolved. How do you know when to employ a trend-following indicator (such as a moving average) or an overbought/oversold oscillator such as stochastics? Moving

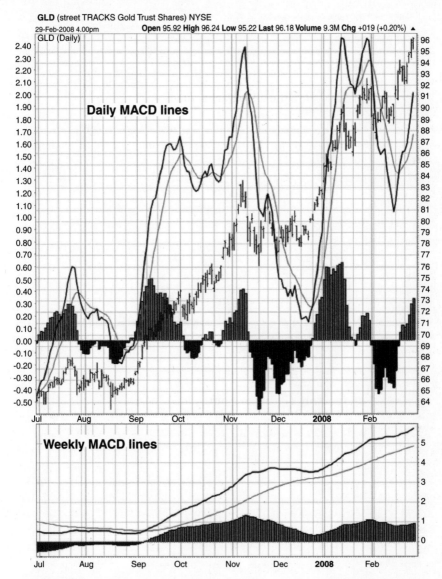

FIGURE 6.6 The daily MACD lines turned negative for gold during the last two months of 2007. The weekly lines, however, stayed positive throughout that downside correction. Longer-term investors should focus more on the weekly MACD lines. *Source:* StockCharts.com.

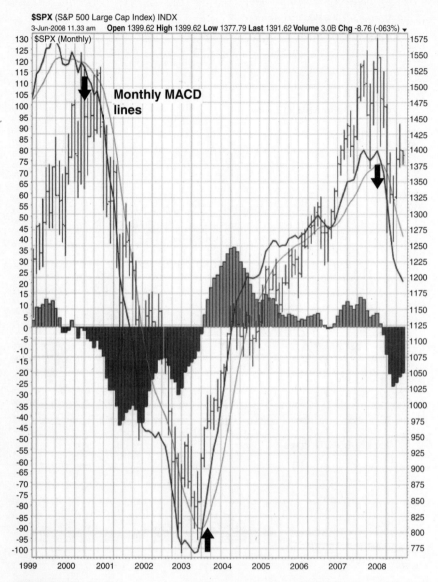

FIGURE 6.7 Only three monthly MACD signals have taken place since 2000 for the S&P 500 (see arrows). They include a sell signal in 2000, a buy in 2003, and a sell at the end of 2007. Monthly MACD signals are excellent for spotting major turning points.
Source: StockCharts.com.

averages are your friend during a trend, but can be cruel to your bottom line during a trading range environment.

Oscillators work especially well in choppy market environments and at important turning points when a trend is losing momentum. During a strong trend in the stock market oscillators can be more harmful than helpful. Fortunately, there is an indicator that can help resolve this dilemma.

THE AVERAGE DIRECTIONAL MOVEMENT (ADX) LINE

This line is part of a more complex trading system, also developed by Welles Wilder, called *directional movement*. We're only introducing this trading system here to alert you to how it might help solve the previously mentioned problem. Appendix A explains where you can find a more in-depth explanation of the entire system. The idea behind directional movement is to determine whether a market is in a *trending* or *nontrending* mode.

First, two lines that measure buying and selling pressure are generated. They are called +*DI* (positive directional indicator) and −*DI* (negative directional indicator). A bullish environment exists when the +*DI* line is greater than the −*DI* line. From these two lines, a third line is generated called the *average directional movement* (ADX) line. The ADX line is basically derived from the difference between the +*DI* and −*DI* lines.

A rising ADX line tells us that a market is in a trending mode. A falling or flat ADX line reflects a trading range environment. An ADX line fluctuates from below 20 to above 40. An ADX line which has fallen below 20 implies low volatility and the absence of any trend (favoring a nontrending approach). An ADX line that suddenly rises above 20 often signals the beginning of an important trend (and the application of trend-following techniques). An ADX that has risen too far above 40 and starts to drop usually signals that the trend has exhausted itself and that it may be time to switch from a trend-following system back to one which emphasizes a more volatile market environment.

Try using the average directional movement line as an overall filter to help determine which type of indicator is most suitable in the current market environment. A rising ADX line favors moving averages; a falling ADX line favors oscillators. The ADX line can be used on daily and weekly charts, although weekly signals are more significant (see Figure 6.8).

FIGURE 6.8 The downturn in the weekly ADX line in May 2006 (first line) signaled the start of a sideways consolidation in gold that lasted for more than a year. The ADX upturn during September 2007 (second line) signaled the start of a new upleg. *Source:* StockCharts.com.

SUMMARY

The moving average convergence divergence—MACD—indicator combines the best features of a moving average crossover system with the ability to determine overbought and oversold conditions such as an oscillator. Employing a histogram greatly enhances the value of the MACD lines by enabling the trader to anticipate signals even before they happen. Although these signals can be used on daily and weekly charts, the latter are considered to be more important. As in the case of other computerized indicators, it is suggested that you begin with the default values of 12, 26, and 9. As you gain more experience with this and other indicators, you can begin experimenting with other numbers. The average directional movement—ADX—line can be helpful in determining which set of indicators to employ at a given time—trend-following (moving averages) or countertrend (oscillators). It's generally a good idea to combine various indicators to enhance their value. Combine MACD lines with RSI and stochastics, for example. Be creative. No indicator is perfect. Combining some of the better ones and ensuring that they agree with one another will greatly improve your chances for success.

Linkage

CHAPTER 7

Market Linkage

The visual—or charting—approach to investing has traditionally emphasized a single-market approach. A stock trader, for example, would study the price charts of the stock market or individual common stocks with little consideration of outside market influences. It was considered sufficient to study the price charts of the market in question along with its own set of internal indicators. The same attitude was true of traders in other asset classes. Bond traders studied bond charts, while commodity traders charted the commodity markets. Currency traders limited their chart work to the currencies they were trading. That is no longer the case. Chart analysis has taken a major evolutionary step over the last decade by emphasizing a more universal intermarket approach. I like to think that my book, *Intermarket Technical Analysis* (John Wiley & Sons, 1991) and its subsequent edition *Intermarket Analysis: Profiting From Global Market Relationships* (John Wiley & Sons, 2004) helped move things in that direction.

Some understanding of how the different asset classes interact with each other is important for at least two reasons. First, such an understanding helps you appreciate how other financial markets influence whichever market you're interested in. For example, it's very useful to know how bonds and stocks interact. If you're trading stocks, you should be watching bonds (for reasons that will be explained later). If you're a bond trader, you should be monitoring the direction of stocks. Very often, chart action in one market will give you a clue about another. For example, a jump in bond prices is often associated with a drop in stock prices. In another illustration of how one market impacts on another, a falling U.S. dollar is usually associated with rising commodities. And, as you'll see later in the chapter, the direction of the dollar also helps determine the relative attractiveness of foreign stocks compared to those in the United States.

A second reason why it's important to undertand intermarket relationships is to help with the asset allocation process. There was a time when investors' choices were limited to bonds, stocks, or cash. Asset allocation models were based on that limited philosophy. Over the last decade, however, investment choices have broadened considerably. Since 2002, commodities have become the strongest asset class of all and are now being recognized by Wall Street and the investing public as a viable alternative to bonds and stocks. This is especially true when bond and stock gains appear limited. The growing availability of *exchange-traded funds* (ETFs) has made investing in commodity markets as easy as buying a stock on a stock exchange. The same is true for currency markets. Up until recently, currency trading was limited to professional interbank traders and futures specialists. This is no longer the case. A new family of mutual funds and exchange-traded funds has put currency trading within easy reach of the average investor. Why is that to your benefit? From the start of 2002 to the start of 2008, the U.S. dollar fell 35 percent to a record low. At the same time, the euro and Canadian dollar gained 70 percent and 61 percent respectively. During those same six years, commodity markets rose 110 percent. By comparison, U.S. stocks rose 15 percent and Treasury bonds 12 percent. Which of those four asset classes would you have preferred to be in?

THE ASSET ALLOCATION PROCESS

My main purpose here is to show you how the major financial markets interact with each other and how you can use that information in the asset allocation process. Let's start with one of the best-known intermarket principles: the inverse relationship between the U.S. dollar and commodity markets. Figure 7.1 compares the two markets over a decade. What should jump out at you is the simple reality that both markets usually trend in opposite directions. The U.S. Dollar Index (which measures the dollar against six foreign currencies) started dropping sharply at the start of 2002 and continued dropping for the following six years. By the start of 2008, the U.S. dollar had fallen to the lowest level in its history. At the same time that the dollar started dropping in 2002, the Reuters/Jefferies CRB Index (which is a basket of 19 commodity markets) started a six-year ascent that took it to an all-time high in early 2008. One of the reasons for their inverse relationship is that commodities are priced in dollars. As a result, a falling dollar makes them more expensive. Another reason is that a falling dollar is

FIGURE 7.1 The major uptrend in commodities started in 2002 as the U.S. Dollar Index began a major decline. Commodity prices and the dollar trend in opposite directions.
Source: StockCharts.com.

inflationary, which is usually manifested in rising commodity prices. Gold, for example, is considered to be a leading indicator of inflation. The visual investor with some knowledge of how the two markets interact with each other (and some knowledge of charting) could have spotted the important trend changes in those two markets and acted accordingly. Fortunately, there are several trading vehicles (which we'll discuss in succeeding chapters) to help you do that.

THE RELATIVE STRENGTH RATIO

Before I can show you how to spot significant shifts from one asset class to another, it's necessary to introduce a technical tool that is indispensable for that purpose, the *relative strength* (RS) line. It's usually plotted at the bottom of stock charts in newspapers and charting services. The line is derived by dividing the price of an individual stock (or a market sector) by the S&P 500. When the RS line is rising, the stock (or sector) is outperforming the market. When the RS line is falling, the stock (or sector) is doing worse than the market. It's generally better to buy stocks (or sectors) with rising RS lines and avoid those with falling RS lines. In other words, the relative strength line is a simple ratio of any two markets (charting services make it very easy to plot a ratio). In fact, I generally use the term *relative strength ratio* in my market reports. In my view, the relative strength ratio is the single most valuable tool in the asset allocation process. In a later chapter, you'll also see its value in implementing sector rotation strategies.[*]

2002 SHIFT FROM PAPER TO HARD ASSETS

The relative strength ratio can be used to compare different asset classes. Figure 7.2 divides the CRB Index of commodity prices by the S&P 500 (the usual benchmark for the U.S. market) over nearly three decades. In the 20 years between 1980 and 2000, the falling commodity/stock ratio meant that stocks were the preferred asset class. That started to change in 2000, however, but didn't become clear until 2002. During 2002, the CRB/S&P ratio broke a down trendline that had lasted for two decades. (Figure 7.2 uses a log scale which is more suitable for long-term analysis). The upside break of that major trendline in the ratio during 2002 signaled a generational shift out of stocks (paper assets) and into commodity markets (hard assets). By early 2008, the commodity/stock ratio had risen to a five-year high. In the

---

[*]The relative strength (RS) line is not to be confused with the Relative Strength Index (RSI) covered in Chapter 5.

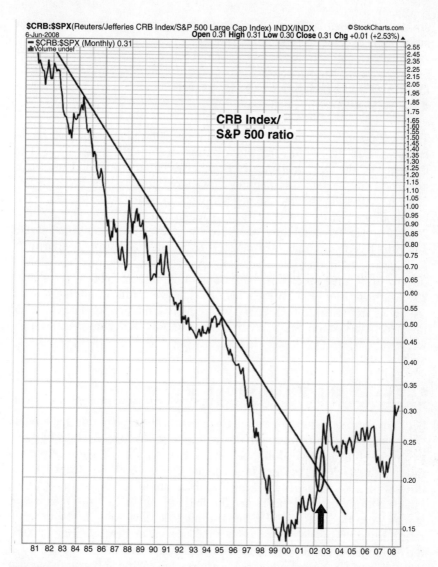

FIGURE 7.2 A ratio of the CRB Index divided by the S&P 500 turned up in 2002, which ended a 20-year period of stock market dominance. Since 2002, hard assets (commodities) have done much better than paper assets (bonds and stocks). *Source:* StockCharts.com.

six years between 2002 and 2008, gains in commodity markets outpaced stock gains by a factor of seven to one.

COMMODITY/BOND RATIO ALSO TURNED UP

The major shift to commodities starting in 2002 didn't come just at the expense of stocks. Figure 7.3 plots a ratio of the CRB Index divided by the price of the 30-year Treasury Bond. The commodity/bond ratio also bottomed during 2002 after declining for more than 20 years. From 1980 to 2000, paper assets (bonds and stocks) were in major bull markets, while commodities (hard assets) were in a major decline. Between 2000 and 2002, however, the pendulum started to swing away from bonds and stocks and back to commodities. During 2000, stocks started dropping sharply in anticipation of a possible recession. As a result, commodities started turning up against stocks in 2000. Bonds rallied from 2000 to the end of 2002 as stock prices fell. By the end of 2002, however, the bond rally started to stall as stocks bottomed. That's when the commodity/bond ratio turned up in decisive fashion. Six years after the 2002 bottom in commodities, they were still the strongest asset class.

TURNS IN THE BOND/STOCK RATIO

Let's now turn our attention to the relationship between bonds and stocks. Once again, the relative strength ratio is the best way to spot which of those two competing assets is doing better at any given time. Figure 7.4 plots a ratio of the 30-year Treasury bond divided by the S&P 500 from 1990 to the start of 2008. The arrows show important shifts in their relative performance. During most of the 1990s, the falling bond/stock ratio meant that stocks were the better performer. During 2000, however, the bond/stock ratio turned up (as stocks entered a major bear market). During 2000 to the end of 2002, bond prices rose as stocks fell. When stocks turned up in the spring of 2003, the bond/stock ratio started falling and swung back in favor of stocks. During an economic slowdown or recession (as occurred in 2001), bond prices usually do better than stocks as the Fed lowers short-term rates to stabilize the economy. Bond yields usually drop as well. That makes Treasuries a safe haven in a slowing economy and a falling stock market. (Bond prices rise as yields fall). When the stock market turns back up (as in 2003), investors switch out of bonds and back into stocks. Fortunately, those major turning points are easily spotted on relative strength ratios, and give investors a guide as to which of the two asset classes to overweight at any given time.

FIGURE 7.3 A ratio of the CRB Index divided by Treasury bond prices also turned up in 2002. The break of the trendline signaled a major shift from bonds to commodities.
Source: StockCharts.com.

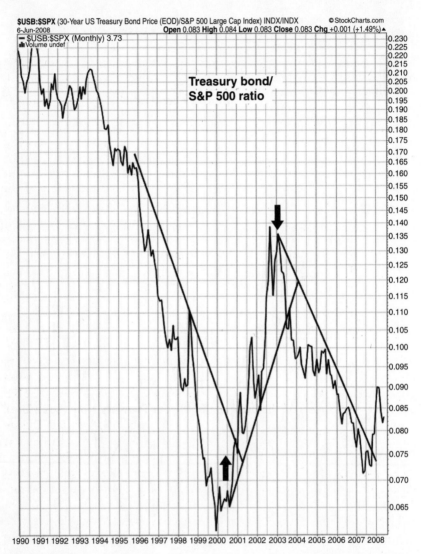

$USB:$SPX (30-Year US Treasury Bond Price (EOD)/S&P 500 Large Cap Index) INDX/INDX   © StockCharts.com
6-Jun-2008   Open 0.083 High 0.084 Low 0.083 Close 0.083 Chg +0.001 (+1.49%)▲

— $USB:$SPX (Monthly) 3.73
▲ Volume undef

Treasury bond/
S&P 500 ratio

1990 1991 1992 1993 1994 1995 1996 1997 1998 1999 2000 2001 2002 2003 2004 2005 2006 2007 2008

FIGURE 7.4 A ratio of Treasury bond prices divided by the S&P 500 is an excellent way to determine which of the two assets is showing the stronger performance. *Source:* StockCharts.com.

2007 RATIO SHIFTS BACK TO BONDS

Figure 7.5 shows the bond/stock ratio since 2000 more clearly. In this case, however, I've used the price of the 10-year Treasury note price as the numerator in the ratio. Figure 7.5 shows the bond/stock ratio favoring bonds from 2000 through 2002 and stocks between 2003 and 2007. In mid-2007, however, the ratio swung back in favor of bonds. During that summer, subprime mortgage problems first surfaced in the mortgage and banking sectors (together with a sharp slowdown in the housing industry) which threatened to undermine the U.S. economy and end the four-year bull market in stocks. That prompted the Fed to start lowering short-term interest rates during the second half of 2007 to stabilize the economy and the stock market. As usually happens in times of financial stress, money rotated out of stocks and into the relative safety of Treasuries. Fortunately, the upturn in the bond/stock ratio that started in the summer of 2007 was pretty easy to spot on the ratio chart.

BONDS RISE AS STOCKS FALL

I mentioned earlier in the chapter that one market usually rises when another falls. Figure 7.6 shows that negative interaction occurring between bond and stock prices during 2007. Figure 7.6 overlays the price of the S&P 500 (daily price bars) on the price of the 10-year Treasury Note (solid line). During the first half of 2007, stock prices rose as bond prices fell. During July, however, the stock market fell as subprime fears started to surface. Bond prices turned up immediately. A second stock drop during October gave the bond uptrend another boost. When one market (like stocks) drops, another one (like bonds) rises. The trick is to move out of the one turning down and into the one moving up. But you have to be able to spot the turn first. You can do that by using the visual tools available to you, along with some understanding of the intermarket principles that make that rotation happen.

FALLING U.S. RATES HURT THE DOLLAR

Let's widen the intermarket net a bit wider during 2007 to explain the ripple effect that took place between short-term interest rates and the U.S. dollar. One of the reasons that bond prices started to rise in summer 2007 was that long-term yields were dropping (bond prices and yields trend in

FIGURE 7.5 A ratio of Treasury notes divided by the S&P 500 shows three major turning points in relative performance between those two assets since 2000. *Source:* StockCharts.com.

FIGURE 7.6 An example of bond and stock prices trending in opposite directions during 2007. Bond prices (solid line) turned up during July 2007 just as stocks were peaking.
Source: StockCharts.com.

opposite directions). One of the reasons bond yields were dropping was the Fed's lowering of short-term rates to combat a weakening economy (and a falling stock market). When the Fed lowers short-term rates aggressively (and foreign central bankers don't), one usual side effect is a weaker U.S. dollar. Figure 7.7 shows a close correlation during 2007 between the two-year T-note yield (solid line) and the price of the U.S. Dollar Index (daily price bars). Both started to fall together during July and continued to drop into first quarter 2008 (pushing the U.S. currency to a record low). So here's another intermarket relationship to consider. Whenever the Fed lowers short-term rates to combat a possible recession, the U.S. dollar usually suffers as a result. How does an investor capitalize on that knowledge? One way is to invest in a commodity market that usually rises when the dollar falls. The commodity that does that most often is gold.

FALLING DOLLAR PUSHES GOLD TO RECORD HIGH

While it's true that a falling U.S. dollar benefits most commodity markets, the one that's most closely linked to the greenback is gold. Part of the reason is that traders often view gold as an alternate currency. Figure 7.8 compares the price of bullion (solid line) to the U.S. Dollar Index (daily bars) throughout 2007 and into early 2008. The two markets are almost a perfect mirror image of one another. The two arrows in the middle of the chart show that bullion started climbing sharply during August 2007 just as the dollar started dropping. Both moves were the direct result of the Fed's lowering of short-term rates. By first quarter 2008, the dollar was trading at a record low and bullion at a record high. Why buy gold instead of a foreign currency? Both rise when the dollar is falling. The reason is because gold usually rises faster than the world's currencies during a bull market in bullion. Prior to 2002, the last time that happened was during the 1970s. In the six years following the 2002 peak in the dollar, and a corresponding bottom in gold, the dollar lost 36 percent. At the same time, the world's three strongest currencies gained 81 percent (Australian dollar), 70 percent (euro), and 60 percent (Canadian dollar). By contrast, the price of gold rose 246 percent. (Crude oil was an even better bet with a six-year gain of 401 percent). Another reason for favoring commodity investments is that investors have easy access to stocks tied to commodities. Gold and energy shares were pretty good bets in the years after 2002. So let's widen the intermarket net even further to consider stocks tied to commodity markets.

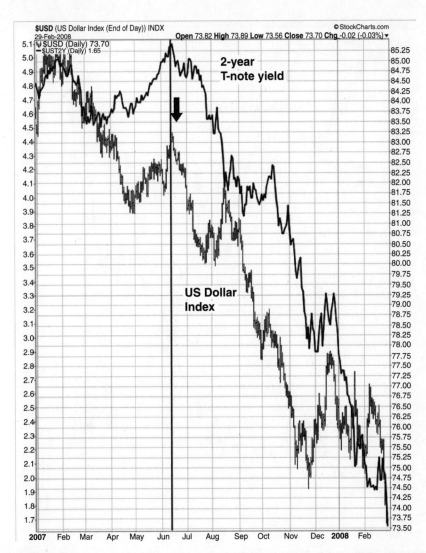

FIGURE 7.7 The U.S. dollar fell along with U.S. interest rates starting in June 2007. Both were a reaction to subprime mortgage problems and expectations for a weakening economy. That had a positive impact on bond prices and commodities. *Source:* StockCharts.com.

FIGURE 7.8 Gold prices turned up during summer 2007 as the U.S. Dollar Index dropped. Gold is one of the biggest beneficiaries of a falling dollar.
Source: StockCharts.com.

COMMODITY-RELATED STOCKS

Although I'm going to deal with the matter of choosing the right market sectors and industry groups in a later chapter, this is a good spot to introduce the idea that many stocks are tied to the fortunes of commodity markets. That offers another way to participate in an uptrend in commodity markets. Entering 2008, the five-year performance record for stock sector mutual funds showed gold-oriented funds in first place with a cumulative gain of 30.5 percent. A close second was natural resource funds (which are mainly energy stocks) with a gain of 30.3 percent. Those gains were three times larger than any other sector funds. When commodities are the strongest asset class, it makes sense that stocks tied to those commodities will be stock market leaders. This is another reason to keep an eye on the direction of commodity markets

Figure 7.9 compares the price of crude oil (bars) to a relative strength ratio of the Energy Sector SPDR (XLE) divided by the S&P 500 since 2002. Notice the tight correlation between the two lines. In mid-2004, crude oil rose above $40 (left scale) to hit a record high. Within four years, it had reached $140 a barrel. During those four years of rising energy prices, Energy stocks as a group gained 181 percent. That made them the market's strongest sector by a wide margin. To give you an idea of how much of a margin, the next three top sectors were Utilities (+79 percent), Basic Materials (+61 percent), and Industrials (+40 percent). Energy stocks rallied nine times more than the S&P 500 during those four years. We'll cover sector trends in more in-depth in a later chapter. My intention here is simply to show that the direction of commodities and currencies give clues as to which parts of the stock market to overweight at any given time.

FOREIGN STOCKS ARE LINKED TO THE DOLLAR

Let's widen the net even further to include foreign stocks. Another reason to keep an eye on the trend of the U.S. dollar is because its direction helps determine when foreign stocks are more or less attractive than U.S. stocks. Figure 7.10 helps make that point. The falling bars show the major descent in the U.S. dollar starting in 2002. The rising solid line is a ratio of the Morgan Stanley World Stock Index (ex-USA) divided by the S&P 500. The ratio shows how foreign developed stock markets have done "relative" to the U.S. stock market. It also shows that foreign stocks did much better than U.S. stocks since 2002 when the dollar started dropping.

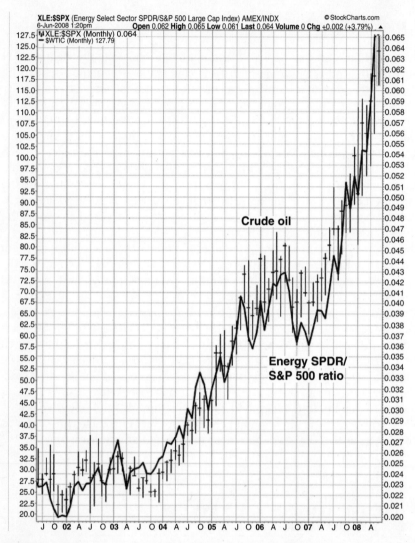

FIGURE 7.9 The relatively strong performance of energy shares (solid line) was closely tied to rising crude oil prices (price bars). Commodity-related stocks have done especially well during the major uptrend in commodity markets.
Source: StockCharts.com.

FIGURE 7.10 A falling dollar since 2002 has helped foreign stocks outperform the U.S. market. A falling dollar favors foreign investments for U.S. investors. *Source:* StockCharts.com.

At their respective peaks in fourth quarter 2007, foreign stocks doubled the performance of the S&P 500 (+160 percent versus +80 percent) from their 2003 bottom. That shows that U.S. investors need to take currency trends into consideration when planning global investments. One of the reasons for the stronger performance of foreign stocks from 2003 to 2007 is that foreign stocks are quoted in their local currencies. When they're quoted in terms of a weaker U.S. currency, foreign gains are even bigger for U.S. investors. Conversely, weaker foreign currencies (a stronger dollar) hurt U.S. foreign investments. The general rule of thumb is this: A falling dollar favors foreign investments, while a stronger dollar favors U.S. investments.

COMMODITY EXPORTERS GET BIGGER BOOST

Not all foreign markets rise equally. Not only does a falling dollar favor foreign stocks, but it also favors those countries' stocks that are commodity exporters. That's because they get a double boost from a falling dollar and rising commodities (which is a side effect of a falling dollar). In the five years from 2003 through 2007 as commodity prices were rising, the top overseas stock fund was Latin America (+51 percent). Emerging markets (of which Latin America is a big part) came in second at +34 percent. The main reason for the strong global performance in Latin America was the fact that it was a big exporter of commodities at a time when commodities were red hot. Brazil's gains, for example, were largely tied to the rising fortunes of oil, metals, and steel. (Most of the foreign demand for those commodities came from China.) Figure 7.11 compares Brazil's six-year performance to rising commodity prices (see Figure 7.11). The rising price bars show the CRB Index of commodity prices. The solid line is a ratio of the Brazilian Bovespa Stock Index divided by the Dow Jones World Stock Index. The close correlation between the two lines is obvious. Canada and Russia also benefit from rising commodity markets. During the early months of 2008, global stock prices fell while commodities rose. The only three markets that gained were Brazil, Canada, and Russia.

GLOBAL DECOUPLING IS A MYTH

Most of the major global stock markets are pretty closely correlated. In other words, major bull and bear markets are usually global in scope. Currency and commodity trends may help determine which ones do better

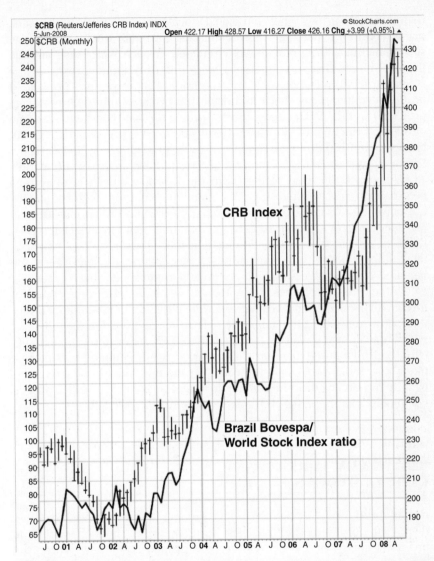

FIGURE 7.11 Rising commodity prices helped make the Brazil stock market one of the strongest in the world. Commodity exporters do well during a commodity uptrend. They do worse in a commodity downturn.
Source: StockCharts.com.

than others at various times, but global stocks generally trend in the same major direction. When the U.S. stock market started to weaken during the second half of 2007, a new theory circulated through Wall Street and the financial media that foreign stocks were relatively immune from a U.S. stock market drop and possible U.S. recession. That theory was predicated on the mistaken belief that U.S. housing and related subprime mortgage problems were U.S. and not a foreign problem. That theory violated one of the key principles of intermarket analysis which is based on tight global linkages. And it didn't take long for it to be proven wrong. Between the fourth quarter of 2007 and the first quarter of 2008, many of the world's stock markets fell even further than the U.S. market. Little more was heard about *global decoupling*. That simultaneous drop in global stocks, however, raises some caveats on foreign investing. Foreign markets can provide excellent diversification in a global "bull" market, especially when the U.S. currency is weak. During a global "bear" market, however, most stock markets will eventually start to decline. At such times, the benefits of global diversification are greatly diminished. That's especially true if the U.S. dollar starts to strengthen, which diminishes the appeal of foreign investments for U.S. investors. The direction of commodity prices does, however, have some influence over which markets fall the most and which hold up better. During the first half of 2008, for example, commodity exporters did better than other global markets while commodity importers like China, India, and Japan did worse. By the third quarter of 2008, however, a 25 percent drop in commodities and a rise in the dollar pushed commodity exporters like Brazil and Russia into major declines.

RISING YEN THREATENS GLOBAL STOCKS

During spring 2007, I worked on a video product to educate investors about the benefits of intermarket analysis. To dramatically show how action in one asset class could effect another, I explained how the Japanese yen could be used as a *contrary indicator* for global stocks. Here's why. For several years, Japanese interest rates had been the lowest in the world (near zero). As a result, the Japanese yen was the weakest of the world's major currencies. That precipitated the so-called "yen carry trade," when global investors borrowed yen (sold it short) at very low interest rates and used that cheap money to buy higher-yielding assets elsewhere in the world. As a result, an inverse relationship developed between a weak yen and rising global stocks. I concluded that the global bull market depended on a continuing weak yen to provide cheap global liquidity. I also suggested that any sudden rise in the yen could threaten the bull market in global stocks. A rising yen would force global traders to buy the yen back (cover their short positions) and sell global assets elsewhere. And that's just what happened later in 2007.

Figure 7.12 compares the Japanese yen/U.S. dollar relationship (candlesticks) to the Dow Jones World Stock Index (solid line) during 2007. During the first half of that year, the yen fell as stocks rose (as had been the case for several years). During July, however, the yen started to rally sharply. By comparing the two arrows, you can see that the yen upturn coincided exactly with the start of a topping process in global stocks. By first quarter 2008, the yen had risen to the highest level in three years against the U.S. dollar as global stocks tumbled. It seemed far-fetched to claim that the direction in one currency market could influence the direction of the world's stock markets. That unusual example, however, demonstrates the value of intermarket analysis and why I recommend blending intermarket principles with traditional charting methods.

REVIEW OF 2004 INTERMARKET BOOK

For those of you seeking a more comprehensive explanation of intermarket principles, I recommend that you consult my book *Intermarket Analysis: Profiting From Global Market Relationships* (John Wiley & Sons, 2004). That earlier work examines in detail the intermarket events leading up to and following the stock market top that started in 2000, as well as the upturn that began during spring 2003. The book you're reading now deals with market trends since then, including intermarket events surrounding the stock market top of 2007. Another reason that I recommend consulting the earlier intermarket book is because many of the trends discussed in this book (like the major decline in the dollar and the ensuing bull market in commodities) were actually described when that book was written during 2003. I point that out simply to demonstrate that these trends are not being written about with the benefit of hindsight. They were pointed out as they were starting. As an example, Chapter 10 in the earlier book, entitled "Shifting From Paper to Hard Assets," is similar to one of the headlines in this chapter. Another reason for studying past market events is because some of the trends that took place near the end of 2007 and the start of 2008 were repeats of what happened eight years earlier. In both time periods, bond prices rose as stocks fell. During 2008, as in 2001, the Fed started lowering rates aggressively to support the economy and stocks. In both instances, the dollar fell and commodities rose. Those who studied past downturns knew that global stocks usually fall together. 2007 proponents

FIGURE 7.12 The upturn in the Japanese yen (candlesticks) during the summer of 2007 signaled the end of the "yen carry trade" and contributed to the peak in global stocks.
Source: StockCharts.com.

of global decoupling weren't market historians. Market history has a way of repeating itself. The only way to benefit from that history is to study it.

SUMMARY

This chapter is intended to explain how the various financial markets interact with each other. Those markets include bonds, stocks, commodities, and currencies. (We discuss housing and real estate in a future chapter.) Foreign markets are also part of the mix. Rather than focus on the economic reasons between those linkages, I've tried to show how the use of a simple technical tool like the relative strength ratio can be indispensable in spotting when the relationship between two markets is changing. The ability to do that is very helpful in deciding whether to overweight bonds, stocks, or commodities at any given time. Or, when to favor foreign shares. A second goal in this chapter is to make you aware that a new generation of mutual funds and exchange-traded funds has made investing in nontraditional asset classes like commodities and currencies very easy for the average investor. You can now buy a rising commodity or foreign currency by simply buying a stock on a stock exchange (through an ETF). There's always a bull market somewhere. Entering 2008, global stocks were entering a bear market. At the same time that stock prices were falling, however, rising trends were seen in bond prices, commodities, and foreign currencies. The trick is to buy what's rising (no matter what the market), and avoid what's falling. The simple tools described in this book can help you do that.

During the second half of 2008, foreign currencies like the euro started to tumble on signs of weakening global economies. That pushed the U.S. dollar higher and caused a downturn in commodities on fears of a global recession. Traders began talking about "global contagion." That was a big change from their talk a year earlier on "global decoupling."

CHAPTER 8

Market Breadth

The previous chapter showed that commodities were the strongest asset class going into 2007 and had been so for several years. That reality favored investments in commodities and stocks tied to those commodities (like energy and gold shares), which remained stock market leaders throughout 2007. In this chapter, we're going to study the other side of the equation by looking at stock market groups that started to underperform the U.S. stock market during the second half of that year. At the same time, we're going to study the negative impact those weak groups had on *market breadth*, which gave early warning signs that the stock market was peaking as 2007 drew to a close. We start by examining obvious warning signs in the most popular indicator of stock market breadth, which is the NYSE advance-decline line. Near the end of the chapter, you learn about other useful breadth indicators that show that the last market move into new highs during 2007 was on weak footing.

MEASURING MARKET BREADTH WITH NYSE AD LINE

Market breadth usually refers to the number of NYSE stocks that are rising versus those that are falling on any given day. If there are more advancing stocks than decliners, market breadth for that day is positive. More declines than advances translate into a negative breadth day. There are several ways to measure market breadth. The most popular is the NYSE *advance-decline line*. The AD line is simply a running cumulative total of advancing stocks minus declining stocks. When the line is rising, there are more advances than declines and the market is in an uptrend. Market analysts usually compare the advance-decline line to an index of stock prices. The reason for doing that is to ensure that both lines are trending in the same direction. At market tops, the advance-decline line usually turns down before the price index. A warning sign of a possible market top is given when the AD line is falling while the market price is still rising. That's exactly what happened during the second half of 2007. Let's start by studying the trend of the NYSE advance-decline itself.

NYSE AD LINE VIOLATES MOVING AVERAGE LINES

Figure 8.1 charts the NYSE advance-decline line during 2007. The AD line peaked during the June–July period and started falling from there. A second peak occurred during October which fell short of its July peak (more on that later). The AD line then fell below its August low to initiate a new downtrend. The two lines drawn on that AD line are the 50- and 200-day moving averages (which were explained in Chapter 4). Two things happened on Figure 8.1 that were bearish for the AD line and the market. The first was its drop below the 200-day moving average during November (see circle). (Although it had dipped below the 200-day average during August, it bounced quickly back over it). The downside crossing during November was the first decisive break of that long-term support line since the bull market started in spring 2003. The second bad thing that happened was the 50-day moving average crossing below the 200-day line during the same month (see arrow). That was also the first time that bearish signal had been given in four years. Those bearish moving average signals gave ample warning that market breadth had started to deteriorate in a serious way during fourth quarter 2007 before that trend damage became evident in the major market indexes.

ADVANCE-DECLINE SHOWS NEGATIVE DIVERGENCE

One of the most important features in studying the advance-decline line is seeing how it's trending in relation to its main stock index. As long as both lines are rising together (which had been the case since 2003), the market uptrend is healthy. When the AD line starts to drop before the price index, a "negative divergence" is created. (Chapter 5 discussed the importance

FIGURE 8.1 The NYSE advance-decline line started to weaken noticeably during the second half of 2007 and warned of a stock market peak. Bearish moving average signals during November confirmed the downturn in the AD line.
Source: StockCharts.com.

of negative divergences in oscillator analysis). That negative divergence is usually a warning that the stock market uptrend is on weak footing. Figure 8.2 compares the trend of the NYSE advance-decline line to the NYSE Composite Index during 2007. Both lines peaked together during June and July before falling into August. Up to that point, things looked okay. The NYSE Index then started a rally that took it to a new record high during October. Unfortunately, the NYSE AD line failed to do so. It fell well short of its July high (first arrow). That's when the trouble started. That lack of upside confirmation by the AD line created a negative divergence which warned that the record high by stock prices was being driven by a smaller number of stocks than before. From that point, the AD line led the NYSE Index down from its October high. That pattern of "lower highs" by the NYSE AD line gave an early warning that the market was peaking. That demonstrates why market analysts pay attention to the advance-decline line. And why you should too.

WHERE THE NEGATIVE DIVERGENCES WERE LOCATED

It's also instructive to know which groups were the ones "diverging" from the rising stock market from the August bottom to the October top and the ones leading the market lower during the second half of 2007. The reasons for knowing that are twofold. One is to show the trader which groups to avoid. The other reason is because certain market groups have a history of turning down first at a market top. Knowing that they are the ones leading the market lower adds to the bearish warning. Figure 8.3 shows the five weakest market groups during the second half of 2007. None of those groups reached new highs during fourth quarter 2007 along with major stock indexes. Listed in order from the strongest to the weakest, the five groups were transports, small caps, financials, retailers, and homebuilders. Not only were those groups leading the market lower that year, but each had a history of turning down before market tops.

Small cap stocks have a history of turning up first at market bottoms (like 2003) and turning down first at market tops (like 2007). In the final stage of a bull market, investors rotate out of riskier small cap stocks into more stable large caps as a defensive maneuver. Another factor working against small caps during 2007 was the plunge to a record low by the U.S. dollar. A weak dollar generally favors large multinational stocks that do a lot of foreign business (for the same reason that weaker dollar favors foreign stocks). Another weak 2007 group, financial stocks, are also traditionally viewed as leading indicators for the rest of the market. In other words,

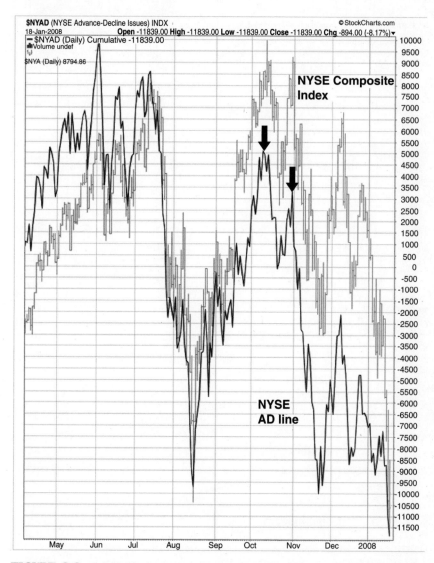

$NYAD (NYSE Advance-Decline Issues) INDX
18-Jan-2008 **Open** -11839.00 **High** -11839.00 **Low** -11839.00 **Close** -11839.00 **Chg** -894.00 (-8.17%)▾
— $NYAD (Daily) Cumulative -11839.00
Volume undef
$NYA (Daily) 8794.86
© StockCharts.com

NYSE Composite Index

NYSE AD line

FIGURE 8.2 A bearish divergence is clearly visible between the NYSE advance-decline line (solid line) and the NYSE Composite Index (price bars) during October and November 2007. The AD line usually turns down before the major market indexes. *Source:* StockCharts.com.

FIGURE 8.3 The transports, small caps, financials, retailers, and homebuilders led the major market indexes lower during the second half of 2007.
Source: StockCharts.com.

they turn up first at bottoms and turn down first at tops. During 2007, financial stocks turned down with a vengeance. Transportation stocks are another group that has a history of turning down first at market tops (more on that later). This brings us to retailers and homebuilders.

RETAIL STOCKS START TO UNDERPERFORM DURING 2007

Consumer spending accounts for two-thirds of the U.S. economy. That being the case, the trend of retail stocks tells us a lot about the health of the economy. But not just the *absolute* trend of retail stocks. Their *relative* trend is also important. And it was the collapse in their relative performance during 2007 that made it clear that consumers were starting to rein in their spending. The price bars in Figure 8.4 shows the trend in the S&P Retail Index during the bull market that lasted from 2003 through 2007. The weekly price bars show that retail stocks bottomed in the first half of 2003 (along with the rest of the stock market) and hit a record high during the first half of 2007. They then started falling during the second half of that year as the rest of the market continued rising (producing the negative divergence referred to earlier).

The real story in Figure 8.4, however, is the relative strength ratio of the Retail Index divided by the S&P 500 (solid line). (Comparison between a relative strength ratio and price bars is much more revealing when the ratio is overlaid right over the price bars.) Notice, for example, that retail stocks led the S&P 500 higher from spring 2003 to mid-2005. That's not unusual in the early stages of a bull market. Relative strength by retail stocks tells us that consumers have turned more optimistic on the economy and are spending more freely. That's why retail leadership is usually good for the economy and the stock market. That's also why retail underperformance is bad.

Up until the start of 2007, retail stocks either led the market higher or at least matched the S&P 500 performance. That started to change during the first half of that year. Starting in first quarter 2007, a serious "negative divergence" developed between the ratio and the trend of retail stocks. While the Retail Index hit a record high, its relative strength ratio fell well short of its earlier peaks (see falling trendline). That was the first visual evidence that retail stocks were starting to underperform the rest of the market. Then things got even worse. The relative strength ratio started dropping sharply during the second quarter and, by the third quarter, had fallen to the lowest level in four years. That was a serious sign that retail stocks were in trouble. It was also a sign that consumer spending was starting to slow, which

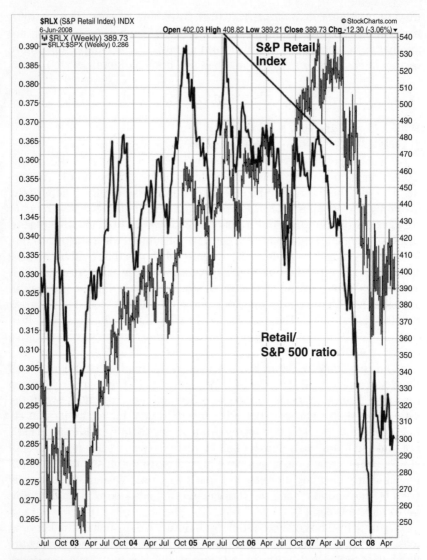

FIGURE 8.4 The breakdown in the Retail Index/S&P 500 ratio (solid line) during 2007 showed that retailers were starting to underperform the rest of the market. *Source:* StockCharts.com.

would have negative implications for the economy and the stock market. Let's consider why that happened.

RETAILERS AND HOMEBUILDERS WERE LINKED

Throughout 2007, one of the mantras repeated over and over again in the financial media was that the U.S. economy was still pretty healthy. Economists claimed that the fallout from a weakening housing sector wasn't having much of a negative impact on retail spending or the rest of the economy. As a result, there wasn't much concern about the downturn in housing infecting the economy or the stock market. Unfortunately, visual analysis told a very different story. Figure 8.5 shows weekly price bars for the PHLX Housing Index. The chart shows that homebuilding stocks actually peaked in the middle of 2005, but really started dropping during the first half of 2006. They fell even more sharply during the second half of 2007. One of the reasons for looking at market charts is that financial markets have a way of "discounting" economic fundamentals before those fundamentals become generally known. The peak in housing stocks during 2005 and their downturn in early 2006 (which was so clear on the charts) gave two warnings. One warning was that it was time to exit homebuilding stocks that had been market leaders since 2000. A second warning was that a weaker housing sector could have negative implications for the rest of the economy. That warning, by the way, was given anywhere from one to two years before subprime problems surfaced in summer 2007, and was largely ignored by the financial community.

Figure 8.5 shows that another piece of conventional wisdom was wrong which was that the housing downturn wasn't spreading to other parts of the economy. The solid line in Figure 8.5 is the same Retail/S&P 500 ratio shown in Figure 8.4. We're overlaying the retail relative strength ratio on top of the Housing Index. The close correlation between the two lines is striking. Notice, for example, that the retail relative strength line peaked in the middle of 2005 right along with the Housing Index (see circle). They fell together during the first half of 2006 and throughout 2007. Figure 8.5 makes it clear that the start of the downturn in the relative performance of retail stocks (which is itself a leading indicator of retail spending) was closely linked to the downturn in homebuilding stocks and the housing sector. The chart clearly shows that housing weakness was infecting an important part of the stock market and the economy. And all of the leading warning signs were clearly visible to the visual investor.

FIGURE 8.5 A comparison of the Housing Index (price bars) and the Retail/S&P 500 ratio (solid line) shows that both peaked together during 2005 and 2006 and fell together during 2007. That showed that housing problems were hurting retail spending.
Source: StockCharts.com.

CONSUMERS ARE ALSO SQUEEZED BY RISING OIL

During 2007, consumers were being hit from two different directions. Not only was the price of their homes falling for the first time in their lifetime, but energy prices were soaring to record heights. Figure 8.6 overlays the Retail/S&P ratio (solid line) on weekly price bars of crude oil. From the start of 2006 to spring 2008, the two lines show a generally inverse correlation. In other words, they trended in opposite directions. A surge in oil prices near the start of 2007 was especially negative for retailers for the rest of that year (see arrows). A doubling of crude oil from $50 at the start of 2007 to $100 at the end of the year accompanied a 2007 plunge in the performance of retail stocks (a falling ratio). As was the case with the relationship between retailing and housing, the financial community held to the mistaken belief that rising oil prices weren't having a negative impact on the consumer. Visual investors knew better. Rising oil prices didn't just hurt the relative performance of retail stocks. It also accounted for the 2007 drop in transportation stocks which led to another one of the negative divergences referred to earlier. And that brings us to the Dow Theory.

DOW THEORY

The venerable Dow Theory is one of the oldest approaches in market analysis (having been first defined by Charles Dow at the start of the twentieth century). It was Charles Dow who invented the first two stock indexes, which were the Dow Industrials and Transports. At first, the transports were limited to railroads. In time, however, airlines and truckers were added to the transportation index. Dow reasoned that, in a healthy economy, industrial and transportation stocks should be rising together. After all, the industrial companies made the products while the transportation companies moved them to market. One couldn't function without the other. Although he intended his idea to be used mainly as an indicator of economic trends, it later became adapted to the stock market itself. In its simplest form, Dow Theory holds that the Dow Jones Industrial and Transportation averages must rise together in an ongoing bull market. If one of them lags too far behind the other, or forms a serious negative divergence from the other, a stock market peak may be at hand. One of the first danger signs occurs when one of the two hits a new high and the other doesn't. That's just what happened during 2007. And it probably had something to do with soaring oil prices.

FIGURE 8.6 A comparison of rising crude oil prices (bars) and a falling Retail/ S&P 500 ratio (solid line) during 2007 shows that energy costs were hurting retail spending.
Source: StockCharts.com.

TRANSPORTS DON'T CONFIRM INDUSTRIAL HIGH

During the bull market from 2003 to 2007, industrial and transportation stocks rose pretty much in tandem. That changed in a big way during 2007. Figure 8.7 shows the Dow Industrials and Transports rising together into mid-2007. During July and August of that year, however, transportation stocks (solid line) fell further than the industrials (price bars). At first, that didn't seem too serious. During October, however, the Dow Industrials rose to a new record high while the transports didn't even come close to matching that. While the industrials were at a new high during October 2007, the transports were trading nearly 10 percent below their summer high (see falling trendline). That negative divergence between the two Dow averages during the fourth quarter of 2007 was a Dow Theory warning that the market uptrend was in trouble. There were probably two reasons for that.

One of the reasons for the sudden drop in transportation stocks was rising oil prices. For reasons that should seem obvious, transports are especially vulnerable to rising oil. Airlines and truckers use huge amounts of fuel in their operations. Although railroads can pass most of their fuel costs on to their customers, even they couldn't withstand the type of soaring fuel costs that occurred during 2007 when oil doubled in price.

Another factor hurting transportation stocks was a weakening economy (resulting from a housing depression). That's because the transports are considered to be economically sensitive stocks. That means they're tied to the business cycle. As such, they're especially vulnerable to early signs of a slowing economy. If demand for goods starts to drop, there are fewer goods to transport. And as Charles Dow predicted a century before, the downturn in transportation stocks during the second half of 2007 turned out to be a bad sign for the economy (and the stock market). The stock market is considered to be a leading indicator of the economy. Historically, stocks usually peak six to nine months before the economy. Since the stock market started peaking in July 2007, the time target for an economic downturn was during first half 2008. By mid-2008, most economists acknowledged the likely start of a U.S. recession.

PERCENT OF NYSE STOCKS ABOVE 200-DAY AVERAGE

I promised you a look at a couple of other useful market breadth indicators that warned of a market top during the second half of 2007. The first of those is the percent of NYSE stocks that are trading above their

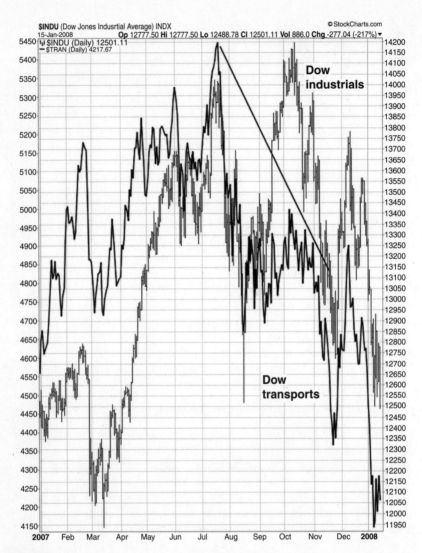

FIGURE 8.7   The Dow transports (solid line) failed to confirm the new high by the Dow industrials (price bars) during the fourth quarter of 2007 and gave a Dow Theory sell signal. Transportation weakness was tied to rising fuel costs and a slowing economy.
Source: StockCharts.com.

200-day moving average. You may recall my mentioning in Chapter 4 that the 200-day moving average acts as a major support line during uptrends. Any serious downside violation of that line warns that the stock, or market in question, has entered into a bear market. We can of course apply the 200-day moving average to the major market indexes like the Dow Industrials or the S&P 500. All of those fell below their 200-day line during fourth quarter 2007. I started this chapter by showing the NYSE advance-decline line doing the same (only earlier). By the time the major market indexes fall below their 200-day averages, however, a lot of profits have already been lost. That's why market breadth indicators are so useful. They tell us in advance that a market is in trouble, and give much earlier warnings that it may be time to take some profits or some other type of defensive action.

Some chart services include an indicator that measures the percent of NYSE stocks that are trading above their 200-day averages. Figure 8.8 compares that indicator to the NYSE Composite Index during 2007. As is normally done with market breadth indicators, the idea is to compare the direction of the two lines. In a healthy uptrend, both lines should be rising together. Figure 8.8 shows, however, that the percent of stocks over their 200-day average (solid line) started dropping sharply in the middle of the year. That negative divergence between the two lines was especially noticeable when the NYSE Composite Index hit a record high during October of that year and the breadth indicator didn't even come close to doing so (see arrow). While the NYSE was hitting a new high, only two-thirds of its stocks were still in uptrends. That weakening in the breadth indicator warned the visual investor that the stock market rally wasn't to be trusted. And that warning proved to be very timely. But there's more to this indicator.

As important as the direction of this breadth indicator is, there are other factors to consider. The vertical scale along the right side of Figure 8.8 gives us the actual percentage of stocks trading over their 200-day average. Readings over 70 percent usually warn of a dangerously overextended market. By early 2007, the indicator had reached 85 percent. When that happens, a first warning of a market drop is given when the percent line falls back below the 70 percent line. During that July, the indicator fell to 65 which put it below its March low and at the lowest level in 10 months (see circle). That breakdown warned that the overextended market was starting to weaken.

The 40 percent line separates bull markets from bear markets. The percent line fell below that level during August 2007 and again during the fourth quarter. That was the first move below that support line since the bull market started more than four years earlier. At the time, the drop in the major market indexes was still relatively small. In one of my market reports written during that period, I asked the following question:

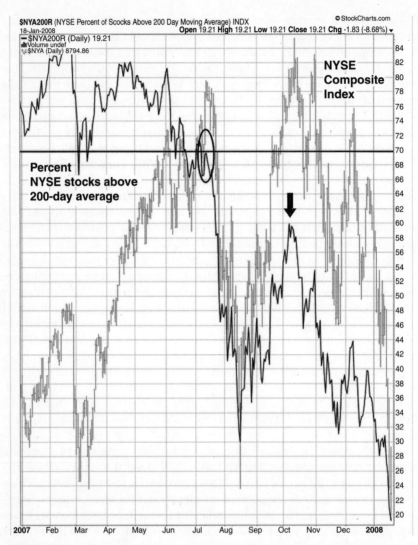

$NYA200R (NYSE Percent of Scocks Above 200 Day Moving Average) INDX   © StockCharts.com
18-Jan-2008   **Open** 19.21 **High** 19.21 **Low** 19.21 **Close** 19.21 **Chg** -1.83 (-8.68%) ▾
— $NYA200R (Daily) 19.21
📊 Volume undef
📈 $NYA (Daily) 8794.86

NYSE
Composite
Index

Percent
NYSE stocks above
200-day average

FIGURE 8.8 The percent of NYSE stocks over their 200 day averages (solid line) weakened noticeably during the second half of 2007 and signaled a weaker stock market.
Source: StockCharts.com.

How can a bull market exist in the NYSE Composite Index if nearly two-thirds of the stocks in that index are in bear markets? After all, the stock market is a market of stocks. And most of those stocks started falling well before the major market indexes. During the first quarter of 2008, the percent line traded as low as 20 percent. Readings below 30 percent usually warn that the market is due for a rebound. To signal the start of a new bull market, however, the percent line has to rise back over 60 percent.

This is a good spot to point out one of the fallacies of just following a major market index like the NYSE Composite Index, and why breadth indicators are so valuable in spotting market tops. Most major market indexes are capitalization weighted. That means that bigger stocks are given greater weight in the daily calculation of each index. I suggested earlier in the chapter that small-cap stocks usually fall faster than large-cap stocks in the early stages of a market downturn. There are more small- and midsize stocks than there are large-cap stocks. As a result, the large-cap dominated stock indexes reported in the media each day tell us more about what the large-cap stocks are doing. And they're usually the last ones to fall at a market top. The breadth indicators being described in this chapter tell us what most of the other stocks are doing. That's why breadth indicators usually start dropping before the major market indexes. And that's what gives them their forecasting value.

NYSE BULLISH PERCENT INDEX

This next breadth indicator is also intended to tell us what the majority of stocks are doing as opposed to the major market indexes—the NYSE Bullish Percent Index (BPI). To explain this indicator, however, refer back to one of the chart types mentioned briefly in Chapter 3, the point-and-figure chart. One of the values of the P&F chart is that it gives specific buy and sell signals. The BPI measures the percent of NYSE stocks that are in point and figure uptrends. The "line" version which is similar to the others that you've seen in this chapter is shown in Figure 8.9.

Figure 8.9 shows the NYSE Bullish Percent Index (solid line) plotted over the NYSE Composite Index price bars during 2007. It looks very similar to the chart in Figure 8.8. And its interpretation is also similar. The idea again is to compare the direction of the two lines. And, once again, a major negative divergence is visible during October 2007. The percentage scale along the right vertical side of Figure 8.9 is also similar to the one shown in the preceding figure. Readings over 70 percent warn of an overbought market, while readings below 30 percent are considered to be

FIGURE 8.9 The NYSE Bullish Percent Index (solid line) also showed a serious negative divergence from the NYSE Composite Index during fourth quarter 2007. *Source:* StockCharts.com.

oversold. This breadth indicator had fallen to 40 percent by November of
that year. That meant that only one-third of the big board stocks were in
point-and-figure uptrends. At the same time, the NYSE Composite Index
was down only 10 percent from its October high, which signaled nothing
more than a normal market correction. Obviously, the breadth indicator
was painting a bleaker picture than the major market indexes.

POINT-AND-FIGURE VERSION OF BPI

Most traders who use the NYSE Bullish Percent Index prefer to use its
point-and-figure version. That seems only fitting since the BPI is based on
P and F signals (see Figure 8.10). Figure 8.10 shows the point-and-figure
version of the NYSE Bullish Percent Index over several years. Each box

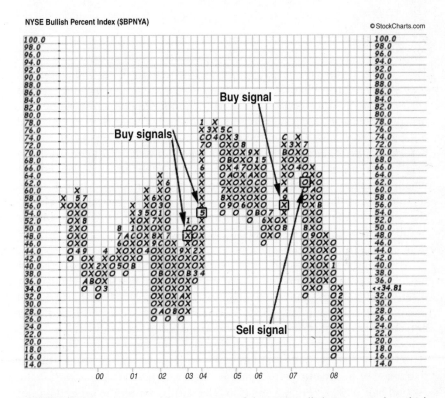

FIGURE 8.10 A point-and-figure version of the NYSE Bullish Percent Index which
measures the percent of NYSE stocks in P&F uptrends. A sell signal was given during
July 2007 at 62 percent before falling to the lowest level in eight years.
Source: StockCharts.com.

is worth two percentage points (see percentage scales). A point-and-figure chart is composed of alternating X and O columns. An X column represents rising values, while each O column represents falling values. A P&F buy signal occurs when an X column exceeds a previous X column. Buy signals occurred in November 2002, May 2003, and August 2006. A sell signal occurs when a O column falls below a previous O column. Figure 8.10 shows a sell signal given during July 2007 when the O column fell to 62 percent and undercut its previous O column low at 64 percent. That sell signal took place after the BPI fell from overbought territory over 70 percent, which gave the bear signal more significance. (The numbers in some of the boxes are the start of new months—7 starts July and 8 begins August. The letters A, B, and C represent October, November, and December.) During August 2007, the BPI fell to 44 percent which was below its 2006 bottom and the lowest reading since 2003. That was bear market territory.

SUMMARY

This chapter deals with the subject of market breadth. These indicators tell the visual investor what the majority of stocks are doing and not just the large-cap stocks that dominate the major market indexes. These market breadth indicators are especially important at spotting market tops and bottoms. Their value lines in the fact that they generally change direction before the major market indexes. That's especially true of market tops. The best known measure of market breadth is the NYSE advance-decline line which measures the number of advancing stocks on the big board minus the number of declining stocks. In a healthy uptrend, the AD line should rise along with the major indexes. During 2007, the NYSE AD line starting to fall sharply during the second half of the year and gave early warning of impending stock market weakness.

Most of those negative divergences were spotted in market groups that have historically turned down first at market tops. They include consumer discretionary stocks, financials, small cap stocks, and the transports. Visual comparisons showed that selling in retail stocks was caused by a falling housing market and rising oil prices. Transportation stocks fell as a result of the doubling in oil prices during 2007 and gave a Dow Theory sell signal. Dow Theory holds that industrial and transportation stocks should rise together in a healthy stock market. They stopped doing that during the second half of 2007. Small caps also fell sharply during the second half of 2007 as they usually do at market tops. Financial stocks started tumbling in mid-2007 as subprime mortgage problems started to surface. Within eight months of their 2007 top, financial stocks had lost more than 30 percent of their value. All of those warning signs showed up in the various market breadth indicators long before the market started to fall.

Two other market breadth indicators covered herein are the percent of NYSE stocks trading over their 200-day moving averages and the NYSE Bullish Percent Index. The BPI measures the percent of NYSE stocks in point-and-figure uptrends. The interpretation of both indicators is essentially the same. Readings over 70 percent signal an overbought market, and a drop below 40 percent warns of a new bear market. Both breadth indicators started to fail badly during the second half of 2007 and warned that the stock market was headed for a drop. That's why visual investors should be watching them.

By October 2008, exactly one year after peaking, the S&P 500 had lost more than a third of its value. Financial stocks were worth only half of their early 2007 values. Foreign stocks did even worse. Foreign developed markets had fallen 40 percent and emerging markets 50 percent.

CHAPTER 9

Relative Strength and Rotation

T he idea of using relative strength analysis was introduced in Chapter 7 to show how to spot which asset classes were moving into a leadership role and which were lagging behind. That chapter concentrated on relative performance between bonds, stocks, commodities, and foreign stocks. It also showed that commodity-related stocks were top performers in 2007. Chapter 8 expanded the use of relative strength to show which market groups were market laggards during 2007. Whether one is dealing with asset classes or market sectors, the principle of relative strength is the same. That is, to invest in asset classes or sectors that are showing the best relative strength, and to avoid those displaying relative weakness. The ability to plot relative strength lines (or ratios) makes it relatively easy to track trends in relative performance and to spot when trend changes are taking place. The goal of this chapter is to expand even more on the use of relative strength analysis, and to show how flexible a tool it can be in the hands of the visual investor.

USES OF RELATIVE STRENGTH

Relative strength is an extremely simple but powerful tool. It simply compares how one asset is performing relative to another. This is accomplished by constructing a ratio between two competing assets. In other words, one asset is divided by another. The resulting *relative strength* (RS) line is then plotted along with the respective price chart. In Chapter 7, we showed the CRB/Treasury Bond ratio. By dividing an index of commodity prices by bond prices, the direction of the ratio line tells which of the two assets is stronger. If the ratio is rising, the numerator (the CRB Index) is the stronger of the two. If the ratio line is falling, the denominator (Treasury bonds) is stronger. A rising CRB/Treasury bond ratio also favors stocks tied to commodities like basic materials, precious metals, and natural resources. A falling CRB/Bond ratio favors interest-sensitive shares like financials. In recent years, commodity prices have been stronger than both bonds and stocks, and commodity-related shares have been market leaders.

Relative strength analysis can be applied to any two assets. Its most common usage in financial charts is to compare an individual stock to the S&P 500 to see if the stock is doing better or worse than the general market. It's usually better to be in those stocks that are doing better (with rising RS lines). Another way to use relative strength is to compare an individual stock to its market sector or industry group. That way you can tell which stocks are the strongest and weakest within their own group. The idea is to be in the strongest stocks. Another popular use is to compare stock sectors (and industry groups) to the general market to determine which groups are outperforming and underperforming the market. As will be shown later in the chapter, you can even apply relative strength analysis to two market sectors to see which is the stronger.

TOP-DOWN ANALYSIS

Top-down analysis refers to three stages (or layers) of decision making in the stock market. The first step is to determine if the market's current climate is conducive to stock investments. That would certainly be the case during a bull market or a correction in a bull market. That might not be the case during a prolonged bear market. The second step is to determine which market sectors or industry groups are showing relative strength. If you are committing funds to the market, the goal is be buying relative strength and avoiding relative weakness. There are lots of mutual funds and exchange-traded funds to allow you to buy and sell market sectors and industry groups. If you're a sector trader, that's as far as you need to go. If you're stock picker, there's a third step. Once you've isolated the groups that you wish to buy (which should be the strongest ones), you then have to find the individual stocks in those groups that are the strongest. In other words, you want to buy the strongest stocks in the strongest sectors. Relative strength analysis allows you to do that. But there's more to the equation than just relative strength.

RELATIVE STRENGTH VERSUS ABSOLUTE PERFORMANCE

As important as relative strength is, it's not the only consideration. There's also the question of absolute performance. In a bull market, for example, you're trying to find groups or stocks that are rising faster than the general market. That's where you get the most "bang for your buck." In a bear market, however, some groups or stocks may show relative strength but absolute weakness. That means that they're falling slower than the rest of the market. All you're doing in that situation is losing your money more slowly. In a falling market, it's certainly better to be in groups that are losing the least money. However, I prefer to look for situations that are showing both absolute and relative strength. To do that, you have to combine relative strength performance with chart analysis of the markets you're following. Make sure the market you're considering is in an uptrend first. Then consider its relative strength. Relative strength in a rising asset is better than relative strength in a falling asset.

Let's show an example of the difference between absolute and relative performance. The weekly price bars in Figure 9.1 show the Semiconductor (SOX) Index over a five-year period. From the middle of 2003 to the end of 2007, the SOX Index basically trended sideways. While no money was made during those three years, none was lost either. Or was it? The solid line in Figure 9.1 is a relative strength ratio of the SOX Index divided by the S&P 500. That line fell from the start of 2004 to the end of 2007. In other words, the SOX Index underperformed the market during those four years.

While the group's absolute performance was flat, its relative performance was weak. That raises an obvious question. Why hold an underperforming asset when there's money to be made elsewhere? Although no money was actually lost by holding the semiconductor shares during most of that period, there was an "opportunity cost." Investors lost the opportunity to profit from other sectors of the market that rose during that same period. So, in a sense, semiconductor shareholders did lose money by holding an underperforming asset. They paid for being in the wrong group at the wrong time.

By comparison, gold shares showed the right combination of absolute performance and relative strength. The price bars in Figure 9.2 show the Gold & Silver (XAU) Index rising from 2001 to 2008. Its relative strength line rose as well. Not only did precious metal shares rise during those years, they rose much faster than the rest of the stock market. That's a winning combination.

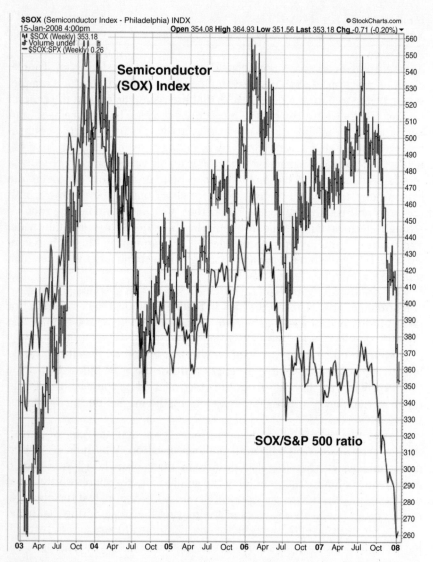

FIGURE 9.1 The relative performance of the Semiconductor (SOX) Index from 2004 to 2008 (solid line) was much worse than its absolute performance (price bars). It's not a good idea to stick with an underperforming asset.
Source: StockCharts.com.

FIGURE 9.2 The PHLX Gold & Silver (XAU) Index rose steadily from 2001 to 2008. Its relative strength line (solid line) rose as well. That's a good combination of relative strength and an actual price uptrend.
Source: StockCharts.com.

USING RELATIVE STRENGTH BETWEEN STOCKS

When an investor decides to invest in a stock market group, he or she has two choices. One is to buy an entire basket of stocks either through a sector mutual fund or an exchange-traded fund. A second choice is to buy a stock (or stocks) within the group. Let's start by assuming that the group itself is a market leader. This is always the best place to start. Gold stocks certainly qualified as market leaders during 2006 and 2007.

But not all gold stocks rose equally. Figure 9.3 plots the relative strength ratios of Barrick Gold and Newmont Mining versus the Gold & Silver Index (XAU) during 2006 and 2007. That tells us what the two stocks did relative to precious metal stocks in general. It's clear that the relative strength line for Barrick Gold rose while the RS line for Newmont Mining fell during those two years. In other words, Barrick was a gold leader, while Newmont was a gold laggard.

Barrick Gold rose 55 percent during those two years (versus +35 percent for the XAU). By painful comparison, Newmont Mining actually lost 7 percent. There are two morals to that story. One is that relative strength analysis is extremely helpful in isolating leading stocks in a market group (and avoiding laggards). A second moral is that it's usually simpler to buy the entire group to take advantage of its market leadership position. If you choose to buy an individual stock, make sure it's a group leader.

COMPARING GOLD STOCKS TO GOLD

Gold shares often rise faster than the commodity in a commodity uptrend. That was the case during the first four years of the bull market in gold from 2002 to the end of 2005. That wasn't the case, however, during 2006 and 2007 (see Figure 9.4). Here again, relative strength analysis comes into play. Figure 9.4 plots a ratio of gold divided by the XAU Index from 2005 to spring 2008. The ratio turned up at the start of 2006 and rose for the next two years during which time the commodity did better than the shares. Not that the performance of gold stocks wasn't good. The XAU Index gained 35 percent during 2006 and 2007, which was twice as much as the S&P 500 (17 percent). Gold itself, however, gained 62 percent during 2006 and 2007. That made the commodity a stronger investment than gold shares during those two years. That may have been due to the launching of exchange-traded funds that allowed direct purchase of the commodity. Nonetheless, the use of relative strength analysis helped investors hoping to profit from the bull market in gold to maximize their profits by favoring the commodity over its related shares from 2006 into 2008.

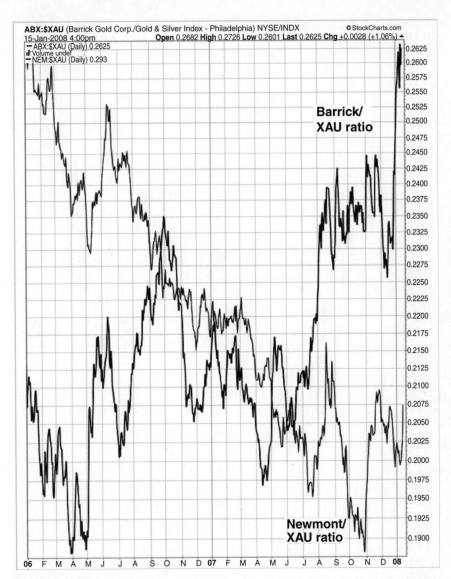

FIGURE 9.3 Barrick Gold and Newmont Mining are plotted relative to the XAU Index during 2006 and 2007. Barrick was clearly a gold leader while Newmont was a laggard. It always better to pick a leader in a strong group.
Source: StockCharts.com.

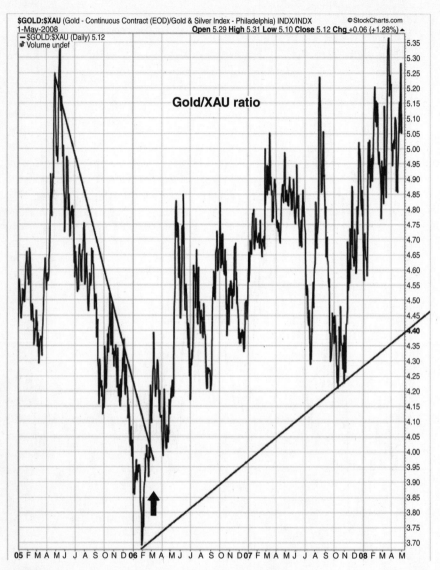

FIGURE 9.4 The gold/XAU ratio shows that bullion did better than gold shares during 2006 and 2007. Investors can use relative strength analysis to determine whether to buy a commodity or its related shares.
Source: StockCharts.com.

HOW TO SPOT NEW MARKET LEADERS

It's one thing to write about market leaders that have been rising for several years such as gold stocks or stocks tied to commodities in general. It's another thing to spot new emerging market leaders. And it's usually not that hard to do that. Figure 9.5 plots a relative strength ratio of the Consumer Staples Sector SPDR (XLP) divided by the S&P 500 from mid-2001 to mid-2008. After rising throughout the bear market that started in 2000, the staples/S&P 500 ratio peaked at the end of 2002 and fell until spring 2006, when it started to bounce. After rallying during most of that year, the ratio retested the 2006 low during summer 2007 and started to rise sharply. The pattern traced out by the Consumer Staples ratio was a very obvious "double bottom" reversal pattern as explained in Chapter 3. That bullish pattern was completed during fourth quarter 2007 when the ratio broke out to a four-year high. There are several important messages revealed by that RS line.

One message has to do with the nature of the Consumer Staples sector. The group is composed of stocks that are defensive in nature. In other words, they tend to do better when the economy and stock market are in trouble. That's because the group includes basic necessities such as food, beverages, and household products. People need to buy those products in good times and bad. As a result, investors usually rotate toward those defensive stocks when they sense that the stock market and the economy are weakening. Because of that, Consumer Staples usually underperform the S&P 500 during bull markets and outperform during bear markets. The peak in the staples ratio in the fourth quarter of 2002 coincided exactly with the end of the bear market that started two years earlier (the staples/S&P ratio had risen from the start of 2000 to the end of 2002). The defensive group became a market laggard from the end of 2002 until mid-2007 as the bull market continued. The ratio upturn in the second half of 2007, however, sent two messages. One was that it was time to rotate back into Consumer Staples. Another was that the five-year bull market in stocks was in jeopardy along with the U.S. economy.

WHERE THE MONEY CAME FROM

There are usually two parts to sector rotation. Money usually rotates out of one market sector and into another. Figure 9.5 shows one part of the sector rotation that started in summer 2007, when Consumer Staples suddenly attracted a lot of money and began a new period of market leadership. Figure 9.6 shows where some of that money rotating into Consumer Staples came from. The two trends in Figure 9.6 are the Consumer Staples

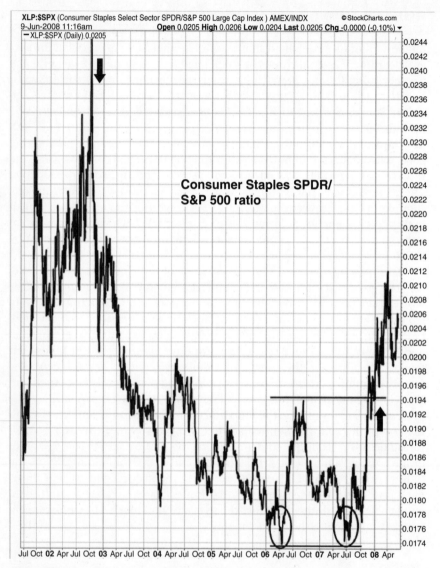

FIGURE 9.5   The Consumer Staples SPDR/ S&P 500 ratio completed a bullish double bottom during the second half of 2007. That signaled that it was a good time to rotate into that group. It also signaled that investors were turning more defensive. *Source:* StockCharts.com.

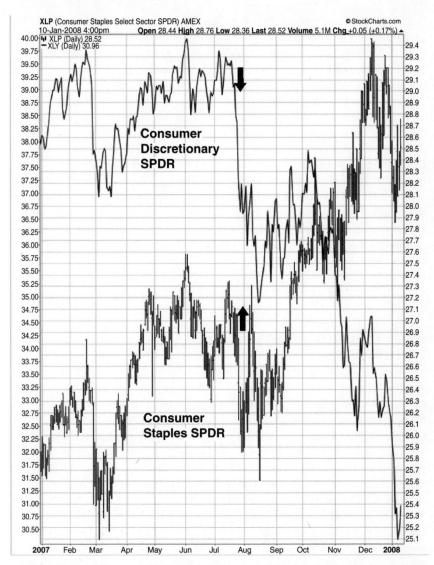

FIGURE 9.6 A comparison of these two ETFs shows that money rotating out of consumer discretionary stocks during the summer of 2007 was moving into Consumer Staples.
Source: StockCharts.com.

Sector SPDR (price bars) and the Consumer Discretionary Sector SPDR (solid line). The interplay between the two market sectors is unmistakable. When subprime mortage problems started to surface in July 2007, fear started to spread that contagion from a collapsing housing sector would bring down the stock market and the economy along with it. That fear was reflected in a 10 percent drop in stock prices during that summer.

Another manifestation of that fear, however, was the rotation out of consumer discretionary stocks (which includes retailers) that are considered to be economically sensitive into economically resistant stocks like Consumer Staples. That was a clear message that investors were turning defensive for the first time since the bull market in stocks started in spring 2003. The good news for the visual investor was that the rotation that started in the middle of 2007 was easily spotted on the charts of the two competing sectors. Figure 9.6 also demonstrates how the interplay between competing market sectors offers clues about the state of the stock market and the economy.

SPOTTING ROTATION BACK INTO LARGE CAPS

Another choice that investors have to make is whether to favor large-cap stocks or small caps. Although both groups usually trend in the same direction, they don't do so at the same rate. In the six years from 2000 to the middle of 2006, small-cap stocks rose 100 percent while large caps were basically flat. Obviously, small-cap stocks were a better investment during those years. How can you tell, however, when that trend is changing? When is it time to switch back into large-cap stocks? Once again, the best way to do that is by using relative strength analysis. Figure 9.7 plots a ratio of the S&P 500 Large Cap Index divided by the S&P 600 Small Cap Index over a four-year period from the start of 2004 to the start of 2008. The downtrend to the left of the chart shows the last phase of the decline that actually started in 2000 during which time large-cap stocks underperformed small caps. Things changed in the spring of 2006.

Figure 9.7 shows the large-cap/small-cap ratio bottoming in the spring of 2006 (see circle). The change in trend was confirmed by the breaking of the down trendline (which extended all the way back to 2000). That made it clear that it was time to start lowering one's exposure to small-cap stocks and to start favoring large caps. That switch could have been easily accomplished by using mutual funds or exchange-traded funds.

FIGURE 9.7 The large-cap/small-cap ratio shows the rotation from small caps to large caps during 2006. Large caps usually do better in the latter stages of a bull market.
Source: StockCharts.com.

TREND CHANGES ARE EASY TO SPOT

As Figure 9.7 demonstrates, trendlines are very effective on ratio charts. Simple trendline analysis is one of the easiest ways to spot important trend changes in relative strength ratios (and some simple chart-reading skills). (You can also apply moving averages.) The fact that it's relatively easy to spot ratio trend changes brings up an important point. There's no point in sticking with an underperforming asset when there's a better performing asset elsewhere. That's especially true when it's relatively easy to tell when the underperforming asset is starting to do better.

During the five-years from spring 2003 to the start of 2008, small-cap stocks gained 97 percent versus 62 percent for large caps. Those figures seem to support a continuing preference for small caps during that entire time span. From mid-2006 to January 2008, however, large caps gained 8 percent versus a 6 percent loss for small caps. During those 18 months, large caps beat small caps by nearly 15 percent. That's the time period that began with the upturn in the large-cap/small-cap ratio in Figure 9.7. Investors who stuck with a fixed weighting of small caps versus large caps missed both trends. They missed out on the greater profit opportunities in small caps from 2000 to 2006 and then the greater profits offered by large caps after mid-2006. Simple trendline analysis of the large-cap/small-cap ratio would have kept you in small caps from 2000 to mid-2006 and in large caps after that. There's no reason to miss out on those profit opportunities.

ROTATION WITHIN MARKET SECTORS

Relative strength analysis can also be used to determine which industry groups to favor within a market sector. Market sectors include many different industry groups. It's important to make sure you're in the right ones. In the four years from the start of 2004 through the end of 2007, energy was the market's top performing sector with a gain of 198 percent (versus an S&P 500 gain of 34 percent). That made energy a good place to be. But not all groups within the energy patch did equally well. During those four years, oil service stocks gained 227 percent and were energy's top group. Natural gas stocks rose 161 percent and were the weakest part of the energy patch. Those numbers suggest that oil service stocks were the best place to be in the energy sector during those four years. But let's look a little deeper to see if that was the case for the entire four year period.

Figure 9.8 plots a ratio of the Oil Service Holders (OIH) divided by the S&P Energy Sector SPDR (XLE) from 2004 through 2007. (The Energy SPDR offers a broader cross-section of energy stocks.) While it's true that

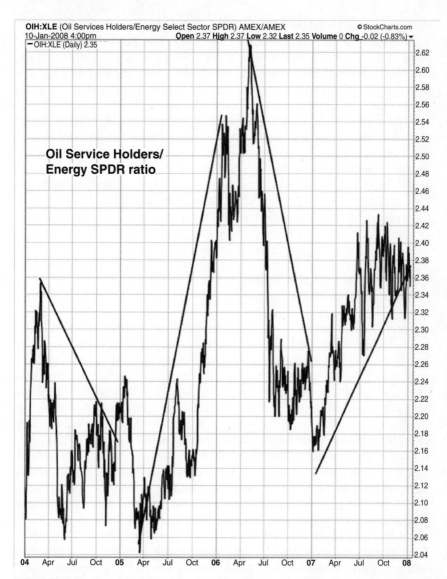

FIGURE 9.8 The Oil Service/Energy SPDR ratio shows that oil service stocks did better during 2005 and 2007. A ratio helps determine which ETF is the stronger bet. *Source:* StockCharts.com.

oil service stocks did better than the energy sector over those four years, that superior performance was very uneven. In fact, oil service stocks saw most of their gains in only two of those four years which were 2005 and 2007. And most of the oil service gains were concentrated in 2005. The falling ratio in 2004 and 2006 shows that oil service stocks were much weaker parts of the energy patch during those two years.

Although Figure 9.8 is too long-range to use for shorter-time timing purposes, I'm showing it here to demonstrate that what appears true on the surface (oil service stocks were the top energy performers over the four-year period), the reality was that they were underperformers for half of that time. You would have done better buying the Oil Service Holders in 2005 and 2007 and the Energy SPDR during 2004 and 2006. And you could have accomplished that easily by using those two exchange-traded funds.

CHINESE STOCKS LOSE LEADERSHIP ROLE

Chapter 7 touched briefly on the idea of using relative strength analysis to determine whether foreign stocks or U.S. stocks were acting better. A relative strength ratio of foreign stocks divided by the S&P 500 rose from 2002 through 2007 which favored investment in foreign shares. That was due in large part to a falling U.S. dollar. That period of foreign strength, however, ended in 2007. Relative strength analysis can be applied to a wide variety of exchange-traded funds that cover foreign markets. Relative strength ratios are especially helpful in spotting when a foreign market is doing better and when it's not. China is a good example of a major trend change to the downside (see Figure 9.9). In the two years starting in 2006, the Chinese stock market was by far the strongest in the world. From the start of 2006 until the fourth quarter of 2007, the Shanghai Stock Exchange Composite Index rose over 400 percent. During that same period, the FTSE/Xinhua China iShares (FXI) rose 250 percent. By contrast, the Dow Jones World Stock Index gained 35 percent. That dramatic outperformance by Chinese stocks took a big detour starting in the fourth quarter of 2007.

Figure 9.9 plots a ratio of the Chinese iShares divided by the Dow Jones World Stock Index from the start of 2007 to the spring of 2008. The solid line is a 50-day moving average that is helpful in spotting turns in the ratio line. The Chinese/world ratio had been rising since the start of 2006. The ratio peaked in October 2007, however, and fell for several months. The downside violation of the 50-day average during the fourth quarter warned that Chinese stocks were starting to underperform other global stocks. The

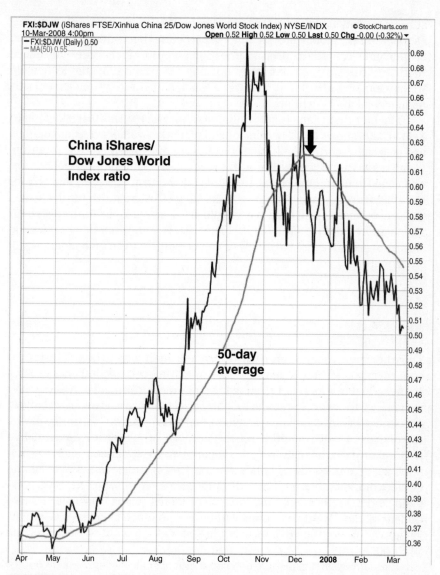

FIGURE 9.9 A ratio of China iShares (FXI) divided by the Dow Jones World Stock Index shows Chinese stocks underperforming badly in the five months after October 2007. By October 2008, the FXI had lost more than 50 percent. *Source:* StockCharts.com.

subsequent numbers bore that out. In the twelve months following the October peak, global stocks fell 40 percent. The Chinese iShares fell 50 percent. The sharp drop in the China/world stock ratio starting in fourth quarter 2007 gave an early warning that Chinese global leadership was no longer a safe bet. It was also a warning that foreign leadership was no longer a safe bet either.

The fact that Chinese stocks fell much further than other global markets in 2008 shows the downside of global market volatility. Asian markets are generally more volatile than the U.S. or European stocks. In an uptrend, that increased volatility works in favor of Asian shares which tend to rise faster than other markets. In a global downturn, however, that greater volatility works against Asian markets which often fall much further. China was a good example of that. We'll explore the use of ETFs for foreign markets in more depth in Chapter 12. Figure 9.9 is simply intended to demonstrate how relative strength analysis can be applied to an individual foreign stock market.

SUMMARY

The whole purpose of using relative strength analysis is to help investors to concentrate their funds in asset classes, market sectors, industry groups, or individual stocks that are showing superior performance. A secondary purpose is to avoid (or underweight) assets that are showing relatively weak performance. Relative strength (or ratio) analysis is the best way to compare any two entities for the purpose of measuring their relative performance. Ratio analysis can compare two asset classes (such as commodities versus bonds or bonds versus stocks), stock sectors versus the broader market (such as gold and energy shares versus the S&P 500), competing stock sectors (such as Consumer Staples versus Consumer Discretionary stocks), industry groups within sectors (such as oil service shares versus the Energy sector), or individual stocks versus their sector or the S&P 500.

Ratio analysis can also be used on a global scale to determine whether foreign shares are more or less attractive than those in United States, and which foreign markets are showing the best relative performance. Ratio analysis has an endless number of uses in comparing any two financial markets. The top-down approach to investing means determining the trend of the stock market first, then isolating better-acting sectors and industry groups, and then the strongest stocks within those sectors. It's always a good idea to combine relative strength with strong absolute performance.

The first three sections of this book present the basics of charting, explain some of the more useful trend indicators, and offer some intermarket principles to help understand the nature of market and sector rotation. This chapter examined in more depth the valuable concept of relative strength and rotation. Armed with these tools and insights, we're now ready to devote ourselves to the question of how best to apply these principles through the use of mutual funds and exchange-traded funds.

Mutual Funds and Exchange-Traded Funds

CHAPTER 10

Sectors and Industry Groups

T he preceding chapters provided you with the necessary tools to perform visual analysis of the financial markets. That material deliberately avoided an exhaustive description of available market indicators to stress those that are the most useful. This focus also provided you with selected visual tools that can be used across a broad spectrum of markets and asset classes. With so many investment choices available to today's investor, both on a domestic and a global scale, a relatively simple system is needed in the search for superior performance.

This chapter breaks the stock market down into sectors and industry groups. It's often been said that the stock market is a market of stocks. It's equally true to say that the stock market is a market of groups. It is important to know what they are and how to measure their performance because they don't always do the same thing at the same time. Some market groups rise faster than others. Some fall while others rise. Most people would probably agree that the single most important question relating to stock investing is whether it's a good time to put new funds into the market (or take some out). An equally important question is "where" in the market to put your money.

One thing that stock investing has in common with real estate is that "location" is very important. In this case, however, this means the location of your money within the stock market. Being in the right sectors and industry groups can enhance your overall performance. Being in the wrong ones can hurt it. We've already covered relative strength investing through the use of ratio analysis. This chapter adds a few more visual tools to help in your search for winning market groups.

DIFFERENCE BETWEEN SECTORS AND INDUSTRY GROUPS

Standard & Poor's divides the stock market into nine sectors that are further subdivided into 88 industry groups. There is a difference between a "sector" and an "industry." A sector is a much broader category such as Basic Materials, which includes several industry groups such as aluminum, chemicals, copper, gold mining, paper and forest products, and steel. Other sectors include Consumer Staples, Consumer Discretionary, Energy, Industrials, Financials, Health Care, Technology, Transportation, and Utilities. Each of those sectors has its own industries. It's important to know what industries are included in each sector and well as which stocks are included in each industry.

Sam Stovall, chief investment strategist for Standard & Poor's Equity Research, has written extensively on how sectors act at different stages in the business cycle. The sector rotation model in Figure 10.1 is based on the rotational sequence described in Stovall's *Standard & Poor's Guide to Sector Investing* (McGraw-Hill, 1996). Cyclicals and Technology are early cycle leaders while Energy is a late cycle leader. The latter is due to a buildup of inflationary pressures from rising energy prices. Consumer Staples and Health Care are favored early in an economic contraction, while Financials do best late in a contraction.

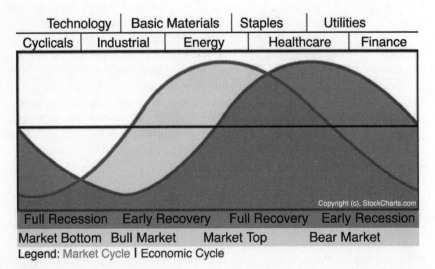

FIGURE 10.1 This sector rotation model shows how market sectors perform throughout the business cycle. The model also shows that stocks change direction before the economy.
Source: StockCharts.com

That model can be useful in several ways. If you know where we are in the business cycle, you can adjust your sector strategies accordingly. Most of the time, however, it's the other way around. Rotating sector leadership often tells us where we are in the business cycle. Since the stock market is also tied to the business cycle, the sector rotation model also tells us something about the current condition of the stock market. The model also shows that stocks lead turns in the economy.

PERFORMANCE CHARTS

Performance charts are visual tools that help the investor discover market leadership. Figure 10.2 shows two of top performing market sectors during 2007 and two of the weakest. That was a period when the economic expansion and stock market rally were both in their fifth years and starting to weaken. The two leading sectors shown in Figure 10.2 are Energy and

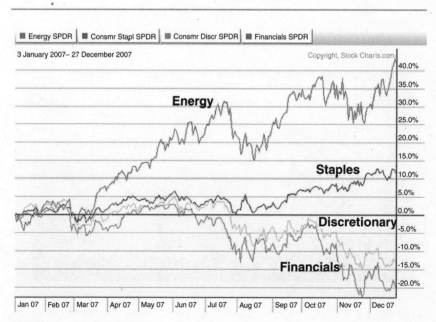

FIGURE 10.2 This performance chart shows that Energy and Consumer Staples were 2007 leaders while Consumer Discretionary and Financials were the weakest sectors.
Source: StockCharts.com

Consumer Staples (in that order). The two weakest were Financials and Consumer Discretionary. That's a recipe for a lower stock market and a slowing economy.

Figure 10.3 shows the same data in bar format and arranges the best and worst sector performers during 2007 in descending order. Those above the zero line were in the black while those below the zero line in the red. That chart shows the top four 2007 performers to be Energy, Basic Materials, Utilities, and Consumer Staples. If you check the diagram in Figure 10.1, you'll see that those four sectors are usually market leaders in the late stages of an economic expansion and early stages of an economic contraction. As the economy starts to slow, money moves into more defensive sectors such as Consumer Staples and Utilities. That rotation is usually associated with a weak stock market. That negative rotation is further characterized by relative weakness in Financials and Consumer Discretionary stocks (which include autos, retailers, and homebuilders). That was certainly the case during the second half of 2007.

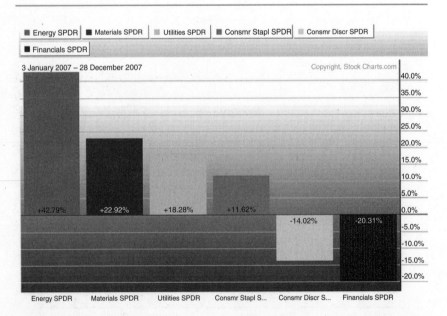

FIGURE 10.3 Performance bars show top sectors during 2007 to be Energy, Materials, Utilities, and Consumer Staples. The weakest were Consumer Discretionary and Financials. That's a recipe for a weak stock market.
Source: StockCharts.com

SECTOR CARPETS

One of the most user-friendly visual tools that I use to help isolate market leaders is the *market sector carpet*. You won't get the full impact of the carpet here because it's shown in grayscale. On your computer screen, however, it's in color. I'm including it to alert you to its existence and to explain how to use it. Figure 10.4 shows the S&P sector carpet for the two months between April and June 2008. (You can adjust the time period to one day, one week, or one or two months.) The boxes in Figure 10.4 show the nine S&P sectors over that two-month time span. On a computer screen, each box is shown in varying shades of green and red. The greener the sector box, the stronger the sector. The redder the sector box, the weaker the sector.

Although you can't see the actual colors here, you can still read the percentage changes on the top of each box. The list on the far right shows the four top and four bottom sectors during those two months based on percentage changes. The top four sectors were Energy (+11 percent), Technology (+7 percent), Utilities (+5 percent), and Industrials (+1 percent).

FIGURE 10.4 The S&P market sector carpet shows Energy to be the strongest sector (+11 percent) during second quarter 2008. Financials were the weakest (−9 percent).
Source: StockCharts.com

The four weakest were Financials (−9 percent), Consumer Discretionary (−3 percent), Materials (−1.6 percent), and Health Care (−1.3 percent). The sector carpet showed you where market leadership was coming from and gave you a starting point from which to dig deeper.

USING MARKET CARPET TO FIND STOCK LEADERS

The sector carpet does more than just tell you which market sectors have been the strongest over the selected period of time. It can also tell you which stocks were market leaders within each leading sector. Energy was the top performing sector over the two months in question. By clicking on the Energy carpet, you're shown another carpet which ranks the stocks within that leading sector. Figure 10.5 ranks the top five percentage gainers in the Energy sector over the same time span. The top percentage gainer was Peabody with a two-month gain of 33 percent. Just because a stock shows up on the sector leader board doesn't make it a good investment.

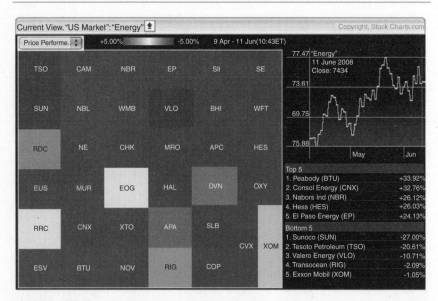

FIGURE 10.5 The S&P market sector carpet shows Peabody to be the strongest energy stock during second quarter 2008. Four other leaders are shown in the box to the right.
Source: StockCharts.com

You still have to look at its stock chart to determine that. (You can instantly view a chart by simply clicking on the name of any stock.) But you're already starting your search by looking at five stock leaders within a top-performing sector. The other energy leaders were Consolidated Energy (+32 percent), Nabors (+28 percent), Hess (+26 percent), and El Paso Energy (+24 percent). It's been estimated that at least half of a stock's performance is determined by its particular sector. That being the case, the search for a winning stock is made a good deal easier by first locating the strongest sectors. The same is true for industry groups.

INDUSTRY GROUP LEADER

Performance rankings can also be used to isolate leaders among industry groups. Figure 10.6 shows which industry groups were marker leaders and laggards during the second half of 2007. Two of the top industry leaders were gold and oil service stocks, subsets of the Basic Material and

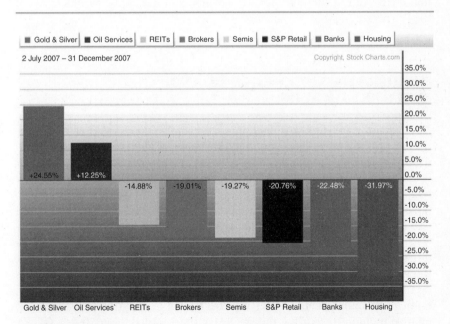

FIGURE 10.6 Performance bars show precious metal stocks and oil services to be the strongest industries during second half of 2007. The weakest were homebuilders, banks, retailers, semiconductors, brokers, and real estate investment trusts (REITS). *Source:* StockCharts.com

Energy sectors. By contrast, the weakest were homebuilders, banks, retailers, semiconductors, brokers, and REITS. Figure 10.6 shows which industry groups did best during the last six months of 2007 as the stock market was weakening. And which ones were leading the market lower.

SECTOR TRENDS NEED TO BE MONITORED

Keep in mind that sector trends need to be monitored on a regular basis. You can't just "buy and hold" a sector like you can the stock market. What worked during one six-month period (or quarter) may not work during the next. That's where performance charts and market sector carpets come into play. It's generally a good idea to review those visual tools at least once a week to see if some of the leaders are starting to slip in the rankings or if some of the laggards are starting to move up. Also keep in mind that these tools are simply screening devices to ensure that you're always dealing with market leaders. The next step after that is to look at the actual charts of the sectors, industry groups, and individual stocks to see if they're acting in a bullish fashion.

INFORMATION ON SECTORS AND INDUSTRY GROUPS

Most of the group indexes used in sector analysis are listed as exchange traded options on various stock exchanges. As such, the data is readily available and easily charted. If you wish to know what's in each index (which is a good idea), the exchange where it's traded is usually the best source. The three biggest options exchanges are the American Stock Exchange (AMEX.com), the Chicago Board Options Exchange (CBOE.com), and the Philadelphia Stock Exchange (PHLX.com). Although the Philadelphia Exchange has the fewest listings, some of its offerings are among the most popular in the industry. They include the KBW Bank Index (BKX), the Gold/Silver Index (XAU), the Housing Index (HGX), the Oil Service Index (OSX), the Semiconductor Index (SOX), and the Utility Index (UTY). Some of the more popular stock indexes traded on the American Stock Exchange include the Airline Index (XAL), the Biotechnology Index (BTK), the Gold Bugs Index (HUI), the Gold Miners Index (GDX), the Natural Gas Index (XNG), the Oil Index (XOI), the Pharmaceutical Index (DRG), and the Broker/Dealer Index (XBD).

SPOTTING NATURAL GAS LEADERSHIP

The AMEX Natural Gas Index was one of the stock market's strongest performers during the first quarter of 2008. Natural gas stocks gained 7 percent versus a 6 percent loss for the S&P 500 during those three months. That being the case, natural gas would have been a good place to be looking for market leadership. The sector carpet showed that Energy was the top performing sector during February and March 2008. The AMEX Natural Gas Index gained 12 percent during that period versus 7.5 percent for the entire sector. That made natural gas a leader within that leading sector. Figure 10.7 shows the AMEX Natural Gas Index reaching a record high in spring 2008. The rising relative strength ratio below the chart divides the Natural Gas Index (XNG) by the Energy Sector SPDR (XLE). The rising ratio during that first quarter shows natural gas stocks doing much better than the energy sector as a whole during those three months and emerging as new energy leader. Natural gas remained the top energy sector during the first half of 2008.

NATURAL GAS COMPONENTS

Stock pickers had one more step to take in looking for a marker leader during first quarter 2008. That was to locate the strongest stock in the natural gas group. The Market Carpet revealed that EOG Resources was the top percentage energy gainer during those same two months. EOG was also the most heavily weighted stock in the Natural Gas Index. You could have found that out by going to AMEX.com and clicking on the Natural Gas Index. By then selecting "Show Index Components," you would see a list of 15 natural gas stocks in order of their relative weighting in the XNG (starting with the biggest). EOG had a top weight of 8 percent. The next five were Southwestern (7.9 percent), Devon (7.2 percent), Apache (7.2 percent), Chesapeake (7.1 percent), and XTO Energy (6.8 percent). All six natural gas stocks were energy leaders at the time.

There are several reasons for finding out which stocks are in an index. One is simply to obtain a list of potential market leaders. Another is to see which stocks carry the most influence in the index. Those are usually the bigger ones. They usually warrant a closer look. In a market climate that favors larger stocks (such as first quarter 2008), it's advantageous to be able to combine relative strength with size. In the case of EOG, you had the best of all worlds. Not only was EOG the biggest stock in the XNG. It was also the strongest stock in the strongest industry in the strongest sector.

FIGURE 10.7 Natural gas stocks became new energy leaders during fourth quarter 2007 and the first half of 2008. Notice the upturn in the XNG/XLE ratio.
Source: StockCharts.com

The weekly price bars in Figure 10.8 show EOG Resources achieving a bullish breakout during fourth quarter 2007 and surging to a record high during first quarter 2008 (see circle). The solid line below the chart is a ratio of EOG divided by the Natural Gas Index (XNG). From the start of 2006 until the fourth quarter of 2007, EOG had been a natural gas laggard. The upturn in its relative strength ratio during the fourth quarter gave an early hint of more explosive leadership to come in first quarter 2008. The trick was to spot those changes. These tools made it easier to do that.

CBOE VOLATILITY (VIX) INDEX

Let's not leave the subject of group indexes without including the Chicago Board Options Exchange (CBOE) Volatility Index (VIX). The VIX is a measure of market expectation of near-term volatility for the S&P 500. It can be traded on the CBOE as a futures contract and an option. Most people in the industry, however, use the VIX as a contrary market indicator—it's a good one.

The most important thing to remember about the VIX is that it's a "contrary" indicator. That means that it trends in the opposite direction of the S&P 500. In other words, a rising VIX Index is bad for stocks, while a falling VIX is good. Figure 10.9 shows how well it worked in the eight years since 2000.

The solid line in Figure 10.9 is the VIX, while the prices bars are the S&P 500. You can see their inverse relationship very clearly. After rising during the bear market that started in 2000, the VIX peaked during fourth quarter 2002 (down arrow) just as the bear market for the S&P 500 was ending. The VIX then fell for the next four years, which coincided with rising stock prices. In mid-2007, however, the VIX rose to a four-year high (see circle) and signaled that the era of low market volatility had ended. That upside breakout by the VIX during summer 2007 also coincided with the start of a topping process in the S&P 500.

Figure 10.10 compares the VIX (bottom line) to the S&P 500 (top line) from the start of 2007 through mid-2008. During July 2007, the VIX rose above 18 for the first time in four years (circle) and continued to rise into August. That upside breakout coincided with a drop of 10 percent in the S&P 500 during that same month (see arrows). A second VIX upturn in October coincided with a second S&P peak. The third VIX upturn during January 2008 coincided with another downturn in the S&P 500, which pushed it into a 20 percent loss by mid-March. While each upturn in the VIX coincided with a market drop, each pullback in the VIX coincided with a market bounce.

The VIX turned down sharply in March 2008 (see Figure 10.10) and dropped into mid-May. While the VIX was dropping during that second

FIGURE 10.8 EOG Resources became the natural gas leader starting in fourth quarter 2007. The upturn in the EOG/XNG ratio made that very clear.
Source: StockCharts.com

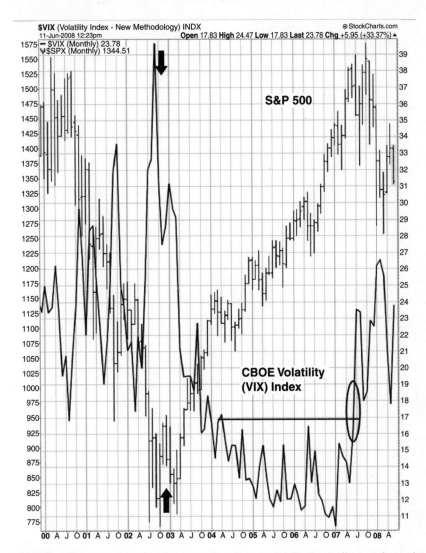

FIGURE 10.9 The CBOE Volatility (VIX) Index (solid line) usually trends in the opposite direction of the S&P 500 (bars). The upside breakout in the VIX during summer 2007 (see circle) warned of rising volatility and lower stock prices.
Source: StockCharts.com

FIGURE 10.10 The VIX Index (lower chart) and the S&P 500 (upper chart) trended in opposite directions from the start of 2007 to mid-2008. The May 2007 upturn in the VIX coincided with another major stock decline.
Source: StockCharts.com

quarter, the S&P 500 rallied enough to regain half of its prior losses. The sharp bounce in the VIX off its October low in mid-May, however, coincided with another downturn in the S&P 500.*

There's more to the VIX than just its direction. Historically, VIX readings over 40 generally coincided with market bottoms (as in 2002), while readings below 20 usually coincided with market peaks (as in 2000). Those numbers shifted downward during the last bull market. During 2005 and 2006, the VIX traded in a narrow range between 10 and 18. Each upturn from 10 coincided with minor market pullbacks. The upside breakout in the VIX during summer 2007 signaled that the VIX was moving on to higher levels and gave the first real danger signal for stocks in five years.

Besides acting as a good contrary indicator for stocks, the CBOE Volatility Index also offers a way to hedge against a falling market. When stocks fall, the VIX usually rises. You can buy a futures contract or an option on the VIX and profit from that rise. Those vehicles allow you to actually benefit from rising volatility and a weak market.

SUMMARY

This chapter explains the importance of market sectors and industry groups. The stock market is divided into nine sectors and nearly 90 industry groups. Investors familiar with those stock categories, and who know how to measure their performance, can greatly improve the overall performance of their portfolio. Fortunately, there are visual tools that make the task of finding group leaders relatively easy—performance charts and market sector carpets. Performance charts allow the investor to compare the relative performance of any number of market indexes. Being in the right sectors (and out of the wrong ones) is very important. Figure 10.11 shows why it's important to be able to tell the difference between the two. From June 2007 to June 2008, the Energy SPDR (bars) gained 50 percent while the Financials SPDR (solid line) lost 36 percent. Both of those SPDRs are exchange-traded funds that we cover in more depth in Chapter 12. Their existence has greatly simplified sector trading.

Being in the right industry groups is also important. Figure 10.12 compares the AMEX Natural Gas Index (bars) to the PHLX Semiconductor Index (solid line) between June 2007 and June 2008. During these 12 months, natural gas stocks rose 66 percent while semiconductors lost 17 percent. Obviously, natural gas was a much better place to be than semiconductors

---

*From that May low, the VIX rose to the highest level since 1987 by October 2008. From its May peak, the S&P fell to the lowest level in five years by that October.

FIGURE 10.11 From the summer of 2007 until mid-2008, the Energy SPDR (bars) soared while the Financials SPDR (line) collapsed. That shows why it's important to be in the strongest sectors and out of the weakest ones.
Source: StockCharts.com

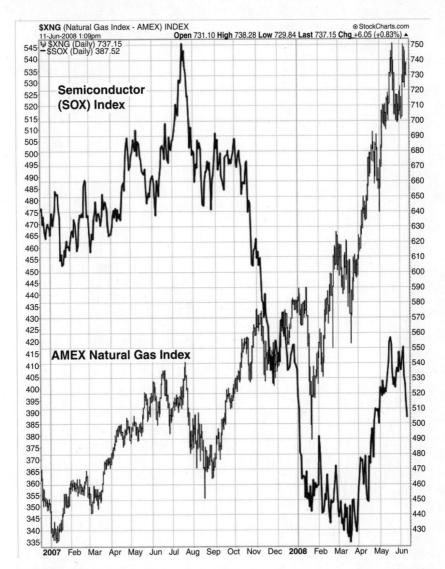

FIGURE 10.12 Natural gas stocks rose sharply from the summer of 2007 through mid-2008 while semiconductors fell. It's always better to be in the group that's rising.
Source: StockCharts.com

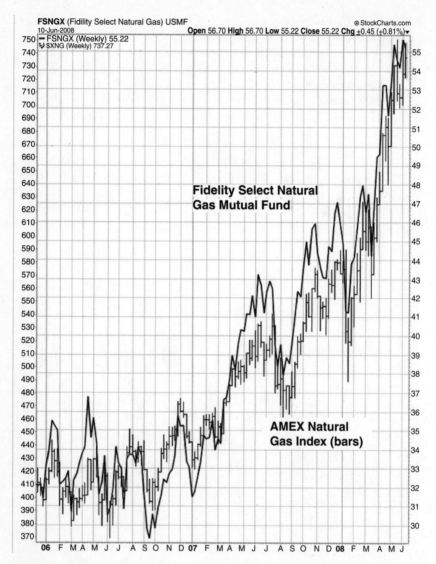

FIGURE 10.13 A close linkage is seen between the AMEX Natural Gas Index (bars) and the Fidelity Select Natural Gas Mutual Fund (line) from 2006 to 2008. Sector mutual funds usually track their sector benchmarks pretty closely.
Source: StockCharts.com

during that year. The two indexes in Figure 10.12 are index options. If you're an option trader, you can buy and sell them directly. There are two other ways to trade them. One is to pick an ETF that matches up with one of the indexes (such as Semiconductor Holders). A second choice is to pick a sector mutual fund that matches up with the one you wish to trade.

There's usually a pretty close correlation between stock indexes and their related trading vehicles (either ETFs or mutual funds). Figure 10.13 overlays the AMEX Natural Gas Index (bars) over the Fidelity Select Natural Gas Fund (solid line) from the start of 2006 to mid-2008. It's hard to tell the two lines apart because they track each other so closely. The natural gas mutual fund was one of Fidelity's top sector performers during that period of time. That leads us to our next chapter, which shows how to implement various trading strategies by utilizing mutual funds.

CHAPTER 11

Mutual Funds

C hart analysis of mutual funds is an additional step. A trader can analyze the various industry and sector indexes to find which ones he or she wishes to invest in and then simply match them up to a suitable mutual fund. The mutual fund industry is so vast that you can find anything you wish to trade in the bond and stock markets. Most mutual funds are also indexed to some market benchmark. All you really need to do is analyze the benchmarks and then match them up with the appropriate fund. Chart analysis can also be performed on the mutual funds themselves if you wish to go a step further. There are at least two reasons for doing so.

One is for purposes of confirmation. A buy or sell signal on an index chart should be confirmed by a similar signal on the mutual fund that corresponds to that index. A second reason is because index charts and mutual funds are not always "perfectly" correlated. Sometimes action in the mutual fund chart will lead the group index, and sometimes it's the other way around. If you're a mutual fund investor, it's usually a good idea to make sure that the mutual fund chart looks reasonably similar to the group index that attracted you to the mutual fund in the first place. The good news is that most of the visual tools described in this book work very well on mutual fund charts.

WHAT WORKS ON MUTUAL FUNDS

As is the case with most markets, it's not necessary to do an exhaustive analysis of mutual fund charts. Simple trend-following techniques like trendlines, support and resistance levels, and moving averages work quite well. *Moving average convergence divergence* (MACD) and the MACD histogram can also be used to good effect. Most oscillators can also be employed to spot overbought and oversold conditions and positive and negative divergences. Price patterns like "double tops and bottoms," "head and shoulders," and "triangles" can be spotted on mutual fund charts. And, of course, relative strength analysis applies equally well on charts of mutual funds. There are some minor limitations, however, when charting open-end mutual funds.

OPEN- VERSUS CLOSED-END FUNDS

There are two types of mutual funds. Both types allow investors to buy and sell baskets of stocks, but in different ways. The *closed-end mutual fund* has a fixed amount of shares and is traded like any other stock on a stock exchange. That being the case, closed-end mutual funds can be charted like any other stock. The *open-end mutual fund* takes in new cash from investors at any time and is usually purchased through a fund family such as Fidelity or Vanguard. Since most of our work in this book is directed at the open-end fund, it's necessary to point out some chart limitations in dealing with that vehicle.

CHARTING ADJUSTMENTS ON OPEN-END FUNDS

Some minor adjustments have to be made when doing chart analysis of open-end mutual funds. The first has to do with the price. Only one price is available on a daily basis—the *net asset value* (NAV) that is released after the close of business each day. The NAV tells us what the fund is actually worth, based on the closing values of the stocks included in the fund. There is no opening price and no high and low range for the day. As a result, line charts that connect closing prices are used in place of bar charts. (It isn't possible to construct candlestick charts either because that technique requires an opening price along with high and low prices).

Virtually all of the indicators described in this book can still be used because they are based primarily on closing prices. (One exception is the stochastics oscillator, which uses the daily price range.) The RSI oscillator, however, can still be used to measure overbought and oversold readings. Traditional momentum and *rate of change* (ROC), as well as the MACD indicators, can also be used. Volume analysis, however, isn't possible on open-fund mutual funds. That's because volume figures are not released with the daily NAV values. This, however, doesn't prevent you from checking the volume figures for the stocks or group on which the fund is based.

BLENDING FUNDAMENTAL AND TECHNICAL DATA

Although this book deals primarily with the charting (or visual) aspects of mutual fund analysis, investors should be aware of the fundamental (or economic) background that effects the various financial markets and their related mutual funds. Morningstar provides a unique rating system that takes into account fund profitability and risk. Investors might limit their visual analysis to funds that have the highest (four or five star) Morningstar ratings, for example. Or the visual investor might check Morningstar ratings to obtain more details on a fund that looks attractive from a charting standpoint. That way the investor has both the fundamental and technical factors working together. Sometimes it works the other way around. If you find a highly rated mutual fund, be sure to check its chart first to make sure that the timing of your purchase or sale is right.

RELATIVE STRENGTH ANALYSIS

Earlier chapters extolled the merits of relative strength analysis and its particular importance in choosing the right sectors and industry groups. The same holds true for mutual funds themselves. Relative strength analysis adds an important dimension to market analysis by telling us how one fund is performing relative to the rest of the market or how its performance compares to other fund competitors in the same category. Mutual fund rankings are readily available in the financial press and on the Internet which include general stock funds, international stock funds, and specialized stock funds. Those rankings can be done weekly, monthly, quarterly, or yearly. The same is true for general bond funds, government bond funds, international bond funds, specialized and municipal bond funds. There are lots of sector funds to choose from. Fidelity Investments list at least 40 specialty or select (i.e., sector) portfolios.

TRADITIONAL AND NONTRADITIONAL MUTUAL FUNDS

Fidelity Investments is one of the biggest mutual fund families. Others include Vanguard and T. Rowe Price. All offer a broad array of mutual fund offerings that allow the investor exposure to the stock market through broad index funds and the ability to divide the market up into categories based on size (small cap versus large cap), style (growth versus value), or region (domestic versus foreign). There are a wide variety of bond funds to choose from as well. In addition, there are a large number of sector mutual funds for investors who wish to fine-tune their stock portfolios even further. Our interest in this chapter lies mainly with sector funds. Since Fidelity has the biggest selection of sector funds (at least 40), that's where we're going to focus most of our attention. All of the aforementioned fund families are considered to be traditional mutual funds. Over the last decade, however, a number of newer fund families have started offering "nontraditional" mutual funds offerings.

By nontraditional, I refer to mutual funds that offer exposure to commodity and currency markets. While traditional bond funds match the performance of bond prices, some newer funds are based on the direction of bond yields. We'll show one of those newer funds later in the chapter. *Inverse mutual funds* have also become increasingly popular. These funds, which are designed to move in the opposite direction of some market benchmark, allow investors to profit in falling markets. We'll have more to say on that a little later. The good news is that all of these traditional, and nontraditional, mutual funds lend themselves very nicely to visual market analysis.

KEEP IT SIMPLE

The accompanying charts apply some of the tools of chart analysis directly on open-end mutual fund charts representing various stock market sectors and industry groups. In most cases, only one or two visual tools (or indicators) are drawn on the charts. I've done that simply to show that it's not necessary to get too fancy with your visual analysis. A couple of simple chart tools is usually all you need. There's also a more subtle message on the mutual fund charts. The upside and downside breakouts are pretty easy to spot. So are the important changes in trend that take place. In my experience, the best market moves are usually fairly obvious. The real trick is to make sure that you see them.

200-DAY MOVING AVERAGE AND HOUSING

All of the charting tools included in the following charts have been explained in earlier chapters. Figure 11.1, for example, applies a simple

FIGURE 11.1 The July 2007 drop below the 200-day moving average (circle) warned of a serious downturn in this housing mutual fund.
Source: StockCharts.com.

200-day moving average to the Fidelity Select Construction/Housing Fund from the start of 2007 into the first month of 2008. It's no secret that the housing sector had a very bad 2007. In fact, this particular housing fund fell 30 percent from its June 2007 high to its January 2008 low. That made it one of that year's weakest sector funds. The visual investor could have avoided most of those losses by simply tracking the fund's 200-day moving average. The fund fell below that major support line during July which flashed a major sell signal (see circle).

NATURAL GAS BREAKOUT

Figure 11.2 shows the Fidelity Select Natural Gas Fund from mid-2005 through spring 2008. The main focus on that chart is the very obvious bullish breakout that took place during spring 2007. During April, the fund rose above its spring 2006 highs to achieve a bullish breakout. As further confirmation of that bullish move, the fund dipped right back to its breakout point during August (see circle) before resuming its uptrend. That confirmed the old adage that "old resistance becomes new support." Although several chart indicators also confirmed that bullish action in the natural gas group, they weren't that necessary. That's because the best breakouts are usually the most obvious ones. And that was certainly the case with this fund.

CONSUMER DISCRETIONARY BREAKDOWN

Trendlines are one of the simplest and most valuable of all charting tools. Figure 11.3 is a good example of that. That figure charts the Fidelity Select Consumer Discretionary Portfolio from 2003 to spring 2008. The rising trendline is drawn from the spring 2003 bottom and touches the reaction lows in 2004 and 2006 (up arrows). The more times a trendline is touched, the more reliable it becomes. A good trendline should be touched at least three times as this one was. That's why the decisive break of that four-year support line during October 2007 (circle) was so important. Not only did that signal a substantial downturn in that fund, it occured only a third of the way into the decline. The visual investor had ample warning to step aside. Here again, there's nothing fancy on Figure 11.3. Just a simple trendline was all that was needed.

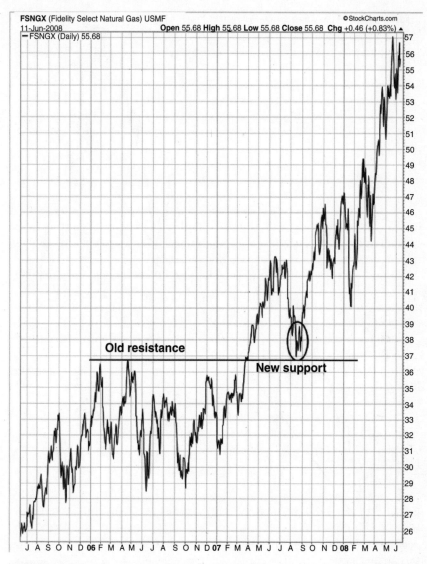

FIGURE 11.2 An example of how old resistance becomes new support. The bullish breakout in this natural gas mutual fund in the spring of 2007 was pretty easy to spot.
Source: StockCharts.com.

FIGURE 11.3 The October 2007 break of four-year support line (circle) signaled a serious downturn in this consumer discretionary mutual fund.
Source: StockCharts.com.

BEAR CROSSING SINKS CHIPS

Figure 11.4 gets a bit fancier, but not by much. That chart uses a 50- and 200-day moving average combination on the Fidelity Select Electronics Fund (which is comprised mainly of semiconductor stocks). There are actually two major sell signals produced on Figure 11.4. The first is the downside violation of the 200-day average during November 2007 (see circle). The second is the downside crossing of the 200-day average by the 50-day (down arrow) a month later. From its summer 2007 top to its spring 2008 bottom, this fund lost 30 percent of its value. The visual trader who spotted the bearish moving average crossing could have avoided two-thirds of those losses. The November violation of the fund's August low also gave a traditional sell signal by violating a previous support low. That's pretty basic charting.

NEGATIVE ROC HURTS TECHNOLOGY

Figure 11.5 shows the Fidelity Select Technology Fund crossing its 40-week (200-day) average twice during 2006. After a downside correction that spring, an upward crossing in September 2006 signaled a new uptrend which lasted more than year. The downward crossing in December 2008 (circle) started a new downtrend. The line at the bottom is a 13-week ROC line. A sell signal occurred in December 2007 (down arrow) when the rate of change fell below zero for the first time in 16 months.

CONSUMER STAPLES HOLD UP OKAY

The darker line in Figure 11.6 plots the Fidelity Select Consumer Staples Portfolio. The lighter line is a ratio of that fund divided by the S&P 500. Although the Consumer Staples fund lost some ground during the first quarter of 2008, it did much better than the S&P 500. Its *relative strength* (RS) line hit a new high in March 2008. Figure 11.6 shows that a Consumer Staples fund is a relatively safer place to be during a market drop.

RETAIL RATIO PLUNGES

While a Consumer Staples fund is a good place to be during a market downturn (and a slowing economy), a retail fund isn't. Figure 11.7 plots a ratio of the Fidelity Select Retailing Fund divided by the S&P 500. During

FIGURE 11.4 This semiconductor mutual fund broke its 200-day average during November 2007. A month later the 50-day also broke the 200-day average. *Source:* StockCharts.com.

FIGURE 11.5 This technology mutual fund broke its 40-week average in December 2007. The 13-week rate of change fell below its zero line for the first time in a year.
Source: StockCharts.com.

FIGURE 11.6 The RS line for this Consumer Staples mutual fund hit a new high in spring 2008. This is why it's considered a defensive fund.
Source: StockCharts.com.

FSRPX:$SPX (Fidelity Select Retailing/S&P 500 Large Cap Index) USMF/INDEX   © StockCharts.com
11-Jun-2008   **Open** 0.02830 **High** 0.02830 **Low** 0.02830 **Close** 0.02830 **Chg** +0.00001 (+0.02%)▲

Fidelity Retail Fund/ S&P 500 ratio

FIGURE 11.7   The RS line for this retailing mutual fund broke a two-year support line during the summer of 2007. That wasn't a good place to be.
Source: StockCharts.com.

summer 2007, the relative strength ratio broke a support line (see circle) drawn under the July 2005 and July 2006 lows. It continued to drop into the start of 2008. In hard times, consumers still need to buy staples. But they can cut back on just about everything else. And they did.

ENERGIZING A PORTFOLIO

One of the reasons consumers were cutting back on retail spending during 2007 and early 2008 was rising energy prices. While this is bad for retail stocks, it's good for an Energy fund. Figure 11.8 shows the Fidelity Select Energy Fund breaking the upper resistance line in a triangular-shaped pattern that formed during first quarter 2008.

LATIN AMERICA LEADS

Mutual funds also offer exposure to foreign markets. As is usually the case here, it's usually best to be in those regions of the world that show the most strength, such as Latin America. Figure 11.9 plots the Fidelity Latin America Fund from the start of 2006 to spring 2008. Notice how each pullback during 2007 and 2008 bounced off the rising support line (which uses a logarithmic scale). One of the reasons why Latin America held up so well was its role as an exporter of natural resources. That made Latin America a beneficiary of rising commodity prices. Falling commodity prices would of course act as a drag on Latin America, which occurred during the second half of 2008 when this fund lost half its value.

REAL ESTATE IS GLOBAL

Global trends can also be seen in stock sectors and industries. Figure 11.10 shows that real estate problems weren't limited to the United States during 2007. That figure plots the Fidelity International Real Estate Fund. The solid line is the 200-day moving average. The inability of that fund to reach a new high during October 2007 was an early sign that the global real estate market was beginning to weaken. Its drop below a falling 200-day average during November was another bearish sign (arrow). It's a bad sign when the 200-day line turns down as it did near the end of that year. Those were warnings to the visual investor that it was a good time to relocate some funds elsewhere. (By October 2008, this fund had lost nearly half its value as subprime problems spread to Europe and elsewhere).

FIGURE 11.8 This energy mutual fund broke out of a triangle formation during April 2008. Price patterns are visible on mutual fund charts.
Source: StockCharts.com.

FIGURE 11.9   Rising commodities helped make Latin America one of the world's strongest regions. The same is true of other commodity exporters. Falling commodities have the opposite effect.
Source: StockCharts.com.

FIREX (Fidelity Intl Real Estate Fund) USMF
11-Jun-2008
Open 11.49 High 11.49 Low 11.49 Close 11.49 Chg -0.19 (-1.63%)▾
© StockCharts.com
■ FIREX (Daily) 11.49
■ MA(200) 13.22

200-day
average

FIGURE 11.10 The drop in this international real estate fund during 2007 shows that housing problems weren't limited to the United States.
Source: StockCharts.com.

PROFUNDS RISING RATES FUND

Traditional bond funds are based on the price of bonds. Bond prices trend in the opposite direction of bond yields. In a climate of falling bond yields, bond prices rise and bond funds profit accordingly. When bond yields start to rise, however, bond funds usually lose money. What's an investor to do then when bond yields are rising? He or she can buy a bond fund that's based on bond yields. One such bond offering is the ProFunds Rising Rates Opportunity 10 Fund (RTPIX). That mutual fund is designed to rise and fall with the 10-year Treasury note yield. Figure 11.11 shows the trend of the fund over a three-and-half-year period starting with 2005. From mid-2005 to mid-2007, the bond yield fund rose steadily for a two-year gain of 15 percent. Treasury prices fell during those two years and most traditional bond funds lost money. From mid-2007 to spring 2008, however, bond yields fell sharply. The downside break of the two-year rising trendline signaled the change in trend. During those eight months, a traditional bond fund would have done much better than this fund.

Entering summer 2008, however, inflation concerns resulting from surging commodity markets started to boost bond yields once again. Figure 11.11 shows the ProFunds Rising Rates 10 Fund breaking its 10-month down trendline after bouncing off chart support at its 2005 low. Rising interest rates would favor this fund over a traditional bond fund which would lose ground as bond prices dropped.

Fortunately, the visual investor has the tools to know when to switch from a bond fund based in price to one based on yield. Figure 11.11 employs nothing more than a couple of simple trendlines and some basic chart analysis. The reasons for showing you Figure 11.11 are twofold. One is to simply alert you to the fact that bond funds do exist that allow you to profit in a climate of rising interest rates. The second point is to reassure you that all of the visual tools that have been described in this book work on bond funds based on price and those based on yield.

PROFUNDS FALLING U.S. DOLLAR FUND

One of the newer developments in the mutual fund industry has been the ability to participate in the trend of the U.S. dollar. Even better is the availability of mutual funds that allow you to profit not only from a rising dollar, but a falling dollar as well. The latter is an inverse fund that trends in the opposite direction of the U.S. Dollar Index. That's very useful to have when the dollar is in a major bear market. Figure 11.12 plots the ProFunds Falling Dollar Fund (FDPIX). The fund is designed to trend in the opposite direction of the U.S. Dollar Index (which measures the dollar

FIGURE 11.11 The ProFunds Rising Rates 10 Fund trends in the same direction of bond yields. It's a good fund to own in a climate of rising interest rates.
Source: StockCharts.com.

FDPIX (Falling US Dollar ProFund) USMF
11-Jun-2008
© StockCharts.com
Open 31.42 High 31.42 Low 31.11 Close 31.29 Chg -0.37 (-1.17%) ▾
▬ FDPIX (Weekly) 31.29

FIGURE 11.12 The ProFunds Falling U.S. Dollar Fund trends in the opposite direction of the U.S. Dollar Index. This inverse fund rises as the dollar falls.
Source: StockCharts.com.

against six foreign currencies). That inverse fund bottomed in 2002 (as the dollar peaked) and then rose steadily for the next six years. From the start of 2002 to spring of 2008, the falling dollar fund gained 60 percent while the U.S. Dollar Index fell a similar amount.

In earlier chapters, several ways were presented to profit from a falling U.S. dollar. One is to buy commodities (or stocks tied to commodities) that usually rise when the dollar falls. Another way is the overweight foreign stocks, which usually do much better with a weak dollar. Or you can buy foreign currencies (more on that in the next chapter). The most direct way to profit from a weak dollar, however, is to buy a mutual fund that actually rises when the dollar falls. ProFunds offers a fund that lets you do that. It also offers a fund that trends in the same direction as the U.S. Dollar Index, which would be more suitable during a dollar uptrend. Of course, the trader needs to be able to tell whether the dollar is in an uptrend or a downtrend. Charting tools help you do that.

COMMODITY MUTUAL FUNDS

Just a decade ago, it was pretty difficult for the average investor to buy commodities outside of the futures markets. Largely as the result of the major uptrend in commodity markets that started in 2002, a number of commodity mutual funds have appeared. One of the first of such funds is the PIMCO Commodity Real Return Fund (PCRAX). This fund is designed to mimic the Dow Jones AIG Commodity Index, and Figure 11.13 plots the PIMCO over the three-year period starting in 2005. A bullish breakout in October 2007 reflected a flood of money moving out of stocks during the subprime mortgage crisis. Commodity mutual funds were the big beneficiaries of that major asset allocation switch. Figure 11.13 shows that the 2007 bullish breakout in the PIMCO commodity fund was pretty easy to spot (see circle).

INVERSE STOCK FUNDS

Bear (or inverse) funds allow investors to make money in falling markets. Fund families like ProFunds and Rydex Investments offer a wide assortment of bear funds that cover domestic and foreign stock markets. Many of them are called *ultra funds* which move 150 percent to 200 percent as far as their underlying index. One such fund is the Rydex Inverse Russell 2000 2X Strategy Fund (RYIZX).

Figure 11.14 shows that small-cap bear fund forming a double bottom between July and October 2007. The ultra bear fund gained 40 percent from

FIGURE 11.13 The PIMCO Commodity Real Return Strategy Fund achieved a bullish breakout during fourth quarter 2007 (see circle) after a period of consolidation. Commodity mutual funds offer investors easy access to commodity markets. *Source:* StockCharts.com.

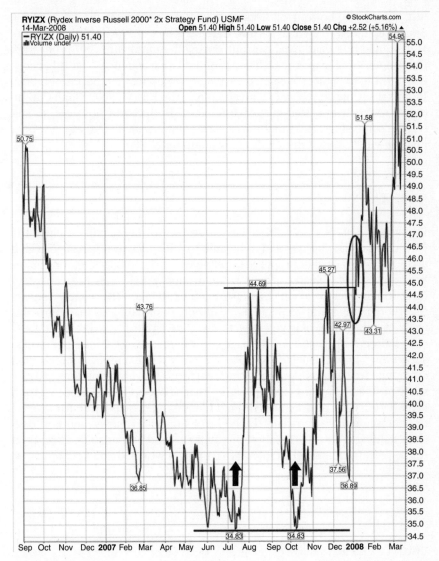

FIGURE 11.14 This inverse small cap fund is designed to rise twice as much as the Russell 2000 falls. The double bottom formed between July and October 2007 led to a 40 percent increase. Inverse funds offer a way to profit from a falling stock market.
Source: StockCharts.com.

its October 2007 bottom to its March 2008 top. By contrast, the Russell 2000 Small Cap Index (on which it's based) fell 20 percent. Not only did investors who bought this small-cap bear fund during the summer of 2007 profit from the drop in small-cap stocks. They profited twice as much. That's because this ultra bear fund is designed to rise twice as fast as the Russell 2000 Index falls. Charting tools can be applied to the Russell 2000 Small-Cap Index or to the inverse Russell 2000 fund itself. Both charts, however, should tell the same story. Bear funds were extremely valuable in the major bear market which started during the fourth quarter of 2007.

SUMMARY

Previous chapters emphasized the importance of being able to chart the various financial markets and to be able to tell which are rising and which are not for purposes of proper asset allocation. The ability to monitor market sectors and industry groups to determine which ones to overweight (and which ones to avoid) has also been explained. This chapter shows that there many traditional and nontraditional mutual funds that allow you to do just about anything you wish to do in the financial markets (and from either direction). That wasn't the case just a decade ago. This chapter also shows that simple visual tools explained in earlier chapters work quite well on mutual fund charts. As good as mutual funds are, however, they provide some problems for the active investor. That's especially true in sector trading where trends may last only a few months. That's also true for inverse mutual funds that are meant to be used as trading vehicles and not long-term holdings. The proliferation of exchange-traded funds has made fund (or basket) trading even simpler. We'll explain why in the next chapter.

CHAPTER 12

Exchange-Traded Funds

Although *exchange-traded funds* (ETFs) first appeared in 1993, they didn't start attracting serious attention until after 2000. By the second quarter of 2008, funds invested in ETFs had reached $612 billion, more than a five-fold increase from eight years earlier. The growth of ETFs represents a huge step in the evolution of the financial markets and has made the task of the visual investor a good deal easier. When I first wrote about intermarket relationships nearly 20 years ago, it wasn't that easy to implement all of the strategies involved. That's because intermarket work encompassed bonds, commodities, currencies, foreign markets, and U.S. stocks. It also included market sectors and industry groups. Outside of the futures markets, it wasn't easy to trade commodities or currencies. Sector trading wasn't that easy either. During the 1990s, the broadening of the mutual fund industry helped a lot. Since 2000, however, the availability of exchange-traded funds has been a giant leap forward.

In the spring of 2008, 683 exchange-trade funds were being offered by 23 fund managers. The three firms that dominate the ETF market are Barclays Global Investors, Vanguard, and State Street. Those three firms account for 85 percent of the ETF market. Of those three, Barclays is the biggest ETF player with 52 percent of the market. Some smaller firms that offer innovative ETF products include Claymore Securities, PowerShares, ProShares, Rydex, Van Eck Global, and Wisdom Tree. Exchange-traded funds exist for major stock indexes, sector and industry groups, and international markets. ETFs also exist for bonds, commodities, and currencies. Every style of stock investing is covered including size (large, midsize, and small) and style (growth and value). Inverse funds are

offered for those who wish to profit from falling markets. Ultra funds offer even greater potential for market movement. International ETFs cover
all of the major stock markets around the globe by country and region.
Emerging market ETFs also exist. There's nothing left out. And the beauty
of ETFs is that they can be traded like any stock on a major stock exchange. That also means that they can be charted like any stock as well.
That's good news for the visual investor.

ETFs VERSUS MUTUAL FUNDS

Mutual funds still offer the simplest way for most investors to participate in
the financial markets. Exchange-traded funds, however, should also have
some place in an investor's arsenal of trading vehicles. That's especially
true for investors who take a more active role in managing their assets.
That's because ETFs offer some advantages over traditional mutual funds.
For one thing, ETFs are considered to be less expensive and more tax-
efficient than mutual funds. The main advantage of ETFs, however, is what
they can do better than traditional mutual funds from a trading standpoint.
Most importantly, ETFs trade like any other stock on a major stock exchange. That means that all of the visual tools described in this book can be
used. That allows more active investors to take quicker positions in the
financial markets and then exit those positions when they wish to do so.
That's especially important in commodity and currency markets as well
as market sectors and industry groups that tend to change direction more
quickly.

Mutual funds discourage frequent trading and penalize investors who
attempt to do so. "Market timing" are bad words in the mutual fund industry. Unfortunately for them, market timing is what this book is mostly
about. That greatly diminishes the value of sector mutual funds for sector
rotation purposes. While an investor might choose to buy and hold a di-
versified stock mutual fund, he or she may not want to do so with market
sectors. That's because sector trends may last for only a few months. The
active investor needs to be able to get into a rising sector as early as possible and rotate somewhere else when the time is right. That involves moving
out of a sector that's starting to fall and into one that's starting to rise. ETFs
make doing that a good deal easier than a sector mutual fund. A trader can
move in and out of an exchange-traded fund as often as he or she wishes.
ETFs also offer more direct exposure to individual commodity and currency markets that isn't available through a mutual fund. The ability to buy
an inverse (bear) ETF for the general market (and some market sectors)
also makes for a complete set of trading alternatives. You can also "short"
an ETF, which you can't do with a mutual fund. While you might want to

use mutual funds for your core holdings with a longer-range focus, shorter-term trading strategies (and hedging needs) are better done with exchange-traded funds. ETFs also trade throughout the day like any other stock.

USING ETFs TO HEDGE

Exchange-traded funds can be especially helpful for those investors who don't like disturbing their core stock market holdings during market sell-offs. Mutual funds discourage investors from moving their funds around too much, which smacks of market timing. If an investor is concerned that the stock market is entering a serious downturn (as in the second half of 2007), he or she can hedge existing stock holdings by buying an inverse (bear) ETF that rises when the market falls. There are several available and sector funds exist that also allow investors to hedge positions in financials, real estate, and other sectors. These allow investors to protect their core stock holdings without actually having to sell them.

Another way for investors to hedge their stock holding is to buy a Treasury bond ETF, which usually rises when stocks fall. During the second half of 2007, bond ETFs rose sharply as stocks fell. So did gold. Exchange-traded funds that cover gold and gold stocks tend to rise when stocks run into trouble. That's especially true when the Federal Reserve lowers short-term rates to combat a weaker economy that usually pushes the U.S. dollar lower. Foreign currency ETFs allow an investor to profit more directly from a falling dollar. Most commodities also rise with foreign currencies.

During the latter half of 2007 and the first half of 2008, rising energy prices cast a pall over the U.S. stock market. An investor could have profited from that trend by buying an exchange-traded fund based on energy markets such as crude oil and natural gas or stocks tied to energy prices. There are any number of ways for the traditional stock investor to protect a stock portfolio (or seek alternative investments outside of stocks) by taking positions in exchange-traded funds. All that's required is the ability to spot those trend changes. Helping you do that is what this book is about.

USING A BEAR ETF

Exchange-traded funds—regular, inverse, and ultra—exist for major stock indexes like the Dow Industrials, the Nasdaq 100, the S&P 500, the S&P MidCap 400, the S&P 600, and the Russell 2000 Small Cap Indexes. That means that you can profit from both a rising and a falling market. Figure 12.1 compares the S&P 500 SPDRs (price bars) to the Short S&P 500 ProShares ETF (bottom line) during 2007. You can see that the funds

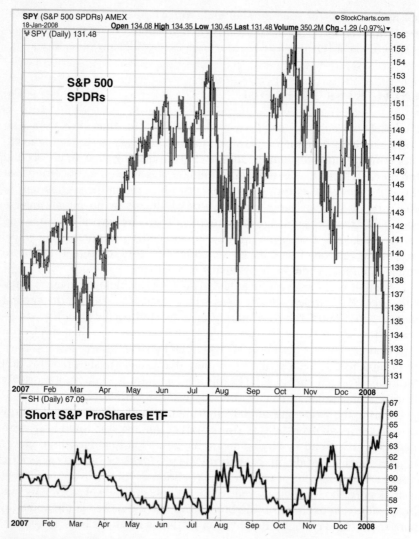

FIGURE 12.1 This chart shows the Short S&P ProShares ETF turning up during 2007 as the S&P 500 SPDRs were turning down. The ETFs mirror each other. *Source:* StockCharts.com.

are mirror images of each other. The short S&P 500 ETF rose during July, October, and December of that year when the S&P 500 SPDRs were dropping (see vertical lines). In the old days (pre-2000), a stock investor might have moved some stock funds to a cash position to protect from a falling market. While that may still be a good way to sidestep a falling market, that same investor in 2007 had an additional way to actually make money as the market was falling. A more aggressive investor might have even chosen an inverse ultra fund that rises twice as fast as the market falls.

Since an inverse fund is a mirror image of the index on which it's based, the same technical indicators can be applied to both. A chart sell signal on the S&P 500 SPDRs, for example, corresponds with a chart buy signal on a short S&P fund. That offers the visual investor another way to confirm one's trading signals. There is one caveat with using an inverse fund, however. Stocks generally spend more time in uptrends than in downtrends. Over an average four-year business cycle, stocks will usually rise three out of the four years. That being the case, a bear fund isn't suitable as a long-term holding. As the name implies, a bear fund is suitable during a bear market (or a severe downside correction). Once the bear market (or correction) has ended, the bear fund should be sold. That's where market timing comes in.

TRADING THE NASDAQ 100

One of the most popular exchange-traded funds is the PowerShares QQQ Trust (QQQQ), which is based on the Nasdaq 100, which includes the 100 largest stocks in the Nasdaq market. An equally popular companion is the PowerShares UltraShort QQQ (QID), which trends in the opposite direction. Figure 12.2 plots the QQQQ over a two-year period surrounding 2007. The solid line is a 200-day moving average. Although the 200-day average is a relatively slow moving indicator, it still proved useful in defining the major trend. The QQQQ rose above the 200-day line in September 2006 and stayed above it until the start of 2008. Many traders use the Power Shares QQQ Trust as a proxy for the technology sector (since it's dominated by large technology stocks). The rising trend showed that technology was a good place to be from fourth quarter 2006 to the end of 2007. The drop below the 200-day line during the first week of 2008 gave visual warning to exit this ETF (or buy the inverse version).

Figure 12.3 plots the ProShares Ultra Short QQQ (QID) which trends in the opposite direction of the Nasdaq 100. That inverse fund achieved an upside breakout during the first week of 2008 as the Nasdaq 100 started to drop. Not only did that bullish move confirm the bearish action in the

FIGURE 12.2 The 200-day average helped define the major trend of the Power-Shares QQQ Trust which tracks the Nasdaq 100 Index.
Source: StockCharts.com.

FIGURE 12.3 The ProShares Ultra Short QQQ broke out to the upside in January 2008 on rising volume as the Nasdaq 100 broke down.
Source: StockCharts.com.

QQQQ, it offered the visual investor a way to profit from the drop in technology stocks and the market in general.

USING SECTOR ETFs

Nine sector SPDRs are traded on the American Stock Exchange (AMEX), which account for the nine sectors that are included in the S&P 500. They include Consumer Staples (XLP), Consumer Discretionary (XLY), Energy (XLE), Financials (XLF), Health Care (XLV), Industrial (XLI), Materials (XLB), Technology (XLK), and Utilities (XLU). These are among the most actively traded vehicles in the ETF universe and, as such, are very suitable for visual market analysis. All of the visual tools explained in this book can be used on them, including volume and relative strength analysis. As explained in earlier chapters, some of those sectors do better than others at various stages in the business cycle. In addition, some of them have generally negative correlations. In other words, some of them fall when others rise. From the start of 2007 to spring 2008, for example, Energy and Materials stocks rose 44 percent and 27 percent respectively and were the market's two strongest sectors. That was mainly due to rising commodity prices.

Rising commodity prices, which carry inflationary implications, are usually bad for financial and consumer discretionary stocks, which include Retailers and Homebuilders. Not surprisingly, those two weak sectors lost 26 percent and 14 percent respectively over the same time span. Retailers are especially vulnerable to rising energy prices and falling home values. Retail stocks fell 20 percent from early 2007 to early 2008. During that same time span, the S&P was about unchanged. The fact that the market ended that period essentially flat demonstrates the value of sector trading.

In late spring 2008, the stock market was trading at about the same level as it started the year before. A lot was happening beneath the surface, however. Commodity-related ETFs were gaining ground, while consumer discretionary and financial stocks were suffering big losses. The astute investor could have benefited by being in the former and out of the latter. Figure 12.4 plots a relative strength ratio of the Materials Sector SPDR (XLB) divided by the S&P 500 from the start of 2007 to spring 2008. The rising ratio testifies to the superior performance of that commodity-related ETF. Only energy sector ETFs (OIH and XLE) turned in a stronger performance.

An investor armed with some charts (and knowledge of how to read them) should have been in those ETFs tied to rising commodities. The

FIGURE 12.4 The uptrend in the Materials SPDR/S&P 500 ratio shows that commodity-related stocks were market leaders throughout 2007 to mid-2008. *Source:* StockCharts.com.

rising trend was clearly visible both in absolute and relative terms. Instead of worrying about the drop in consumer spending (and retail stocks) owing to rising commodity prices, the visual investor could have bought sector (or commodity) ETFs to profit from that rising trend. In addition, the investor could have bought inverse ETFs in those weaker sectors.

INVERSE SECTOR ETFs

Inverse (bear) funds exist for many market sectors and industry groups. The present list includes Basic Materials, Financials, Health Care, Industrials, Oil and Gas, Real Estate, Semiconductors, Technology, Telecommunications, and Utilities. Figure 12.5 shows the UltraShort Financial ProShares (SKF) nearly doubling in price from October 2007 to March 2008. That was during a period when financial shares were losing more than a third of their value during the subprime mortgage crisis. Instead of avoiding the financial sector during those difficult months, the visual investor could have bought an inverse financial ETF. What a great way to turn bad news into good news.

USING TECHNOLOGY AS A MARKET INDICATOR

Earlier in the book I suggested using the action of some market sectors to tell us something about the health of the overall stock market. One of those sectors is Technology. Figure 12.6 plots a ratio of the Technology SPDR (XLK) divided by the S&P 500 SPDRs (SPY) over the span of a year. The rising ratio from spring 2007 to October showed Technology helping to support a rising stock market. After peaking in October 2007, however, the Technology/S&P 500 ratio dropped until it broke a rising trendline at the start of 2008. It continued dropping until March of that year. During the five months that the ratio fell, Technology stocks lost 22 percent while the S&P 500 fell 16 percent.

The ratio in Figure 12.6 offers two messages. One is that the direction of the XLK/SPY ratio tells us whether or not Technology is a good place to be at any given time (that is, when the ratio is rising). Most of 2007 was a good time to be in Technology. The first few months of 2008 were not. The second message has to do with the market itself. As a rule, the stock market does better when the Technology relative strength ratio is rising and Technology is in a leadership role. The market usually struggles when it loses Technology leadership (when the ratio is falling).

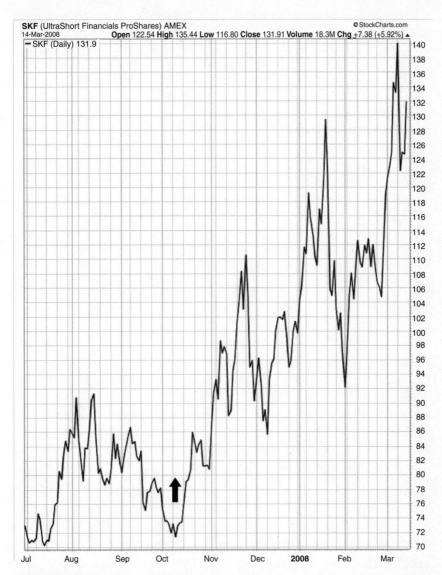

FIGURE 12.5 The Ultra-Short Financials ProShares scored big gains from October 2007 to March 2008 as the financial sector collapsed.
Source: StockCharts.com.

FIGURE 12.6 The Technology SPDR/S&P 500 SPDRs ratio rose during most of 2007 before turning down at the start of 2008. The stock market does better when the ratio is rising and worse when it's falling.
Source: StockCharts.com.

COMMODITY ETFs

Up until the past few years, it was nearly impossible to get involved in commodities outside of the futures markets. That's no longer the case. Exchange-traded funds now exist for commodity baskets as well as a number of individual commodities including Crude Oil (USO), Gold (GLD), Natural Gas (UNG), and Silver (SLV). PowerShares offers an assortment of commodity index ETFs offering exposure to commodity groups such as Agriculture (DBA), Base Metals (DBB), Energy (DBE), and Precious Metals (DBP). PowerShares also offers an ETF that covers a basket of commodities. Figure 12.7 shows the PowerShares DB Commodities Tracking Index Fund (DBC), which is based on the Deutsche Bank Liquid Commodity Index. That index includes futures contracts on six of the most heavily traded commodities in the world. They include crude oil, heating oil, gold, aluminum, corn, and wheat.

Figure 12.7 shows the DBC hitting a new yearly high during September 2007. From August 2007 to May 2008, the commodity ETF gained more than 50 percent. The reason for that was the plunge in stocks that started in mid-2007 and aggressive Fed easing to combat a housing and mortgage crisis. That pushed U.S. interest rates lower and weakened the U.S. dollar. Commodities were the main beneficiaries of those trends.

From the start of 2007 to late spring 2008, energy markets rose 72 percent and were the strongest commodity group. Agricultural commodities came in second with a gain of 43 percent (precious metals were third with a 32 percent gain). Figure 12.8 shows the PowerShares DB Agricultural ETF (DBA) in a rising trend that started in August 2007. The DBA offers investors a way to buy four major farm commodities: corn, wheat, soybeans, and sugar. Two of those commodities (corn and sugar) are being used as energy alternatives. The agricultural ETF offers you another commodity alternative.

FOREIGN CURRENCY ETFs

Commodities are not the only things that rise when the U.S. dollar falls. So do foreign currencies. Fortunately, exchange-traded funds now exist to allow investors to profit from trends in currency markets. One of the most popular is the Currency Shares Euro Trust (FXE) which is based on the trend of the euro. Figure 12.9 plots the FXE during 2006 and 2007 with a 200-day moving average (solid line). The Euro ETF crossed above that line in spring 2006 (thereby issuing a major buy signal) and stayed above that

FIGURE 12.7 The DB Commodities Tracking Index rallied sharply from August 2007 to May 2008. This ETF offers exposure to a basket of commodities.
Source: StockCharts.com.

FIGURE 12.8 The PowerShares Agricultural ETF also scored big gains after August 2007. This ETF offers investors exposure to grain markets.
Source: StockCharts.com.

FIGURE 12.9 The Currency Shares Euro Trust rose sharply from the start of 2006 to the spring of 2008. This ETF offers investors an easy way to buy the euro. *Source:* StockCharts.com.

rising support line for the next two years. During those two years, the euro rose more than 30 percent as the U.S. dollar fell.

In the past, currency trading was limited to banks and financial institutions. This is no longer the case with the development of foreign currency ETFs. Rydex Investments launched the NYSE listed CurrencyShares Euro Trust in 2005. It was the first exchange-traded fund to provide investors with currency exposure. Since then, Rydex has issued seven more CurrencyShares, all of which are traded on the New York Stock Exchange. They include the Australian dollar (FXA), the British pound (FXB), the Canadian dollar (FXC), the Swiss franc (FXF), the Mexican peso (FXM), the Swedish krona (FXS), and the Japanese yen (FXY).

Three things are needed for the visual investor to take advantage of foreign currency trends. One is the ability to read the charts of currency markets. The other is some knowledge of intermarket principles in order to understand that a falling dollar is usually beneficial to two asset classes—commodities and foreign currencies. The third is the existence of ETFs that allow you to buy and sell those markets. You have all three.

BOND ETFs

Less than a dozen bond ETFs were on the market during 2007. By first quarter 2008, that number had expanded to 58. ETFs covering municipal bonds were introduced by Barclays Global Investors, State Street Global Advisors, and Van Eck Global. ProShares introduced two inverse bond funds, ProShares UltraShort Lehman 7–10 Year Treasury ETF (PST) and ProShares Ultra Short Lehman 20+ Year Treasury ETF (TBT). During October 2007, the Lehman International Treasury Bond ETF (BWX) was also launched. Bond exchange-traded funds are offered along the entire yield curve. They include the 1–3 Year T-Bond Fund (SHY), the 3–7 Year T-Bond Fund (IEI), the 7–10 Year T-Bond Fund (IEF), and the 20+ Year T-Bond Fund (TLT). Treasury Inflation Protected Securities are covered by a bond ETF (TIP).

For most investors, the most important thing to remember is that bond prices trend in the opposite direction of bond yields. Bond ETFs rise when interest rates are falling. Figure 12.10 shows the 7–10 Year Treasury Bond Fund (IEF) rising 15 percent from June 2007 to March 2008. During that time, the S&P 500 fell an equal amount. This is because money rotating out of stocks during a period of economic stress usually moves into the relatively safety of Treasuries. That makes bond ETFs a relatively easy way to cushion one's stock portfolio in a falling stock market. Inverse

FIGURE 12.10 The 7–10 Year Treasury Bond ETF rose sharply from summer 2007 to March 2008. Bond ETFs usually rise when the stock market falls. *Source:* StockCharts.com.

bond ETFs allow bond investors a way to profit even when interest rates are rising and bond prices are falling.

INTERNATIONAL ETFs

The earlier edition of this book spent an entire chapter explaining the merits of global investing. This is no longer necessary. American investors have gotten that message and for good reason. From spring 2003 to the end of 2007, the S&P 500 doubled in price (+100 percent). Foreign developed stocks did twice as well as their U.S. counterparts (+200 percent). Emerging markets quadrupled the S&P 500 performance (+400 percent). As explained earlier in the book, a lot of the foreign gains came from a falling dollar, which makes foreign investments more attractive to American investors and American markets less attractive to foreigners. Fortunately, there are several exchange-traded funds that allow American investors to move easily in and out of foreign stocks.

The simplest way to invest in foreign shares is to buy EAFE Index iShares (EFA). (EAFE stands for Europe, Australasia, and the Far East.) Figure 12.11 shows the EAFE iShares in an uptrend from 2003 through the end of 2007 (before turning down in 2008). The relative strength ratio of the EFA divided by the S&P 500 SPDRS (SPY) is plotted on top of that chart. That rising ratio shows that foreign stocks were stronger than U.S. stocks throughout that entire period. That stronger foreign performance ended in 2008.

Figure 12.12 plots the MSCI Emerging Markets iShares (EEM) over the last three years to June 2008. Its relative strength ratio (top of chart) rose as well. The EEM offers investors a simple way to buy into emerging markets in general. There are, however, ETFs that allow for more specialized investments in emerging markets. Figure 12.13 plots the Claymore/BNY BRIC ETF (EEB), which offers exposure to the four biggest emerging markets that are Brazil, Russia, India, and China. It is starting to weaken during summer 2008 (and continued to do so for most of that year).

ETFs now exist for all four BRIC countries. But they don't always trend in the same direction. Figure 12.14 shows Brazil iShares (EWZ) hitting a new high in spring 2008. Part of that strength came from rising commodity prices since Brazil is a big exporter of natural resources (as is Russia). From the start of 2006 to the end of 2007, China was the world's top gainer (+400 percent). Figure 12.15, however, shows the FTSE/Xinhua China 25 iShares (FXI) losing nearly 50 percent of its value from October 2007 to March 2008. Fortunately, most of that downturn could have been avoided. A simple 50-day moving average would have helped the visual investor

FIGURE 12.11 EAFE iShares started to weaken in 2008 after a five-year uptrend. This ETF offers investors a way to buy a basket of developed foreign stock markets. Foreign stocks underperformed the U.S. during 2008.
Source: StockCharts.com.

FIGURE 12.12 This chart shows Emerging Market iShares still in an uptrend but starting to weaken. This ETF offers an easy way for investors to buy a basket of emerging market stocks. By October 2008 the ETF fell to a three-year low and lost 50 percent of its value.
Source: StockCharts.com.

FIGURE 12.13 This ETF offers exposure to the four big BRIC emerging stock markets that include Brazil, Russia, India, and China. The "double top" in spring 2008 led to a fifty percent loss later that year.
Source: StockCharts.com.

FIGURE 12.14 Brazil iShares hit a record high during spring 2008. Commodity exporters (like Brazil and Russia) benefited from rising commodity markets. Falling commodities during the second half of 2008, however, pushed both markets into sharp declines.
Source: StockCharts.com.

FIGURE 12.15 The 50-day average helped spot the downturn in China iShares near the end of 2007. China and India fell especially hard during 2008.
Source: StockCharts.com.

sidestep most of that downturn. A sharp trader could have even made money on the falling Chinese market by buying the ProShares UltraShort FTSE/Xinhua China 25 iShares (FXP).

Canada also benefits from rising commodity prices. From October 2007 to May 2008, the Canadian stock market rose 3 percent while the S&P 500 lost 9 percent. Figure 12.16 plots a relative strength ratio (solid line) of Canada iShares (EWC) divided by the S&P 500. The price bars are the CRB Index. The close correlation between the two rising lines demonstrates that Canada's superior performance was tied to rising commodities. The superior performance of commodity exporters, however, ended in the second half of 2008 when commodity prices tumbled.

It is relatively easy to track the performance of the world's major stock markets. MSCI International offers 20 country ETFs, which include all of the world's major stock markets. A number of ETFs cover geographic regions like Asia, Latin America, and Emerging Europe. Inverse global funds exist as well to take advantage of falling foreign markets. That being the case, all you need is a set of charts and you're all set to span the globe for profitable trading opportunities. You don't even have to leave the American and New York Stock Exchanges to do that.

SUMMARY

This chapter covers the explosive growth of exchange-traded funds since 2000, which have revolutionized the world of trading and investing. Not only are they cheaper than traditional mutual funds, ETFs allow more frequent trading and are more easily charted. ETFs offer the best of two worlds. They offer basket trading similar to what you can get through mutual funds (but in a more flexible way). But they also trade like stocks on U.S. stock exchanges. Since most investors are familiar with stock trading, that makes the transition to ETFs much easier. Sector trading, which is discouraged by mutual funds, is encouraged by exchange-traded funds.

ETFs also offer trading vehicles in nontraditional markets such as commodities and currencies. They also offer easy entry into foreign regions and markets, both developed and emerging. Best of all, they offer inverse funds that rise when markets fall. What more can anyone ask for? It's often been said that there's always a bull market somewhere. All you need to do is find it. Inverse (or bear) funds actually turn downtrends into uptrends in a sort of financial alchemy. That means that there are bull markets everywhere just waiting to be exploited.

Relative strength analysis allows you to identify market sectors that are outperforming (leaders) and those that are underperforming

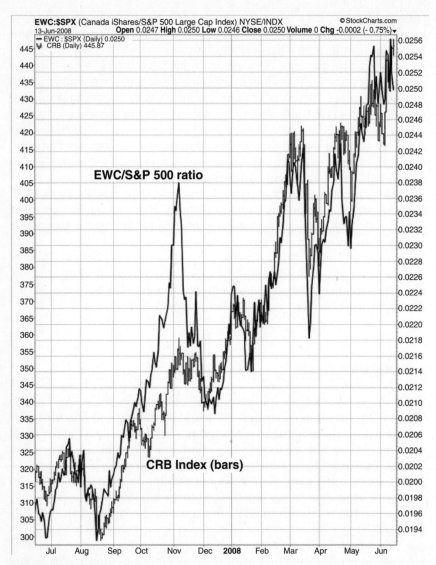

FIGURE 12.16 The Canada iShares/S&P 500 ratio (solid line) rose into mid-2008. That was largely due to rising commodity prices (price bars). Both markets fell together later that year.
Source: StockCharts.com.

(laggards). The main idea in doing that is to buy leading sectors and avoid the laggards. But here's another twist. Instead of avoiding the losers, you can use inverse funds to buy the weakest groups. That way you can profit from both the leaders and the laggards. Broader inverse (bear) ETFs allow investors to profit from a falling stock market (or to hedge existing portfolios). That allows you to avoid market timing restrictions imposed by traditional mutual funds. One of the great benefits of visual (chart) analysis is the ability to scan a lot of markets in a short period of time. This is a big plus in an environment when so many exchange-traded fund alternatives have become available.

Conclusion

WHY IT'S CALLED *VISUAL INVESTING*

This book was written with a number of goals in mind. One was to introduce the reader to visual investing by explaining in simple language some of the charting techniques that professionals have used for decades. A second goal was to show how to use these visual tools for all of the financial markets that include commodities, currencies, bonds, and stocks on both a domestic and a global scale. An emphasis has been placed on using visual tools to implement asset allocation and sector rotation strategies primarily through mutual fund and exchange-traded funds. Calling this approach "visual investing" has two reasons. First, that's just what it is. We look at pictures of markets. The pictures tell us what a market is actually doing. They tell us whether a market is going up or down. That's all that really matters. "Why" a market is going up or down isn't that important.

THE MEDIA WILL ALWAYS TELL YOU WHY LATER

You can pick up your newspaper, turn on your television, read your favorite financial web page and learn why markets did what they did the day before. The reasons seem clear and reasonable. There's only one problem. If the reasons were so clear, then why weren't you told about them while you still had time to act (like the day before yesterday). The main reason they don't warn you is that media experts usually don't know the reasons beforehand. When I worked as the technical analyst for CNBC, I used to get frustrated watching guests explain how a market trend developed because those same guests had often been wrong on that trend. I used to ask the producers why they didn't find guests who got it right. I'd rather hear from someone who got it right than someone who got it wrong. I would also prefer hearing the analysis while something is happening (or before) rather than after the fact when it's too late to do anything about it.

Explaining why things happened in hindsight is easy. That's what the media is best at. Unfortunately, that doesn't do viewers any good.

MEDIA VIEWS KEEP SHIFTING

Media explanations also have an annoying way of shifting with market trends. At 10:00 in the morning, you may be told that an economic report is bullish while the market is rising. After the market closes lower that same day, you may be told at 5:00 P.M. that the same report that was bullish at 10:00 A.M. was really bearish "on closer examination." (Shame on you for not knowing that when you invested your money on their earlier report.) There's a world of difference between "predicting" and "reporting". Reporting on market trends after the fact is interesting but not very helpful. By using the visual tools described in this book, you'll be able to spot market trends and act on them long before the media gets around to explaining to you why they happened. While they explain what happened yesterday, you'll be busy studying your charts for trends that may develop tomorrow. You won't need those so-called experts anymore.

VISUAL ANALYSIS IS MORE USER FRIENDLY

The second reason for using the term *visual analysis* is to lessen the intimidating effect that this form of analysis has had on many investors in the past, under the general heading of "technical analysis." Many investors are turned off by exotic-sounding terminology and incorrectly assume that the techniques are too difficult to grasp. By calling it what it actually is—visual analysis—we hope to encourage a wider understanding and appreciation of these valuable tools among the investing public. Everyone looks at charts. Economists look at charts of economic indicators. Security analysts look at charts of earnings. Even the Fed looks at charts. Why shouldn't you? If you are going to look at charts, however, make sure you know how to read them.

KEEP IT SIMPLE

A consistent theme throughout this book is the need for simplicity. Don't get bogged down trying to master a lot of formulas or esoteric theories. Do the following:

- Concentrate instead on price trends.
- Learn to spot significant support and resistance levels.

- Look for important breakouts or breakdowns.
- Master a few of the more important price patterns.
- Understand the role volume plays in confirming price action.
- Draw trendlines and keep an eye on them after you've drawn them.
- Use moving averages to help keep track of trends.
- Follow a couple of the oscillator systems.
- Learn to tell the difference between markets that are trending and those that are not.
- Watch relative strength.
- Follow one or two of the more popular measures of market breadth.

Before you make any investment, ask yourself this question: "Is the market I'm about to put my money into going up or down?" You'd be surprised how many people have trouble answering that question. The investing community is full of people who keep buying stocks that are falling and selling those that are rising. We have a tendency to make the study of market trend more complicated that it needs to be. Keep it simple.

VISUAL TOOLS ARE UNIVERSAL

The biggest benefits of the visual tools described in this book are their universality and transferability. They can be applied to any market anywhere in the world—and to any time dimension. They can be applied to short-term trading as well as long-term investing. Any market that can be charted can be analyzed with visual tools. That gives the visual investor an enormous advantage over those who prefer to use some form of economic or fundamental analysis. Those two schools of analysis have a number of problems to deal with. The fundamental analyst (who studies company and industry earnings) has a tremendous amount of data to deal with that is company and industry specific. This prevents the fundamental analyst from covering a wide variety of markets. As a result, fundamental analysts are forced to specialize. The visual analyst, by comparison, can follow any market he or she wishes to without having to be an expert on any of them. That's a pretty big advantage.

THE STOCK MARKET LEADS THE ECONOMY

The biggest problem economists face is that they deal with old data. Most economic reports tell us what happened last month or last quarter. They tell us nothing about the future (or the present for that matter). The financial markets, by contrast, are forward looking. The stock market anticipates economic trends at least a half year into the future. The reason we can't use economic forecasting to predict the direction of the stock market is because turns in the stock market "precede" turns in the economy. Historically, the stock market peaks six to nine months before the economy. It also bottoms while the economy is in the midst of a recession. The stock market has an excellent track record in leading turns in the economy—although not every market downturn results in an economic downturn, every economic downturn has been preceded by a market downturn. That being the case, it makes more sense to use the stock market to predict the economy than the other way around. That's because you can't use a lagging indicator (like the economy) to predict a leading indicator (like the stock market). So don't worry too much about what economists say. Follow the market instead.

PRICES LEAD THE FUNDAMENTALS

Market prices are leading indicators of fundamental information. That's why the market is called a discounting mechanism. How many times have you heard on TV, seen online, or read in the press that a stock (or industry group) is fundamentally strong while its price is falling? There is usually a good reason why a stock price is falling, which is that the market believes its fundamentals to be bearish. (If the stock price is rising, the market is saying that its fundamentals are bullish.) Wall Street analysts who tell us different are really saying that they're right and the market is wrong. The market is rarely wrong. I'd rather bet on the market than the opinions of Wall Street analysts.

The stock market is based on the laws of supply and demand. If the demand for a stock (or any market) exceeds its supply, the price will rise. If supply exceeds demand, the price will drop. If the price of a market is rising, chances are good that its fundamentals are bullish. If the price is falling, the fundamentals probably aren't very good. Chart analysis is a shortcut form of fundamental analysis. The price trend of a market revealed on a chart tells us a lot about its fundamentals. Rather than using fundamental data to predict the trend of a market, it makes more sense to use the price trend to predict the fundamentals. So don't be fooled the next time you hear someone say, "The technicals may be bad but the fundamentals are good." If the technicals are bad, the fundamentals are probably just as bad. If you're looking for a market with good fundamentals, find one that's in an uptrend.

SECTOR INVESTING

As I mentioned in the body of the book, stock market investing is a top-down approach. The first step is to determine the direction of the market as a whole to see if it's a good time to commit some funds. You can do that by studying charts of the major market indexes and various market breadth indicators. That, however, is only the first step. One of the most important ideas that I've emphasized in this book is the importance of sector analysis. There is so much that goes on beneath the surface of the stock market having to do with sector and industry group rotation. As we've shown in previous chapters, many market groups often trend in opposite directions. Some are market leaders and others are market laggards.

An investor can dramatically increase his or her overall performance by concentrating funds in stock groups that are market leaders and avoiding groups that are showing relatively weak market performance. Stock pickers would also do well to concentrate their stock picks in the market's strongest groups. Sector trends, however, are usually shorter in duration than major stock market trends. Because of that, sector trends need to be monitored more frequently. The good news is that the visual tools explained in this book make it relatively easy to spot those sector rotations. I happen to believe that sector work is one of the best ways to utilize those charting tools.

EXCHANGE-TRADED FUNDS

The explosive growth of exchange-traded funds over the past few years has greatly simplified our ability to track and trade all financial markets. The ability to move quickly into or out of market sectors and industry groups can now be done with one or two trades. Asset allocation shifts between stocks, bonds, commodities, and currencies can also be done with relative ease. That's been especially helpful in recent years when nontraditional assets like commodities and foreign currencies have been the strongest in the world. The ability to scan the globe for profitable trading opportunities without leaving the American and New York stock exchanges is also pretty neat. And to think that you can even turn downtrends into uptrends with inverse funds. It's all very exciting. That's especially true for the visual investor. All you need now is a computer and a web browser. Appendix A will help you get started.

A YEAR AFTER THE 2007 TOP

The U.S. stock market peaked on October 9, 2007. By the following October, the warning signs shown on the charts during 2007 had come to fruition. Global stock markets were in major bear trends and global economies appeared headed into a global recession. Subprime mortgage problems that had surfaced the previous summer in the U.S. pushed

Lehman Brothers into bankruptcy and necessitated government bailouts or buyouts from other financial firms for those that survived. Things got so bad that a $700 billion government rescue plan was passed on October 3, 2008 to buy mortgage-backed securities from financial firms and remove those toxic assets from their balance sheets. Investor fear forced the government to raise the limits on FDIC protection for bank accounts and guarantee the safety of mutual money market funds.

Then things got worse as subprime problems spread to Europe. A week after the U.S. bailout, Britain announced a bank bailout of its own. Overnight bank lending rates had risen to record highs which froze the global financial system. Stock markets around the world were in freefall. The Federal Reserve, the European Central Bank, and four other central banks lowered interest rates in an unprecedented coordinated effort to ease the economic effects of the worst financial crisis since the Great Depression.

By the second week of October 2008, the S&P 500 had lost more than a third of its value and had fallen to the lowest level in five years. Foreign markets did even worse. Foreign developed stocks fell more than 40 percent while emerging markets lost half of their value. By that time, fears of a global recession had pushed the euro and most other foreign currencies sharply lower. As a result, commodities tumbled. The only relative safe havens during the second half of the 2008 meltdown were treasury bonds, the dollar, and the yen. Not surprisingly, bear market funds were the only big winners.

WARNING SIGNS WERE CLEARLY VISIBLE

It's only natural that a financial writer will use recent market trends to demonstrate how various market indicators work and to explain how those trends developed in the first place. Most of the charts in the preceding chapters deal with market trends surrounding the major peak in global stocks that started during the second half of 2007. And the message is pretty clear. Most of the warning signs were clearly visible on the charts of the various financial markets at least a year before the 2008 panic ensued. Warning signs on housing came even earlier. Just as in 2000, however, the Wall Street establishment relied on outdated economic and fundamental information and ignored the visual warning signs given by the financial markets themselves. Some media headlines described the early stages of the market downturn as a battle between "fear versus fundamentals." It turned out that the fearful sellers were right and the fundamentals were wrong. I suspect that most of those early sellers were visual investors who trusted the message of the markets instead of the one coming from Wall Street.

Getting Started

FIND A GOOD WEB SITE

Now that you're ready to begin your work as a visual analyst, how exactly do you get started? You're going to need at least three things. The first is a computer and web browser such as Firefox, Safari, Opera, or Microsoft Internet Explorer. The second is access to the Internet. The third is a good Internet web site that provides all the necessary market data and the visual tools to organize that information and chart it. Prior to the Internet, the visual investor needed a charting software package as well as access to a data source. The data source provided the necessary market data while the software allowed you to chart it. While some investors still use that approach, the Internet has eliminated the need to collect market data from a separate source. A good web site should include the market data that you want to view and chart. This allows you to chart a market by just typing in its symbol. A good site should also provide you with a list of those symbols or a service to convert company names to their appropriate symbol. Just as the introduction of exchange-traded funds revolutionized the way we can move in and out of the various markets, the Internet has revolutionized the way we go about organizing and charting those markets.

USE THE READERS CHOICE AWARDS

Technical Analysis of Stocks & Commodities is the premier magazine in the field of visual analysis (www.traders.com). It's a great source of articles on that subject, in addition to reviews of books, software, and online products. Each January, *S&C* magazine publishes a bonus issue that includes its "Readers Choice Awards." That poll of the magazine's readers rates various trading-oriented computer services in 20 categories along with their contact information. It is a valuable reference source in looking for products and services with high customer satisfaction.

The 2008 Readers Choice Awards named StockCharts.com "Best Technical Analysis Web Site" for the seventh straight year. Runner-ups included Worden.com, Traders.com, Yahoo!Finance, Investors.com, and Bigcharts.com. MetaStock (Equis International) and TeleChart 2007 (Worden Brothers) were named as the top standalone charting software packages. The "John Murphy Chart Pattern Recognition" (Equis International) was named as the top MetaStock Plug-in. As explained at the end of Chapter 3, that plug-in is designed to scan a database to uncover some of the most common chart patterns that are believed to have predictive value.

STOCKCHARTS.COM

I have been part owner and the chief technical writer for StockCharts.com for several years. As a result, I've had a hand in developing the site and choosing which indicators are employed. In a way, StockCharts.com is an extension of my trading philosophy, and its indicator library offers some insight into which indicators I find most useful. Not only does it offer easy charting of all of the financial markets, it includes all of the indicators described in this book (and a lot that aren't). It also includes a number of visual tools explained in previous chapters such as market sector carpets and performance charts that help the visual investor organize and rank the various markets.

CHARTSCHOOL

StockCharts.com places a lot of emphasis on education. To ensure that its users understand how to interpret the available tools, it features a "ChartSchool" that offers easy explanations of every aspect of technical (or visual) analysis with numerous chart examples. Figure A.1 should give you an idea of how much information the ChartSchool provides. In addition to explaining every aspect of technical analysis, it also includes a "How to Use Our Charting Tools" section. Those tools include the market sector carpets and performance charts used earlier in the book. StockCharts.com also explains how to use its "Stock Scans" page that lists stocks (and mutual

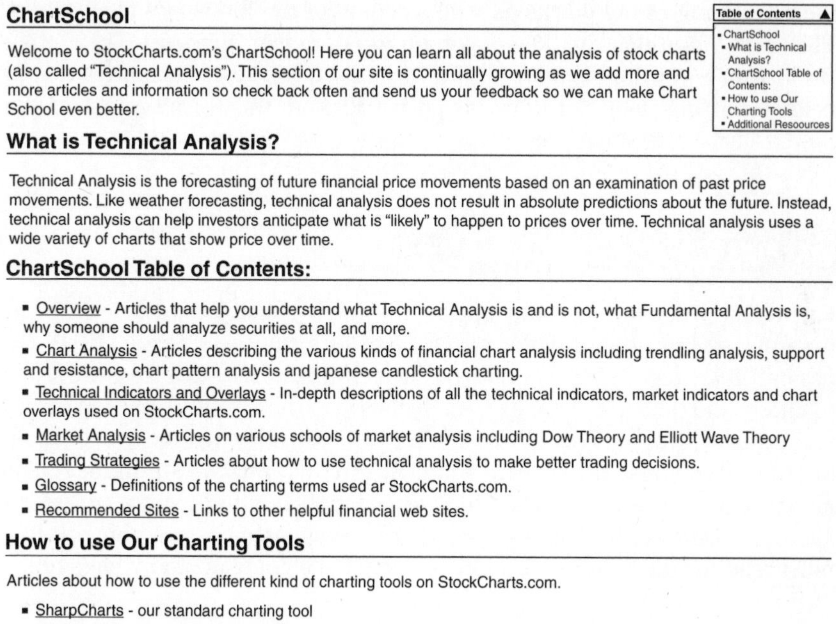

ChartSchool

Table of Contents ▲
• ChartSchool
• What is Technical Analysis?
• ChartSchool Table of Contents:
• How to use Our Charting Tools
• Additional Resoources

Welcome to StockCharts.com's ChartSchool! Here you can learn all about the analysis of stock charts (also called "Technical Analysis"). This section of our site is continually growing as we add more and more articles and information so check back often and send us your feedback so we can make Chart School even better.

What is Technical Analysis?

Technical Analysis is the forecasting of future financial price movements based on an examination of past price movements. Like weather forecasting, technical analysis does not result in absolute predictions about the future. Instead, technical analysis can help investors anticipate what is "likely" to happen to prices over time. Technical analysis uses a wide variety of charts that show price over time.

ChartSchool Table of Contents:

- Overview - Articles that help you understand what Technical Analysis is and is not, what Fundamental Analysis is, why someone should analyze securities at all, and more.
- Chart Analysis - Articles describing the various kinds of financial chart analysis including trendling analysis, support and resistance, chart pattern analysis and japanese candlestick charting.
- Technical Indicators and Overlays - In-depth descriptions of all the technical indicators, market indicators and chart overlays used on StockCharts.com.
- Market Analysis - Articles on various schools of market analysis including Dow Theory and Elliott Wave Theory
- Trading Strategies - Articles about how to use technical analysis to make better trading decisions.
- Glossary - Definitions of the charting terms used ar StockCharts.com.
- Recommended Sites - Links to other helpful financial web sites.

How to use Our Charting Tools

Articles about how to use the different kind of charting tools on StockCharts.com.

- SharpCharts - our standard charting tool

FIGURE A.1   ChartSchool.
Source: StockCharts.com.

funds) that are giving buy and sell signals based on a list of technical indicators on a daily basis (more on that later). Candlestick users can scan the "Candlestick Patterns" list each day for stocks that are forming candlestick price patterns that are believed to have predictive value. Another column lists stocks that are forming point-and-figure price patterns. The ability to scan an entire data base to locate buy and sell signals makes the work of the visual analyst a lot easier than it used to be. The ChartSchool also links to "Recommended Sites" that offer good content and value. DecisionPoint.com is one of the best. I'll show one valuable offering from that web site shortly.

ONLINE BOOKSTORE

The previous edition of this book provided a list of recommended reading and some of the industry's top software packages. The problem with doing that is that lists become quickly outdated as new books and products appear on the market. The StockCharts.com "Online Bookstore" provides a current list of top books, videos and CDs, and software packages. That list includes some of my works as well as some of the industry's top writers. The "New Additions" list keeps you on top of newer offerings. The Online Bookstore is a valuable source of information. StockCharts.com is an excellent starting point for your visual work. And, best of all, most of the StockCharts.com site is free.

INVESTOR'S BUSINESS DAILY

I wouldn't want to leave out one of the most valuable sources of information that I use on a regular basis: *Investor's Business Daily* (IBD). *Investor's Business Daily*—and its online version, *eIBD*—is a treasure trove of charts and tables that are extremely useful to the visually oriented trader and investor. Not only does *Investor's Business Daily* include a large number of charts, it also ranks them according to their relative strength. This is also true of market sectors and industry groups. In other words, *Investor's Business Daily* (IBD) shows you where the smart money is going. It is a must read for those of us who like to see what's going up and what's not.

STOCK SCANS

The StockCharts.com "Stock Scans" page provides a daily list of stocks (which include exchange-traded funds) and mutual funds that are registering buy and sell signals based on a number of technical indicators (see Figure A.2). The market signals are broken down by exchanges [Nasdaq, NYSE, AMEX, TSE (Canadian stocks), and Mutual Funds]. One of the main values I find each day is simply comparing the number of buy and sell signals. The page shown here is based on trading for June 18, 2008. A quick glance shows many more sell signals taking place than buy signals. For example, the NYSE shows 139 stocks hitting new 52-week lows versus only 61 reaching 52-week highs. That shows a bearish bias in the market. On that same day, 76 mutual funds were hitting new highs while 138 hit new lows. By clicking on the mutual fund list, you'd see that virtually all of the mutual fund new highs were in the basic material, commodity, and natural resource (energy) categories. That showed that commodity-related funds were still rising while the rest of the market was falling.

Being able to scan through a list of markets that are giving visual buy and sell signals is a great way to screen for potential candidates for purchase or sale. While a glance at the mutual fund gainers would have told you that commodity stocks were the market's strongest group, a glance at the stock lists could have narrowed the search for commodity leaders. On the list of NYSE stocks, one of the stocks that qualified as a "strong volume

Technical Indicators	Equities					Total	Mutual Funds
	Nasdaq	NYSE	AMEX	TSE	CDNX		
New 52-week Highs	43	61	17	37	14	172	76
New 52-week Lows	163	139	12	17	13	344	138
Strong Volume Gainers	27	4	6	20	39	96	
Strong Volume Decliners	24	13	4	16	10	67	
Bullishs 50/200-day MA Crossovers	12	11	1	3	2	29	41
Bullishs 50/200-day MA Crossovers	5	9	2	1	0	17	22
Bullish MACD Crossovers	23	20	7	7	11	68	7
Bearish MACD Crossovers	22	8	1	3	9	43	1
Overbought with a Declining RSI	4	1	1	3	3	12	2
Oversold with an improving RSI	4	1	0	1	1	7	40
Moved Above Upper Bollinger Band	45	35	11	23	32	146	22
Moved Below Lower Bollinger Band	116	148	13	28	15	320	210
Improving Chaikin Money Flow	41	8	7	27	18	101	
Declining Chaikin Money Flow	49	47	15	12	8	131	
New CCI Buy Signals	57	41	25	38	32	193	50
New CCI Sell Signals	219	317	43	46	43	668	2348
Parabolic SAR Buy Signals	77	43	20	27	24	191	41
Parabolic SAR Sell Signals	122	119	24	25	32	322	10
Stocks in a New Uptrend (Aroon)	19	13	7	26	16	81	7
Stocks in a New Downtrend (Aroon)	70	74	5	17	9	175	18
Stocks in a New Uptrend (ADX)	15	8	3	7	2	35	2
Stocks in a New Downtrend (ADX)	26	43	6	7	5	87	389
Gap Ups	16	1	1	8	33	59	
Brekaway Gap Ups	0	0	0	0	0	0	
Runaway Gap Ups	1	1	1	3	7	13	
Island Tops	0	0	0	0	0	0	
Gap Downs	19	10	1	8	29	67	

FIGURE A.2   Technical Indicators.
Source: StockCharts.com.

gainer" that week was General Steel Holdings. Figure A.3 shows that stock jumping on sharply higher volume. The steel stock also achieved a bullish price breakout. That's a strong combination. And you could have spotted that stock standout with a couple of keystrokes on the Stock Scans page. You still need to study the charts of stocks or funds that you find on those lists to determine if you like the way they're acting. But you've saved yourself a lot of time finding the right charts to look at.

BULLISH PERCENT INDEXES

I explained earlier how to use the NYSE Bullish Percent Index (BPI), which measures the percent of stocks in an index that are on point-and-figure buy signals. At the bottom of its Market Summary page, StockCharts.com shows a list of other bullish percent indexes each day. Figure A.4 shows those BPI values for June 18, 2008. On that day in June 2008, each of the major market indexes showed BPI values below 50 percent. Those values showed that the stock market was still in the bear trend that started

FIGURE A.3   General Steel Holdings, Inc.
Source: StockCharts.com.

			Close	Change	% Chg	
⊞⊠⊟	$BPNYA	NYSE	47.21	-1.34	-2.76%	▬
⊞⊠⊟	$BPCOMPQ	Nasdaq	39.36	-0.28	-0.70%	▪
⊞⊠⊟	$BPOEX	S&P 100	41.00	-2.00	-4.65%	▬▬
⊞⊠⊟	$BPNDX	Nasdaq 100	46.00	0.00	0.00%	
⊞⊠⊟	$BPSPX	S&P 500	43.40	-0.89	-2.01%	▬
⊞⊠⊟	$BPINDU	Dow 30	33.33	0.00	0.00%	
⊞⊠⊟	$BPDISC	Consumer Discretionary	39.43	-1.43	-3.51%	▬▬
⊞⊠⊟	$BPSTAP	Consumer Staples	48.75	-1.25	-2.50%	▬
⊞⊠⊟	$BPENER	Energy	81.18	+1.18	+1.47%	▭
⊞⊠⊟	$BPFINA	Finance	25.27	0.00	0.00%	
⊞⊠⊟	$BPHEAL	Healthcare	53.89	-0.60	-1.10%	▪
⊞⊠⊟	$BPINFO	Info Tech	52.50	0.00	0.00%	
⊞⊠⊟	$BPINDY	Industrial	34.55	0.00	0.00%	
⊞⊠⊟	$BPMATE	Materials	49.41	-1.18	-2.33%	▬
⊞⊠⊟	$BPTELE	Telecom	53.85	0.00	0.00%	
⊞⊠⊟	$BPUTIL	Utilities	61.33	-1.33	-2.13%	▬

FIGURE A.4 Bullish Percent Indexes.
Source: StockCharts.com.

in fourth quarter 2007. The BPI sector readings also contained valuable information. The weakest sectors were Finance (25 percent), Industrial (34 percent), and Consumer Discretionary (39 percent). Those numbers confirmed that financial and consumer discretionary stocks were still the market's weakest groups. By contrast, the strongest group was energy (81 percent). Other groups with readings over 50 percent were Utilities (61 percent), Health Care (53 percent), Telecom (53 percent), and Information Technology (52 percent). Three of those groups are defensive in nature.

Earlier in the book, you may recall that readings in the NYSE Bullish Percent Index ($BPNYA) well below 50 percent put it in bear market territory; and that a move back over 60 percent was necessary to put it in back into a bull market. Figure A.5 shows the $BPNYA rebounding from oversold territory (below 30 percent) during first quarter 2008 before recovering to 60 percent in May of that year. Unfortunately, the $BPNYA turned back down from that resistance barrier at 60 percent (see arrow) and fell back below 50 percent during June. That trend suggested that the market had completed a "bear market rally" between March and May 2008 before turning back down again. The juxtaposition of the sector BPI readings showed two reasons why the spring 2008 market rally failed. It was a combination of weak Financial and Consumer Discretionary stocks (which include homebuilders and retailers) and rising Energy prices (reflected in rising Energy shares).

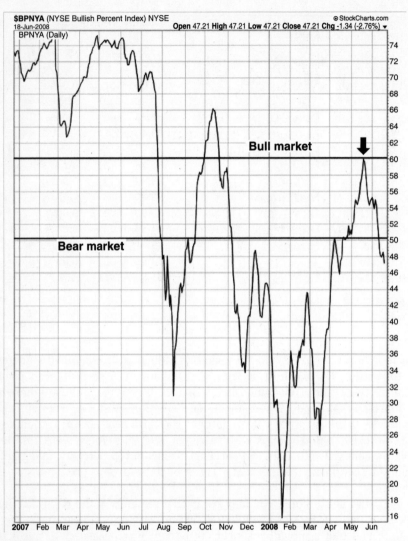

FIGURE A.5 $BPNYA.
Source: StockCharts.com.

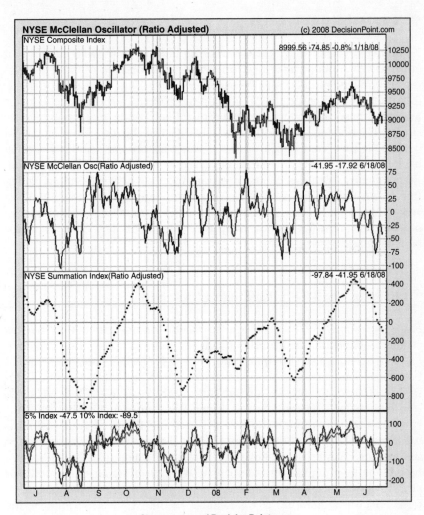

Chart courtesy of **DecisionPoint.com**

FIGURE A.6 NYSE McClellan Oscillator and Summation Index.
Source: DecisionPoint.com.

DECISIONPOINT.COM

I mentioned earlier that StockCharts.com links to other web sites that it considers to contain valuable information to the visually oriented user. Its top recommendation goes to DecisionPoint.com. That charting web site is full of market indicator charts. In addition to charts for each of the major markets, it also shows market indicators for each of the major sub indexes such as the Nasdaq 100 and the Russell 2000. The site also shows advance-decline lines for small-cap stocks as well as market sentiment figures going back to 1978. Over 500 unique charts and data sets are included. Decision-Point.com also includes charts of various industry indices, iShares, Rydex funds, and Fidelity Select Funds. That information greatly facilitates the search for group leaders. Its arsenal of unique market breadth charts is another strong point. Two of my favorites are the NYSE McClellan Oscillator and Summation Index.

McCLELLAN BREADTH INDICATORS

Figure A.6 shows the NYSE McClellan Oscillator and Summation Indexes as they looked on DecisionPoint.com on June 18, 2008. The two indicators (developed by Sherman and Marian McClellan) measure market breadth and are meant to be used together. The NYSE McClellan Oscillator (second line from top) is derived from each day's net NYSE advances (the number of advancing issues minus declining issues). The oscillator is derived by taking the difference between the 19-day exponential moving average (EMA) and the 39-day EMA of the net NYSE advances. When the shorter EMA crosses above the longer, it signals that the short-term breadth momentum has turned positive. When that happens, the oscillator crosses above its zero line. Crossings below the zero line signal that short-term breadth momentum is weakening. As the explanation implies, the McClellan Oscillator is a short-term trading tool.

The Summation Index is a longer-range version of the oscillator. The Summation Index (dotted line) rises when the oscillator is above its zero line and falls when the oscillator is negative. The Summation Index measures long-term market breadth. Figure A.6 shows one year from the June 2007 to June 2008. It shows the Summation Index trading below its zero line for most of that time, which is reflective of a bear market environment for the NYSE Composite Index.

Japanese Candlesticks

J apanese candlestick charts, discussed in Chapter 3, are an alternative to the more traditional bar chart. Considered to be the oldest form of charting in the world, Japanese candlesticks were introduced to the western world by Steve Nison in his book *Japanese Candlestick Charting Techniques* (Prentice Hall, 2002). Many traders find candlesticks more visually attractive than bar charts and believe that candlesticks include more valuable price information. Figure B.1 compares the two forms of charting and shows how the candlestick is constructed. Both charts use the same four pieces of daily information—the open, the high, the low, and the close. (All of the figures in this Appendix are taken from the "Introduction to Candlesticks," which is included in the StockCharts.com ChartSchool).

On the candlestick, the difference between the high and low (the range) is marked by a thin line which is called the *shadow*. The difference between the open and close is marked by a box which is called the *body*. The upper part of Figure B.1 shows a white body and a black body. A white body is formed when the day's closing price is higher than the open (which is considered bullish). A black body is formed when the day's closing price is lower than the open (which is considered bearish). While the color of the box is important, so is its size.

Figure B.2 shows long versus short bodies. Generally speaking, the longer the body (box), the more intense is the buying or selling pressure. Conversely, short candlesticks indicate little price movement and consolidation. Long white candlesticks show strong buying pressure. The longer the white candlestick is, the further the close is above the opening

295

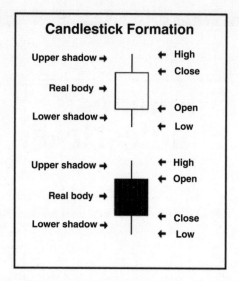

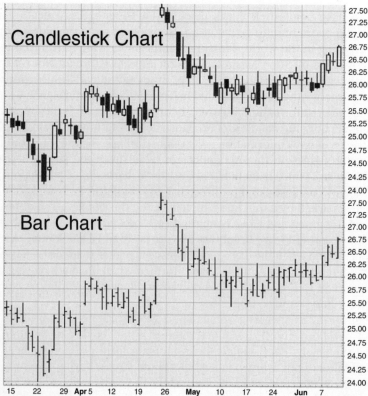

FIGURE B.1 Candlestick Formation, Candlestick Chart, and Bar Chart.
Source: StockCharts.com.

Long versus Short Bodies

Generally speaking, the longer the body is, the more intense the buying or selling pressure. Conversely, short candlesticks indicate little price movement and represent consolidation.

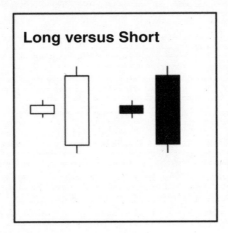

FIGURE B.2 Long versus short bodies.
Source: StockCharts.com.

price. This indicates that prices advanced significantly from open to close and buyers were aggressive. While long white candlesticks are generally bullish, much depends on their position within the broader technical picture. In other words, where the candlestick signals take place within the trend of the market and how other technical indicators look at the time should be taken into consideration. Most of the technical indicators described in this book can be applied to candlesticks.

CANDLESTICK PATTERNS

Candlesticks combine to form price patterns. The Candlestick Pattern Dictionary in Figure B.3 lists 32 different candlestick patterns divided into continuation or reversal patterns (see Figure B.3). Most candlestick patterns encompass two or three days of price action. When used in conjunction with other technical criteria, candlestick patterns can help pinpoint short-term turning points in a market. Figure B.3 shows samples of a few candlestick patterns with esoteric sounding names such as "Abandoned Baby," Dark Cloud," "Doji," "Engulfing Pattern," and "Evening Star." Let's take a closer look at one of them.

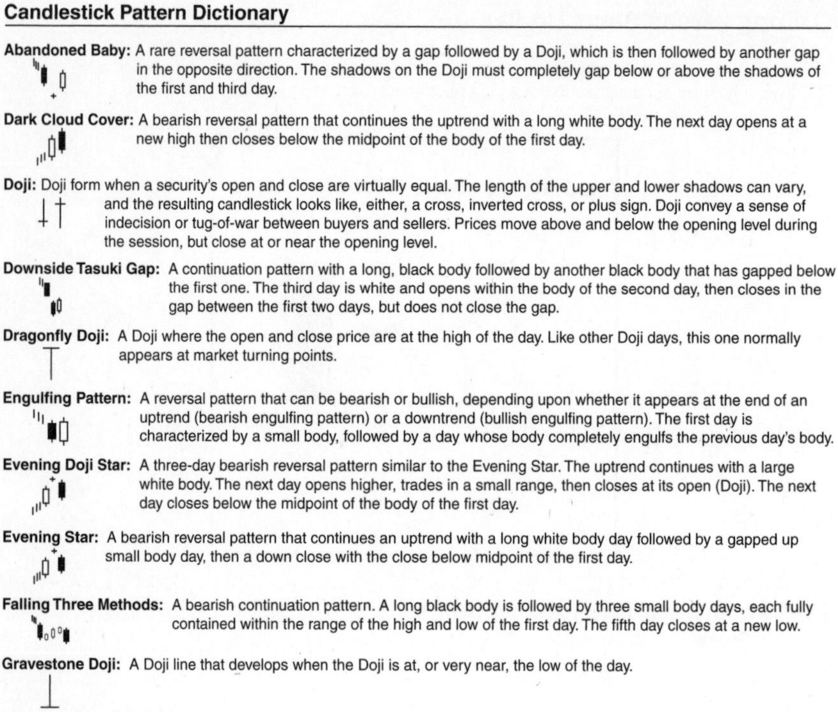

Candlestick Pattern Dictionary

Abandoned Baby: A rare reversal pattern characterized by a gap followed by a Doji, which is then followed by another gap in the opposite direction. The shadows on the Doji must completely gap below or above the shadows of the first and third day.

Dark Cloud Cover: A bearish reversal pattern that continues the uptrend with a long white body. The next day opens at a new high then closes below the midpoint of the body of the first day.

Doji: Doji form when a security's open and close are virtually equal. The length of the upper and lower shadows can vary, and the resulting candlestick looks like, either, a cross, inverted cross, or plus sign. Doji convey a sense of indecision or tug-of-war between buyers and sellers. Prices move above and below the opening level during the session, but close at or near the opening level.

Downside Tasuki Gap: A continuation pattern with a long, black body followed by another black body that has gapped below the first one. The third day is white and opens within the body of the second day, then closes in the gap between the first two days, but does not close the gap.

Dragonfly Doji: A Doji where the open and close price are at the high of the day. Like other Doji days, this one normally appears at market turning points.

Engulfing Pattern: A reversal pattern that can be bearish or bullish, depending upon whether it appears at the end of an uptrend (bearish engulfing pattern) or a downtrend (bullish engulfing pattern). The first day is characterized by a small body, followed by a day whose body completely engulfs the previous day's body.

Evening Doji Star: A three-day bearish reversal pattern similar to the Evening Star. The uptrend continues with a large white body. The next day opens higher, trades in a small range, then closes at its open (Doji). The next day closes below the midpoint of the body of the first day.

Evening Star: A bearish reversal pattern that continues an uptrend with a long white body day followed by a gapped up small body day, then a down close with the close below midpoint of the first day.

Falling Three Methods: A bearish continuation pattern. A long black body is followed by three small body days, each fully contained within the range of the high and low of the first day. The fifth day closes at a new low.

Gravestone Doji: A Doji line that develops when the Doji is at, or very near, the low of the day.

FIGURE B.3   Candlestick Pattern Dictionary.
Source: StockCharts.com.

BULLISH ENGULFING PATTERN

Figure B.4 shows an example of the "Bullish Engulfing Pattern." This bullish pattern consists of two candlesticks, the first black and the second white. The size of the black candlestick isn't that important. The second candlestick, however, should be a long white candlestick which should totally engulf the body of the first black candlestick. The circles in Figure B.4 show two examples of that happening. If that short-term upside reversal takes place in an area of chart support (like a previous low, a trendline, or a moving average), it takes on even more significance. Heavier upside volume also adds to the significance of the pattern. The Bullish Engulfing Pattern is similar to a well-known bar chart pattern which forms when a lower close one day is followed up an upside reversal the following day. The "upside reversal day" takes place when a market opens lower and closes higher the day after a market decline. The wider the price range on the up day, and the heavier the trading volume, the more bullish it becomes.

FIGURE B.4   Bullish Engulfing Pattern.
Source: StockCharts.com.

Candlestick Patterns	Equities					
	Nasdaq	NYSE	AMEX	TSE	CDNX	Total
Bullish Reversal Patterns:						
Bullish Engulfing	91	85	13	11	2	202
Piercing Line	6	7	0	0	1	14
Morning Star	2	4	1	0	0	7
Bullish Harami	9	4	1	0	0	14
Three White Soldiers	3	0	0	1	3	7
Bearish Reversal Patterns:						
Bearish Engulfing	11	64	21	19	3	118
Dark Cloud Cover	9	13	9	9	0	40
Evening Star	0	0	0	2	0	2
Bearish Harami	8	1	0	4	6	19
Three Black Crows	1	0	0	1	0	2
Continuation Patterns:						
Rising Three Methods	0	0	0	0	0	0
Falling Three Methods	0	0	0	0	0	0
Single-Candle Patterns:						
Dragonfly Doji	1	0	0	2	3	6
Gravestone Doji	1	0	0	0	0	1
Hammer	42	31	5	9	17	104
Shooting Star	8	2	1	4	7	22
Filled Black Candles	91	99	18	21	17	246
Hollow Red Candles	99	134	21	38	25	317

FIGURE B.5   Candlestick Patterns.
Source: StockCharts.com.

STOCK SCAN CANDLESTICK PATTERNS

In case you need some help locating candlestick patterns (and you probably will), the StockCharts.com Stock Scans page includes a "Candlestick Patterns" section. Figure B.5 shows what it looks like. Each day, that section lists stocks (and ETFs) that have formed any one of 18 of the more popular candlestick patterns. (Mutual funds don't have candlesticks since they have only one closing price for the day). The patterns are broken down into Bullish Reversal Patterns, Bearish Reversal Patterns, Continuation Patterns, and Single-Day Patterns. Once you click on a stock (or ETF), you'll be shown its candlestick chart along with several technical indicators. That will enable you to determine if its overall chart situation looks promising. As useful as candlesticks are, they should never be used in a vacuum. The best way to use them is to combine them with western charting techniques. That will give you the best of the East and the West.

RECOMMENDED READING

This explanation is meant as a brief introduction to candlestick charts. You'll find a lot more information on how to use them in the StockCharts.com ChartSchool. Another excellent source of information is Steven Nison's *Japanese Candlestick Charting Techniques*, which is now in its second, revised edition. Another excellent book on that subject is *Candlestick Charting Explained: Timeless Techniques for Trading Stocks and Futures* (McGraw-Hill, 1992) by Gregory L. Morris. Morris developed the candlestick scans that are used by StockCharts.com. Both books are available on that site's Online Bookstore.

Point-and-Figure Charting

W hile candlesticks are the oldest form of charting in the world, point-and-figure (P&F) charts are the oldest form of charting in the United States. First developed near the end of the nineteenth century, P&F charts predate the better known bar chart by several years. After falling out of favor in the latter decades of the twentieth century, P&F charting has gained new popularity in recent years. A lot of the credit for that goes to the advent of computer charting and web sites such as StockCharts.com that have made P&F charts more accessible to the investing public and much easier to use. Although most investors still rely more heavily on traditional bar and line charts, P&F charts have enough unique qualities and advantages to recommend their use along with those other chart forms.

In my view, the two biggest advantages of point-and-figure charting are precision and simplicity. Buy and sell signals are very easy to spot and leave little doubt as to their existence. The P&F chart does that by recording successive X and O columns. The X column records rising prices while the O column shows falling prices. Trend signals are given when previous X or O columns are exceeded on the upside or the downside.

Figure C.1 shows the two simplest P&F signals called the *double-top breakout* and *double-bottom breakdown*. A double-top breakout shows the second rising X column exceeding the first rising X column. That buy signal describes a simple upside breakout of a previous resistance level. The double-bottom breakdown shows the second O column falling below the first O column. That sell signal describes a simple violation of a previous support level. As valuable as those simple signals can be, there are several

Double-Top Breakout

		X	← Double-top breakout
	X		X ← Double top
O	X	O	X
O	X	O	X
O	X	O	X
O	X		
O			

Double-Bottom Breakdown

X			
X	O		
X	O	X	
X	O	X	O
X	O	X	O
	O		O ← Double bottom
			O ← Double-bottom breakdown

FIGURE C.1 Double-top breakout and double-bottom breakdown.
Source: StockCharts.com.

other more complicated signals that are believed to carry even more significance.

TRIPLE AND QUADRUPLE SIGNALS

While a double-top breakout shows the last X column exceeding one previous X column, the triple-top breakout shows the last X column exceeding two previous X columns (see Figure C.2). As a result, the *triple-top breakout* is considered to be a stronger signal. The same is true of the *triple-bottom breakdown*. And, as you might expect, the *quadruple-top breakout* is even stronger because three previous X columns are exceeded. In fact, there exist at least 17 different P&F signals with varying degrees of complexity. Figure C.3 shows the list of P&F patterns that are included on the StockCharts.com Stock Scans page. You can scan through the entire list, or you might want to limit yourself to the more significant P&F breakouts.

The P&F Patterns in Figure C.3 are taken from June 19, 2008. By clicking on the "P&F quadruple-top alerts" for the NYSE, I've isolated an upside

Triple-Top Breakout

					X ← Triple-top breakout
	X		X		X ← Triple top
O	X	O	X	O	X
O	X	O	X	O	X
O	X	O	X	O	
O	X	O			
O	X				
O					

Triple-Bottom Breakdown

X					
X	O				
X	O	X			
X	O	X	O	X	
X	O	X	O	X	O
X	O	X	O	X	O
	O		O		O ← Triple-bottom
					O ← Triple-bottom breakdown

FIGURE C.2 Triple-top breakout and triple-bottom breakdown.
Source: StockCharts.com.

P&F Patterns	Nasdaq	NYSE	Equities AMEX	TSE	CDNX	Total	Mutual Funds
P&F Triple-Top Alerts	46	65	11	15	3	140	27
P&F Spread Triple-Top Alerts	8	11	0	3	1	23	6
P&F Ascending Triple-Top Alerts	100	101	14	35	5	255	71
P&F Quadruple-Top Alerts	9	10	2	0	0	21	3
P&F Triple-Bottom Alerts	106	81	7	20	8	222	13
P&F Spread Triple-Bottom Alerts	17	18	1	7	0	43	0
P&F Descending Triple-Bottom Alerts	243	131	23	41	17	455	41
P&F Quadruple-Bottom Alerts	12	15	0	1	0	28	2
P&F Bullish Signal Reversal Alerts	12	33	3	2	0	50	3
P&F Bearish Signal Reversal Alerts	34	14	5	10	1	64	20
P&F Bull Trap Alerts	19	19	2	2	2	44	4
P&F Bear Trap Alerts	18	22	3	3	2	48	2
P&F Bullish Catapult Alerts	6	12	0	4	0	22	1
P&F Bearish Catapult Alerts	7	10	2	2	0	21	1
P&F Bullish Triangle Alerts	7	9	2	3	1	22	3
P&F Bearish Triangle Alerts	16	13	3	6	1	39	0
P&F Long-Tail Down Alerts	16	5	1	2	0	24	2

FIGURE C.3 P&F Patterns.
Source: StockCharts.com.

breakout in Arlington Tankers. Figure C.4 shows that stock having traded up to 22 and achieving a bullish breakout over three previous X columns at 21. By contrast, Figure C.5 shows Wells Fargo suffering a P&F quadruple-bottom breakdown. Figure C.5 shows Wells Fargo have falling down to 26 and undercutting three previous bottoms at 27.

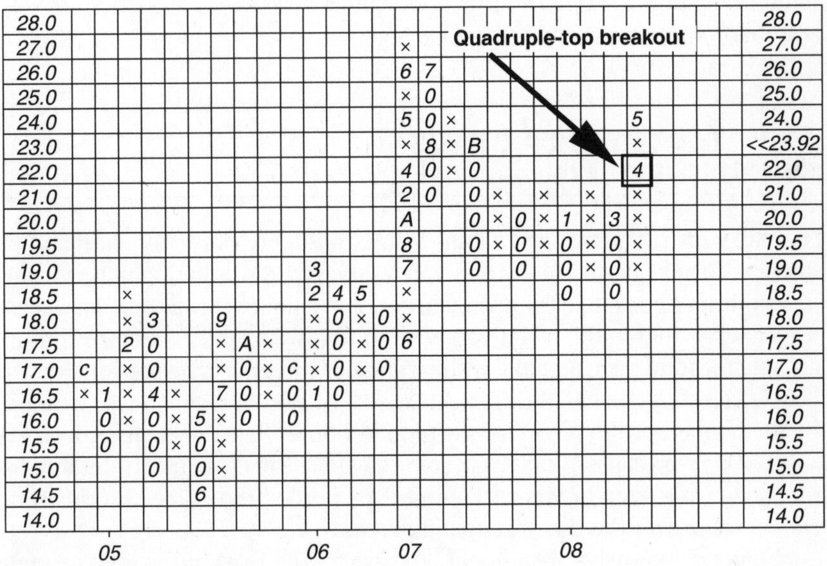

FIGURE C.4 Arlington Tankers, Ltd.
Source: StockCharts.com.

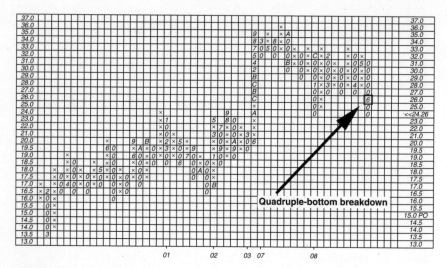

FIGURE C.5 Wells Fargo & Co.
Source: StockCharts.com.

I don't recommend that you make buy and sell decisions based exclusively on those point-and-figure signals. You should also consult the bar chart (or candlestick) to help determine if the bullish or bearish P&F signal is confirmed by other technical criteria. But the ability to scan the various markets for point-and-figure buy and signals is a good place to start your search for winners or losers.

HOW TO VARY P&F CHARTS FOR SENSITIVITY

You can vary the sensitivity of the point-and-figure chart by changing its box size. StockCharts.com offers you a default P&F value, which is based on a traditional box size for each market. You can make that box size larger or smaller to match the trend you wish to follow. A larger box size is more suitable for long-term signals, while a smaller box size is better for shorter-term trades. Or, you can adjust the box size by percentage values (which is the technique I prefer). As I suggested in Chapter 3, a 1 percent box size is suitable in most cases. Traders wishing to make the chart more suitable for long-term trades might want to employ a 2 percent box size. Shorter-term traders can lower the box size to .50 percent.

Figure C.6 shows a .50 percent box size for the Dow Industrials through June 23, 2008. During March of that year, a short-term buy signal was given

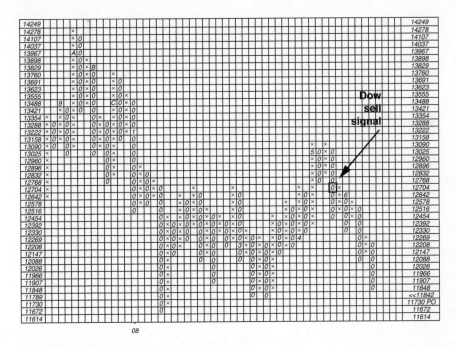

FIGURE C.6 Dow Jones Industrial Average.
Source: StockCharts.com.

at 12330 which lasted for two months. During May, however, the rally faltered and a P&F sell signal was given for the Dow at 12704. (Three additional sell signals were given shortly thereafter.) The chart shows the Dow headed for a test of its 2008 lows, which were broken a month later.

THERE'S NO DOUBT ABOUT P&F SIGNALS

Not every P&F signal is a good one. As is the usually the case, you need to take into consideration the major trend of whichever market you're following. You shouldn't follow every P&F signal blindly, especially if that signal conflicts with your other visual work. The trick is to have as many visual tools (including P&F charts) pointing in the same direction. However, when you are looking for some type of trading signal to confirm a price move, you can't beat the precision of the point-and-figure chart. The first P&F sell signal given by the Dow in May 2008 on Figure C.6 was clear and unambiguous. That sell signal took place after the Dow had recovered

50 percent of its October 2007 to March 2008 decline and after it had failed a test of its falling 200-day moving average. That made the May 2008 Dow sell signal on the P&F chart even more credible. That's just one example of why you should include point-and-figure charting in your visual work.

RECOMMENDED READING

StockCharts.com provides you with lots of information on how to use point-and-figure charts and plenty of help finding P&F price patterns. (Their P&F charts include price objectives on the various price patterns and even allow you to add trendlines, moving averages, and volume.) If you wish to look deeper into the subject, the most comprehensive treatment of point-and-figure trading that I've ever seen is offered by Jeremy du Plessis in his book *The Definitive Guide to Point and Figure* (Horrimon Hovie, 2005). Another excellent book on the subject is *Point & Figure Charting: The Essential Application for Forecasting and Tracking Market Prices*, 3rd ed. (John Wiley & Sons, 2007) by Thomas Dorsey. Both books can be found in the StockCharts.com Online Bookstore.

Index

A

Absolute performance, 187
Advance-decline line, 163–164
 impact, 164, 166
American Stock Exchange (AMEX),
  214, 215
 sector SPDRs, trading, 258, 260
Arithmetic scale, usage, 46
Ascending triangles, 66
Asset allocation process, 140, 142
Asset classes, comparison, 142
Assets, RS analysis, 186
Average directional movement (ADX)
 line, 133
 usage, 133

B

Back-testing, 70–71
 rules, 3
Bands. *See* Bollinger bands
 impact. *See* Monthly charts; Weekly
  charts
 width, importance, 92
Bank accounts, FDIC protection,
  284
Bar charts, 41–42
 pattern, 298
Barclays Global Investors, ETF
  market, 251
Bear ETF, usage, 253, 255
Bearish Reversal Patterns, 300
Bear market rally, completion,
  291
Body
 box, usage, 295

Bollinger bands, 87
 application, 92, 95
Bond ETFs, 267, 269
Bonds, price
 increase, 147
Bond/stock ratio, 144
 2007 level, shift, 147
Brazil, Russia, India, and China
  (BRIC), ETFs
 existence, 269
Breakdown, identification, 281
Breaking support, 18
Breakout, identification, 281
Bullish engulfing pattern, 298
Bullish MACD alignment, positive
  histogram (impact), 130
Bullish Percent Indexes (BPI), 179,
  181, 289, 291
 point-and-figure version, 181–182
Bullish Reversal Patterns, 300
Bull markets, bear market (40 percent
  line separation), 177
Buy decisions, 304
Buy signal, 100, 221, 301

C

Canada iShares (EWC), relative
  strength ratio, 275
Candlestick
 charts, 43
  time adjustment, 46
 patterns, 287, 297
Candlestick Charting Explained
  (Morris), 300
Change oscillators, rate, 99

Channel lines, 34
Charting
criticism, 10
principles, 46
Chartists, problems, 7
Chart Pattern Recognition Software
(Equis International), 71
Charts. *See* Daily charts; Monthly
charts; Weekly charts
future perspective, 8–9
patterns, 52, 54–55, 61
interpretation, 54–55
recognition software, 70–71
speed, 8
types, 41–43
ChartSchool
web site, 286–287
Chicago Board of Exchange (CBOE),
214
volatility (VIX) index, 217, 221
Chinese stocks
decline, 200
leadership loss, 200, 202
Closed-end mutual funds, 228
Closing price, representation, 41
Commodities
baskets, ETFs (usage), 263
exporters, support, 156
increase, 142–144
mutual funds, 247
prices, increase, 258
purchase, 247
Commodity/bond ratio, increase,
144
Commodity ETFs, 263
Commodity-related ETFs, 258
Commodity-related stocks, 153
Commodity Research Bureau (CRB)
CRB/Bond ratio, 186
CRB/S&P ratio, 142
CRB/Treasury bond ratio, 186
Commodity Research Bureau (CRB)
Index, 142
price bars, increase, 155
Computers, availability, 1–2
Consolidation range, 55

Consolidations. *See* Markets
Consumers
discretionary breakdown, 232
discretionary stocks, rotation,
196
oil, impact, 173
Consumer Staples (XLP)
performance, 235
portfolio, 193
Continuation patterns, 52, 54, 300
Contrary indicator, 158, 217
Core holdings, mutual funds (usage),
253
Crossings, examination, 105, 107
Crossover signals, generation, 76
Crossover technique, 123
Crude oil prices
doubling, 173
Currency Shares Euro Trust, 263
Currency trading, limitation, 267
Curving trendline, 76
Cut in half rule, 38

D
Daily charts, 28
timing, 107
Daily signals, weekly signals (blending
process), 125, 128
DecisionPoint, web site, 294
Default value, 103
*Definitive Guide to Point and Figure
The* (du Plessis), 306
Descending triangles, 66
Discounting mechanism, 8–9
Divergences, 97–99. *See also* Moving
average convergence
divergence; Negative
divergences; Relative strength
index
display,
advance-decline, impact, 164, 166
Dollar
foreign stocks, linkage, 152
value, decrease, 147, 150
Domestic stock funds, categorization,
2

Dorsey, Thomas, 306
Double bottom, 52, 54–55, 228
  breakdown, 301–302
  reversal pattern, 193
Double top, 52, 54–55, 228
  breakout, 301–302
Double top and bottom, 52
  usage, 54–55
Doubling technique, 38
Dow, Charles, 173
Dow Jones AIG Commodity Index,
  247
Dow Jones World Stock Index, 159
Down days, loss, 104
Downside crossing, 235
Downside weekly reversal, 38
Down trendline, 31
Dow Theory, 173
du Plessis, Jeremy, 306

E
EAFE Index iShares (EFA), 269
Economic fundamentals, discounting,
  171
Economic slowdown, bond price
  movement, 145
Elliott wave analysis, 36
Emerging market ETFs, 252
Energy
  markets, increase, 263
  stocks, increase, 152
Energy Sector SPDR (XLE)
  relative strength ratio, 153
Envelopes, 87. *See also* Trading
  envelopes
EOG Resources, 215
Exchange-traded funds (ETFs), 2, 140,
  251, 283. *See also* Bond ETFs;
  Commodity ETFs; Foreign
  currency ETFs; International
  ETFs; Inverse sector ETFs
  hedge usage, 253
  impact, 4
  mutual funds, contrast, 252–253
  usage. *See* Bear ETF; Sector ETFs
Exponentially smoothed average, 77

F
Failure swing, 105
Fast stochastics, 112
  slow stochastics, contrast, 110,
    112
Federal Reserve Board, charting
  (usage), 65
Fibonacci ratios, importance, 36
Fidelity International Real Estate
  Fund, 240
Fidelity Investments, portolios, 229
Fidelity Latin American Fund, 240
Fidelity Select Construction/Housing
  Fund, 232
Fidelity Select Consumer
  Discretionary Portfolio, 232
Fidelity Select Electronics Fund, 235
Fidelity Select Funds, 294
50 line, crossing (examination), 107
50-percent retracement, 34
Foreign currency ETFs, 263, 267
Foreign currency trends, visual
  investor actions, 258
Foreign markets, diversification, 158
Foreign stocks
  dollar, relationship, 153, 156
Formation signals, 65–66
40 percent line, separation, 177
40-week average
  usage, 78
FTSE/Xinhua China iShares, increase,
  196
Fundamental analysis, 6
Fundamental data, technical data
  (blending), 229
Fundamentals
  discount, 9
  relationship. *See* Prices

G
Global bull market, diversification,
  158
Global decoupling, 156, 158, 161
Global funds, 2
Global liquidity, providing, 158–159
Global stocks, yen (impact), 158–159

Gold
  consideration, 140–141
  stocks, comparison, 190
Gold-oriented funds, performance, 152
Gold price
  increase, 150
Gold/Silver Index (XAU), 214
Granville, Joseph, 50, 52
Great Depression, 284

H
Halving technique, 38
Hard assets, 142
Head and shoulders, identification,
  222
Head and shoulders bottom, 52, 54, 65
Head and shoulders pattern, 61. *See
  also* Inverse head and shoulders
  pattern
  measurement, 65
Head and shoulders top, 52, 54
Histogram, 128, 130
Homebuilders
  linkage. *See* Retailers
Housing Index (HGX), 214

I
Indicators. *See* Lagging indicators
  classes, 75–76
  combination, 119
  concepts, importance, 4
  usage, 228–229
    selection, 130, 133
Industry groups, 207
  information, 214
  leaders, 213–214
Inflation, impact, 244
Interest-sensitive shares, favoring, 186
Intermarket analysis, 4, 158
  usage, 6
*Intermarket Analysis: Profiting From
  Global Market Relationships*
  (Murphy), 139, 159
Intermarket book (2004), review, 159
Intermarket relationships,
  understanding, 140

Intermarket Technical Analysis
  (Murphy), 139
International ETFs, 252, 269, 275
Internet charting services, availability,
  1–2
Intraday charts, 46
Inverse ETFs, 253
Inverse fund, mirror image, 255
Inverse head and shoulders pattern,
  61
Inverse sector ETFs, 260
Inverse stock funds, 247, 250
Investors
  information, necessity, 3
  performance, improvement, 283
Investor's Business Daily (IBD),
  resource, 288

J
*Japanese Candlestick Charting
  Techniques* (Nison), 295, 300
Japanese candlesticks, 295
Japanese yen/U.S. dollar relationship,
  157

K
KBW Bank Index (BKX), 214
Key reversal day, 38

L
Lagging indicators, 75
Lane, George, 110
Large caps, rotation selection, 196
Large-cap/small-cap ratio, 196
Large-cap stock funds, 2
Latin America
  mutual funds, 240
Lehman Brothers
  bankruptcy, 283–284
Lehman International Treasury Bond
  ETF, 267
Linear scale, usage, 46
Line charts, 43
Logarithmic charts (semilog charts)
  price measurement, 46, 50
Longer-range momentum, 100

Longer-range trend analysis, 31
Long-term analysis, 142
Long-term support line, break,
    164
Long-term trend, 25, 28, 77

M
Major trend, 25
    monitoring, 76
Market analysis
    fundamental analysis, relationship,
        9
    time, importance, 28
    usage, reasons, 5–6
Markets
    accuracy, 9–10
    breadth, 163
        measurement, 163–164
    carpets, 211, 215
        usage. *See* Stocks
    downtrend, example, 128
    extremes, subjectivity, 100
    indicator, technology (usage), 260
    leaders, identification, 193
    linkages, 4, 139
        study, 6
    longer-term trend, 25
    new leaders, identification, 189
    overbought/oversold characteristic,
        75
    potential, 61
    scans, ability, 288–289
    sectors, rotation (presence), 198
    study, reasons, 7
    tendencies, awareness, 34, 36, 38
    timing, discouragement, 252–253
    trends
        action, 10
        importance, 4
    volatility, adjustment, 92
Materials Sector SPDR, 258
McClellan Breadth Indicators, 294
Measuring techniques, 61, 65
Media
    impact, 279–280
    viewpoints, shift, 280

Midsize funds, 2
Momentum, 99–100
    oscillators, 99
    usage, 223
Monthly charts, 28
    bands, impact, 92, 95
    construction, 46
    usage, 107
Monthly signals, examination,
    130
Morningstar, rating system, 229
Morris, Gregory L., 300
Moving average convergence
        divergence (MACD), 77, 228
    alignment, 130
    construction, 121–123
    divergences, 125
    histogram, 128
    improvement, 128, 130
    indicator, 121
        usage, 223
    oscillator, function, 123, 125
    system, study, 123
    trend-following indicator, 123
Moving averages, 75, 76, 110. *See also*
        Shorter moving average;
        Weighted moving average
    combination, 78, 87, 92, 95
    crossing, 235
    lengths, 77–78
    lines, violation, 164
    usage, 281
M pattern, 55
MSCI Emerging Markets iShare
        (EEM), 269
Multinational stocks, 166, 169
Mutual funds, 227–228, 247. *See also*
        Nontraditional mutual funds;
        Traditional mutual funds
    categories, 2
    contrast. *See* Exchange-traded
        funds
    expansion, 1–2
    rankings, 229
    selection, complexity, 1–2
    tools, 222

N

NASDAQ 100, trading, 255, 258
Natural gas
  breakout, 232
  components, 215, 217
  leadership, identification, 215
Natural Gas INdex (XNG), 214, 215
Negative directional indicator (-DI), 133
Negative divergences, 105, 164, 166
  development, 169
  location, 166, 169
Negative ROC, impact. *See* Technology
Negative volume numbers, cumulative total, 52
Net asset value (NAV), 228
New Concepts in Technical Trading Systems (Wilder, Jr.), 100
New York Stock Exchange (NYSE)
  Bullish Percent Index, 179, 181
  Composite Index, 177, 179
New York Stock Exchange (NYSE)
  advance-decline line, 163–164
  moving average violation, 164
19-day exponential moving average (EMA), 39-day EMA (differences), 294
Nison, Steve, 295, 300
Nontraditional mutual funds, 229–230
Nontrending mode, 133

O

Oil, impact. *See* Consumers
Oil Service Holders (OIH), ratio, 198
On-balance volume (OBV), 50, 52
  helpfulness, 54
One-third retracements, 36
Online bookstore, usage, 287–288
Open-end mutual funds, 228
  charting adjustments, 228–229
Opening price, representation, 41
Oscillators, 75. *See also* Momentum; Rate of change
  analysis, negative divergences (usage), 166
  rate. *See* Change oscillators

systems, examination, 281
  usage, 228
Overbought/oversold areas, 113
Overbought/oversold conditions, measurement, 97
Overnight bank lending rates, increase, 284

P

Paper assets, shift, 142
Pattern recognition, 71
Percentage retracement, 34
Percentage weightings, conversion, 77
Performance charts, 209–210
Philadelphia Stock Exchange (PHLX) Housing Index, 171
PIMCO Commodity Real Return Fund (PCRAX), 247
Point and figure (P&F) charting, 301
Point and figure (P&F) charts, 66, 70
  variation, 304–305
Point and figure (P&F) sell signal, 305
Point and figure (P&F) signals, 304–306
Point & Figure Charting (Dorsey), 306
Portfolios
  energizing, 240
  monitoring, 3
Position (determination), weekly signals (usage), 112–113
Positive directional indicator (+DI), 133
Positive volume numbers, cumulative total, 52
PowerShares QQQ Trust (QQQQ), 255
Prices
  action, volume (impact), 281
  determination, 66
  fundamentals, relationship, 282
  information, 46
  objectives, determination, 92
  patterns, 61
    discovery, 41
    height, 61
    identification, 28

range, 41
trends
    concentration, 280
    confirmation, 52
Primary trend, 25
    interruption, 41
ProFund Falling Dollar Fund (FDPIX),
        244, 247
ProFunds Rising Rates Opportunity 10
        Fund (RTPIX), 244
ProShares UltraShort Lehman 7-10
        Year Treasury ETF, 267
ProShares Ultra Short Lehman 20+
        Year Treasury ETF, 267
ProShares Ultra Short QQQ (QID), 255
Pullbacks. *See* Markets

Q
Quadruple bottom breakdown, 303
Quadruple signals, 302–304
Quadruple top breakout, 302

R
Rate of change (ROC)
    interpretation, 100
    oscillators, 99
    usage, 228
Ratio method, usage, 99
Readers Choice Awards, usage,
        285–286
Reading resources, 292, 298
Real body, 43
Real estate, global characteristic, 240
Recession
    bond price movement, 145
    possibility, 158
Regular ETFs, 253
Relative strength index (RSI), 100–101,
        104–105, 107
    divergences, 105
        interpretation, 112
        volatility, 105
    oscillator
        range, 100
        usage, 228–229
    ratio, usage, 104

stochastics, combination, 113, 119
    time spans, usage, 103
    values, modification, 104–105
Relative strength (RS)
    absolute performance, contrast, 187
    analysis, 4, 186
        usage, 229
    line, 142, 181
    performance, chart analysis
            (combination), 187
    ratio, 142
    usage, 185–186, 190. *See also* Stocks
Resistance
    definition, 18
    levels, 18, 280
Retailers
    homebuilders, linkage, 171
Retail ratio, decline, 235, 240
Retail stocks, performance, 169, 171
Retracements. *See* One-third
            retracements; Two-thirds
            retracements
    levels, derivation, 36
Reversal patterns, 52, 54
Rising rates fund, 238
Role reversal, 18, 25
Rotation, 185
Running markets, 112
Russell 2000 Small Cap Index,
            decrease, 250
Rydex Inverse Russell 2000 2X
            Strategy Fund (RYIZX), 247

S
Scales, differences, 50
Scaling, 46, 50
Secondary trend (intermediate trend),
        25
Sector ETFs. *See* Inverse sector ETFs
    usage, 258, 260
Sectors, 207
    carpets, 211–212
    funds, selection, 230
    industry groups, contrast, 208–209
    information, 214
    investing, 282–283

Sectors (*Continued*)
  performers, ranking, 210
  rotation
    components, 193, 196
    trends, monitoring (necessity), 214
Sell decisions, 304
Sell signal, 100, 221, 301
Semiconductor (SOX) Index, 214
Sensitivity, P&F chart variation,
    304–305
70/30 lines, crossing (examination),
    105, 107
Shadow, 43, 295
Shorter moving average, level, 78
Shorter-term analysis, 31
Short-term rates, decrease, 149
Short-term trend, 25, 28
Short-term upside reversal,
    occurrence, 298
Simple average, 76
  weighting/smoothing, 77
Single-Day Patterns, 300
Slow stochastics, 110
Small-cap funds, 2
Small-cap stocks, 166, 169
Standard deviation, 87, 92
Standard & Poor's 500 (S&P500)
  price, doubling, 269
  usage, 153
Standard & Poor's 600 Small Cap
    Index, 196
*Standard & Poor's Guide to Sector
    Investing* (Stovall), 208
Standard & Poor's (S&P)
  Equity Research, 208
State Street, ETF market, 251
Stochastic lines. *See* Semiconductor
    Index
  crossings, 112
Stochastic oscillator, 110–113
Stochastics
  contrast. *See* Fast stochastics
  meaning, 110
StockCharts
  P&F value, offer, 304
  stock scans, 288–289
  web site, 286

Stock market
  decline, 284
  division, 208
  economy, relationship, 281–282
  peak, 283–284
  rotation, relationship, 210
Stocks
  bull market, 145
  holding, hedging, 253
  identification, 215
  leaders (identification), market
      carpet (usage), 212–213
  performance. *See* Retail stocks
  price
    decline, 146–148
  relative strength, usage, 190
  RS, usage, 186
  scan candlestick patterns, 300
  sectors, division, 2
Stovall, Sam, 208
Subprime mortgages, problems, 196
Supply/demand
  consideration, 7–8
  laws, basis, 282
Support
  levels, 18, 280
    violation, 301–302
  test, 18
Symmetrical triangle, 66

T
T. Rowe Price, mutual funds,
    229–230
Technical analysis, 280
*Technical Analysis of Stocks &
    Commodities*, 285–286
Technology
  market indicator, 260
  SPDR (XLK), 260
Technology, negative ROC (impact),
    235
TeleChart, 278
Time
  importance. *See* Market analysis
  information, 46
  selection, 46
Time filter signals, 113

Timing, importance, 13
Top-down analysis, 186
Trading envelopes, 87
  Bollinger bands, contrast, 92
Trading ranges, 55
Traditional mutual funds, 229–230
Transportation stocks, problems,
    175
Transports
  confirmation, 175
Trend-following indicators, 75–76,
    123
  moving average lines, relationship,
    78, 87
Trending
  environment, 78
  mode, 133
Trendlines, 31. *See also* Curving
    trendline
  analysis, 198
  drawing, 66, 281
    process, 31, 34
  support/resistance, 31
Trends, 6
  changes, identification, 198
  definition, 15, 18
  usage, 15
  zig-zags, 34
Triangles, 52, 65–66. *See also*
    Ascending triangles;
    Descending triangles
  identification, 222
Triple bottoms, 52, 55
  breakdown, 302
  usage, 55, 61
Triple signals, 302–304
Triple tops, 52, 55
  breakout, 302
  usage, 55, 61
20-day average, usage, 77–78
20-day moving average, 87
200-day average
  construction, 76
  downside crossing, 229
  NYSE stocks
    relationship, 175, 177, 179
  popularity, 77

200-day line, usage, 77–78
200-day moving average, 177
  housing, relationship, 230, 232
Two-thirds retracements, 36

U
Ultra funds, 247, 253
  potential, 252
Ultra-Short Financials ProShares
    (SKF), 260
Upside reversal day, 298
Upside weekly reversal, 38
Uptrend
  example. *See* Markets
Up trendline, 31
U.S. dollar
  fund. *See* ProFund Falling Dollar
    Fund
  rate, decline, 147, 150
U.S. Dollar Index, 140, 244
U.S. interest rates
  dollar, impact, 147
U.S. Treasury Bond, price, 143
U.S. Treasury Note
  ten-year note, price, 147
  yield
    U.S. Dollar Index price,
      correlation, 150

V
Vanguard
  ETF market, 251
  mutual funds, 229–230
Visual analysis
  chart analysis/technical analysis, 6
  strengths, 9
  usefulness, 280
Visual investing
  benefits, 3
  definition, 5
  nomenclature, reason, 279
  simplicity, necessity, 280–281
Visual tools, universality, 281
VIX. *See* Chicago Board of Exchange
    volatility index
Volatility, 28, 66, 92
  movement, 104

Volume
  analysis, 50–52, 228–229
  usage, importance, 54

W
Web site, selection, 285
Weekly charts, 28
  bands, impact, 92, 95
  construction, 46
  usage, 107
Weekly indicator, appearance, 125
Weekly reversals, 38. *See also*
    Downside weekly reversal;
    Upside weekly reversal

Weekly signals, impact, 112–113
Weekly stochastic indicator, usage, 113
Weighted moving average, 77
Wilder, J. Welles, 100
W pattern, 55

Y
Yen
  carry trade, 158
  increase, 158–159

Z
Zero line, 99, 125
  histogram, relationship, 128